Study Guide

ESSENTIALS OF MANAGERIAL FINANCE

Seventh Edition

Study Guide

ESSENTIALS OF MANAGERIAL FINANCE

Seventh Edition

Eugene F. Brigham
University of Florida

J. Fred Weston
University of California at Los Angeles

THE DRYDEN PRESS
Chicago New York Philadelphia
San Francisco Montreal Toronto
London Sydney Tokyo Mexico City
Rio de Janeiro Madrid

ISBN 0-03-000229-X
Printed in the United States of America
567-066-98765432

Address orders:
383 Madison Avenue
New York, NY 10017

Address editorial correspondence:
One Salt Creek Lane
Hinsdale, IL 60521

CBS COLLEGE PUBLISHING
The Dryden Press
Holt, Rinehart and Winston
Saunders College Publishing

PREFACE

This Study Guide is designed primarily to help you develop a working knowledge of the concepts and principles of managerial finance. Additionally, it will familiarize you with the types of true/false and multiple choice test questions that are being used with increasing frequency in introductory finance courses.

The Study Guide follows the outline of Essentials of Managerial Finance. You should read carefully the next section, "How to Use This Study Guide," to familiarize yourself with its specific contents and to gain some insights into how it can be used most effectively.

We would like to thank Susan Ball, Melissa Davis, Lou Gapenski, Debra Kriebel, and Terry Sicherman for their considerable assistance in the preparation of this Edition, and Bob LeClair for his helpful ideas in prior editions which we carried over to this one.

We have tried to make the Study Guide as clear and error-free as possible. However, some mistakes may have crept in, and there are almost certainly some sections that could be clarified. Any suggestions for improving the Study Guide would be greatly appreciated and should be addressed to Professor Brigham. Since instructors almost never read study guides, we address this call for help to students!

Eugene F. Brigham
College of Business Administration
University of Florida
Gainesville, FL 32611

J. Fred Weston
Graduate School of Management
University of California at Los Angeles
Los Angeles, CA 90024

December 1984

HOW TO USE THIS STUDY GUIDE

Different people will tend to use the Study Guide in somewhat different ways. This is natural, because both introductory finance courses and individual students' needs vary widely. However, the tips contained in this section should help all students use the Study Guide more effectively, regardless of these differences.

Each chapter contains (1) an overview, (2) an outline, (3) some definitional questions, (4) some conceptual questions, and (5) answers to the questions. In addition, all but the first and the last chapters (Chapters 1 and 25) contain a set of problems with solutions. You should begin your study by reading the overview; it will give you an idea of what is contained in the chapter and how this material fits into the overall scheme of things in financial management.

Next, read over the outline to get a better fix on the specific topics covered in the chapter. It is important to realize that the outline does not list every facet of every topic covered in the textbook--the Study Guide is intended to highlight and summarize the textbook, not to supplant it. Also, note that appendix material is clearly marked as such within the outline. Thus, if your instructor does not assign a particular appendix, you may not want to study that portion of the outline.

The definitional questions are intended to test your knowledge of, and also to reinforce your ability to work with, the terms and concepts introduced in the chapter. If you do not understand the definitions thoroughly, review the outline prior to going on to the conceptual questions and problems.

The conceptual questions focus on the same kinds of ideas that the textbook end-of-chapter questions address, but in the Study Guide the questions are set out in a true/false or multiple choice format. Thus, for many students these questions can be used to practice for the types of tests that are being used with increasing frequency. However, regardless of the types of tests you must take, working through the conceptual questions will help drive home the key concepts of financial management.

The numerical problems are also written in a multiple choice format. Generally, the problems are arranged in order of increasing difficulty, and those problems relating to appendix material are clearly marked. Also, note that some of the Study Guide problems are convoluted in the sense that information normally available to financial managers is withheld, and information normally unknown is given. Such problems are designed to test your knowledge of a subject, and you must work "backwards" to solve them. Furthermore, such problems are included in the Study Guide in part because they provide a good test of how well you understand the material, and in part because you may well be seeing similar problems on your exams.

Finally, each Study Guide chapter provides the answers and solutions to the questions and problems. The rationale behind a question's correct answer is explained only where necessary, but the problem solutions are always complete. Note that the problems in the early chapters generally provide both "table-based" and "financial calculator" solutions. In later chapters, only calculator solutions are shown. You should not be concerned if your answer differs from ours by a small amount which is caused by rounding errors.

Of course, each student must decide how to incorporate the Study Guide in his or her overall study program. Many students begin an assignment by reading the Study Guide overview and outline to get the "big picture," then read the chapter in the textbook. Naturally, the Study Guide overview and outline is also used extensively to review for exams. Most students work the textbook questions and problems prior to tackling the Study Guide questions and problems, using the latter as a self-test and review tool. However, if you are stumped by a text problem, try the Study Guide problems first, because their detailed solutions can get you over stumbling blocks.

CONTENTS OF THE STUDY GUIDE

Study Guide

ESSENTIALS OF MANAGERIAL FINANCE

Seventh Edition

CHAPTER 1

THE FINANCE FUNCTION

Overview

Chapter 1 begins with a description of the role and responsibilities of the financial manager and the nature of the finance function within the firm. The goals of financial management are then considered. The conclusion reached is that the primary goal in most publicly owned firms is stock price maximization. Next, the evolution of financial management from 1900 to the present is reviewed. The chapter concludes with a discussion of the organization of the text.

Outline

I. The financial manager has an important role in maximizing the value of the firm.

   A. The main function of the financial manager is to plan for, acquire, and utilize funds to make the maximum contribution to the efficient operation of the organization.

   B. The financial manager must answer questions such as:

      1. Which investments should the firm make?
      2. How should projects be financed?
      3. How should the firm operate its existing resources so as to get the most out of them?

   C. Financial managers interact with capital and money markets, which continuously record the valuation of business firms, and in doing so, assess managerial performance.

II. The specific finance functions are divided between the top financial officers.

   A. The three main financial officers are the treasurer, the controller, and the vice president of finance, with most specific finance functions divided between the treasurer and the controller.

      1. The treasurer handles the acquisition and custody of funds. The treasurer's duties include:

       a. Cash budgeting
       b. Cash position
       c. Credit management
       d. Insurance and pension management
   2. The controller is responsible for accounting, budgeting and control systems including:
       a. Financial statements
       b. Payroll
       c. Taxes
       d. Internal auditing
   3. The treasurer and controller report to the vice president of finance who reports directly to the president and is responsible for general financial policy.

B. Finance committees are used in larger companies.

   1. A committee provides a wider scope of knowledge and judgment, which may be required on major financial policy issues.
   2. Allocation of funds for capital and operating budgets may be more objectively accomplished by a committee.
   3. Key finance subcommittees include:
       a. Capital appropriations
       b. Operations
       c. Pensions
       d. Compensations

C. The finance function is typically close to the top of the organizational structure of the firm because financial decisions are so important to the future well-being of the firm.

III. The goals of financial management are based on the goals of the firm.

A. The goal of financial management is to maximize the value of the firm, and thus maximize the wealth of the firm's stockholders.

   1. Management should seek to balance the interests of owners, creditors, and the other constituencies of the firm.
   2. Changes in the value of a firm's stock provide a good index for measuring a company's performance, hence the performance of the firm's managers.

B. This goal translates into maximizing the price of the firm's common stock. This is not the same as maximizing profits.

C. Maximizing share price reflects the position of the common stockholders as claimants to the residual income of the firm.

      1. This does not imply that managers should seek to improve the value of common stock at the expense of the bondholders.
         a. Riskier investments may benefit shareholders, but cause bond values to fall.
         b. Unless strong signals are given in advance to bondholders that investment and other policies will not be changed to their disadvantage, the returns promised to bondholders must compensate for this risk.

  D. Managers' objectives are tied to the firm's goals.

      1. Compensation is based partly on profits and growth in the firm's stock price.
      2. If compensation is not tied to company performance, managers may place their interest ahead of the interests of stockholders and bondholders.
      3. Shareholders can replace bad managers.
      4. Managers' reputations and their compensation will be affected by the value of their firm's stock.

  E. Social responsibility is an important aspect of the goals of the firm.

      1. Successful value maximization leads to better contributions to society as a whole.
      2. Effects on the external environment--pollution, job safety, product safety--must also be taken into account.
      3. Responsiveness to external constituencies--consumer and other interest groups--may be required for economic survival.
      4. Firms should seek to maximize shareholder wealth within legal and social constraints and to respond to the firms' changing environments and constituencies.

  F. The goal of maximizing profits is narrower than the goal of maximizing the value of the firm.

      1. Maximizing value takes the time value of money into account.
      2. The discount rate or capitalization rate used in seeking to maximize value reflects the risks of the flows that are capitalized while "profit maximization" does not.

IV. The value of the firm is influenced by the risk and profitability of the firm's assets.

  A. A primary policy decision is choosing the firm's product-market lines, or the industries in which the firm will operate.

B. Profitability and risk are then determined by decisions relating to the firm's size, types of equipment, debt level, liquidity position, and so on.

    1. In general, decisions which increase profitability also increase risk; decisions which reduce risk also tend to reduce profitability. For example:

        a. Increased cash holdings reduce risk, but since cash is not an earning asset, this also reduces profitability.

        b. Additional debt increases the rate of return to stockholders, but also increases risk.

    2. The financial manager seeks to find the balance between profitability and risk that will maximize the value of the firm.

V. Financial management has undergone significant changes over the years.

A. During the early 1900s and all through the Roaring Twenties, the emphasis was on legalistic matters such as mergers, consolidations, the formation of new firms, and the various types of securities issued by corporations. During this period capital markets were relatively primitive, and the critical problem firms faced was obtaining capital for expansion.

B. The depression of the 1930s caused finance to focus on bankruptcy, reorganization, corporate liquidity, and governmental regulation of securities markets.

C. During the 1940s and early 1950s, finance continued to be viewed from the outside rather than from within the firm's management. The focus was on the right-hand (claims) side of the balance sheet.

D. In the late 1950s, more sophisticated methods of financial analysis began to be developed.

    1. Capital budgeting and working capital (the left-hand side of the balance sheet) began to receive attention.

    2. Mathematical models were applied to the analysis of inventories, cash, receivables, and fixed assets.

    3. The focus of finance shifted to the insider's point of view as descriptive, institutional materials were deemphasized.

E. The emphasis on improved decision making has continued up to the present time. Attention has focused on quantifying the cost of capital and on ways of raising funds. International finance and mergers have received increased attention, and there has been an increasing awareness of social problems which firms must work to solve. Finally, financial managers have had to deal with a persistent high rate of inflation.

VI. The organization and structure of the seventh edition of Essentials of Managerial Finance reflect the primary goal of stock price maximization.

A. The book deals with the seven major areas of managerial finance.

1. Part I presents basic background material on financial markets, tax laws, and interest rates.
2. Part II covers financial analysis, financial forecasting, and planning and control systems.
3. Part III deals with the key aspects of working capital management.
4. Part IV discusses the time value of money and capital budgeting, under both certainty and uncertainty.
5. Part V deals with the valuation process, measurement of the cost of capital, and decisions regarding the optimum use of financial leverage.
6. Part VI handles the long-run financing decisions of the firm.
7. Part VII deals with special topics in managerial finance such as mergers, reorganizations, small business finance, and international financial management.

B. This Study Guide seeks to outline the material and provide problems with illustrative solutions for the 7th Edition of Essentials of Managerial Finance.

Definitional Questions

1. The main function of the financial manager is to plan for, _____, and utilize funds.

2. The three main financial officers are the _____, _____, and vice president of finance.

3. The _____ handles the acquisition and custody of funds.

4. The controller is responsible for accounting, _____, and _____ systems.

5. Modern financial theory operates on the assumption that the goal of management is the _____ of shareholder _____. This goal is accomplished if the firm's _____ _____ is maximized.

6. Firms should seek to maximize shareholder wealth within the legal and _____ constraints and to respond to the firm's changing _____ and constituencies.

7. The financial manager must balance _____ and _____ in a way that will maximize the value of the firm.

8. In the early 1900s, the finance function concentrated on _____ matters such as mergers, consolidations, and the various types of securities issued by corporations.

9. The _____ of the 1930s caused an emphasis on bankruptcy, liquidity, and _____ regulation of securities markets.

10. During the 1950's, asset management techniques, especially _____ _____, began to be developed and applied to financial decision making.

11. Financial managers had been mostly concerned with _____ and capital in earlier times, but in the late 1950s, attention shifted to _____ analysis.

Conceptual Questions

12. The primary objective of the firm is to maximize earnings per share.

    a. True   b. False

13. Which of the following factors affect stock prices?

    a. Level of projected earnings per share
    b. Riskiness of projected earnings
    c. Timing of the earnings stream
    d. The manner of financing the firm
    e. All of the above factors

14. Which of the following factors tend to encourage management to pursue stock price maximization as a goal?

    a. Shareholders link management's compensation to company performance.
    b. Managers react to the threat of takeovers.
    c. Managers do not have goals other than stock price maximization.
    d. Statements a and b are both correct.
    e. Statements a, b, and c are all correct.

15. The types of actions that help a firm maximize stock price are generally not directly beneficial to society at large.

    a. True   b. False

Answers

1. acquire

2. treasurer; controller

3. treasurer

4. budgeting; control

5. maximization; wealth; stock price

6. social; environments

7. profitability; risk

8. legalistic

9. depression; governmental

10. capital budgeting

11. liabilities; asset

12. b. The primary objective of the firm is to maximize stock price. An increase in earnings per share will not necessarily increase stock price. For example, if the increase in earnings per share is accompanied by an increase in the riskiness of the firm, stock price might fall.

13. e.

14. d.

15. b. The actions that maximize stock price generally also benefit society by promoting efficient, low-cost operations; encouraging the development of new technology, products, and jobs; and requiring efficient and courteous service.

CHAPTER 2

BUSINESS ORGANIZATION AND THE FINANCIAL ENVIRONMENT

Overview

This chapter presents background information on forms of business organization, business securities, income taxes, financial markets and institutions, and interest rates. First, the characteristics, advantages, and disadvantages of the three major forms of business organization are discussed. Then, since all businesses must raise capital to acquire assets, the features of the common forms of capital are discussed. The value of any asset is dependent on the effective, or after-tax, income it produces for its owner. Thus, the federal income tax system as applied to both individuals and corporations is examined. The chapter next examines the functions and types of financial markets and institutions. The manner in which interest rates are determined is of vital importance to firms, as interest rate levels affect a firm's cost of capital and its stock prices. Thus, the determinants of interest rates are discussed next. Finally, Chapter 2 discusses the term structure of interest rates.

Outline

I. The three major forms of business organizations are the sole proprietorship, the partnership, and the corporation.

    A. About 80 percent of businesses operate as sole proprietorships, 10 percent as partnerships, and 10 percent as corporations.

    B. However, when measured by dollar value of sales, corporations have about 80 percent, sole proprietorships about 13 percent, and partnerships about 7 percent.

    C. A sole proprietorship is a business owned by one individual.

        1. It is easily and inexpensively formed and requires no formal charter. It is subject to few government regulations and pays no corporate income taxes.

        2. The sole proprietorship is limited in its ability to raise large sums of capital. The proprietor is subject to unlimited personal liability, and the proprietorship is limited to the life of the individual.

D. A partnership is formed when two or more persons associate to conduct a business enterprise.

1. Partnerships are easy and economical to form as well as free from special governmental regulation. Partnership profits are taxed as personal income to the individual partners in proportion to their ownership.
2. The withdrawal or death of any of the partners dissolves the partnership. A partner's ownership is difficult to transfer, and the individual partners have unlimited liability.

E. The corporation is a legal entity created by a state and is separate from its owners and managers.

1. The corporate form has three major advantages over the other forms of business organization--unlimited life, transferability of ownership through the transfer of stock, and limited liability.
2. A charter must be filed with the state where the firm is headquartered, and by-laws which govern the management of the company must be prepared.
3. Corporations are taxed differently from proprietorships and partnerships.

II. Any business, irrespective of its organizational form, must have assets to operate. The capital raised to acquire these assets comes in two basic forms.

A. Creditors supply debt capital to the firm.

1. Debt capital is obtained mainly by buying on credit from suppliers or borrowing from banks and other institutions.
2. Creditors have first claim against a firm's income, but the claim is limited to the fixed interest charge. Also, creditors have first claim on the proceeds from bankruptcy liquidation.

B. Equity capital is supplied by preferred stockholders and common stockholders.

1. Preferred stockholders have a fixed claim on a firm's income, and preferred dividends must be paid before any dividends can be paid on common stock.
2. Common stockholders have a claim on the residual income remaining after creditor and preferred stockholder claims have been met. Common equity funds are obtained by retaining earnings within the firm and by the sale of new common stock to investors.

III. Income taxes in the United States are progressive; that is, the higher the income, the larger the percentage paid in taxes.

    A. Individuals pay taxes on wages and salaries, on investment income (dividends and interest), and on the profits from proprietorships and partnerships.

        1. Individual tax rates go up to 50 percent, and they may approach 70 percent when state taxes are included.

        2. During an inflationary period such as the 1970s, a progressive tax structure will result in a decline in real after-tax income because a higher percentage of income is paid out in taxes.

        3. Since dividends are paid from corporate income that has already been taxed (at rates up to 46 percent), there is double taxation of corporate income.

        4. To compensate partially for this double taxation, $100 of dividend income ($200 for married couples with jointly owned stock who file joint returns) is excluded from personal income taxes.

        5. Interest on state and local government securities, which are often called "municipals," is not subject to federal income taxes. This is a strong incentive for individuals in high tax brackets to purchase such securities.

    B. Gains and losses on the sale of capital assets receive special tax treatment.

        1. An asset sold for a gain or loss within 6 months of purchase produces a short-term capital gain or loss.

        2. An asset held for more than 6 months, and then sold, produces a long-term capital gain or loss.

        3. Short-term gains are taxed as ordinary income.

        4. For long-term gains, only 40 percent of the gain is taxed as ordinary income.

        5. Gains and losses are netted out before figuring taxes; therefore, losses on one stock can offset gains on another.

        6. Capital gains and losses also apply to corporate income.

    C. Corporations pay taxes on profits.

        1. The tax on corporate income for 1984 consists of five rate categories.
            a. 15 percent of the first $25,000 of taxable income
            b. 18 percent of the next $25,000
            c. 30 percent of the next $25,000
            d. 40 percent of the next $25,000
            e. 46 percent of all income over $100,000

2. Interest and dividends received by a corporation are taxed.
   a. Interest is taxed as ordinary income* at regular corporate tax rates.
   b. 85 percent of the dividends received by one corporation from another is excluded from taxable income. The remaining 15 percent is taxed at the ordinary rate.
3. The tax system favors debt financing over equity financing.
   a. Interest paid is a tax-deductible business expense. Thus, interest is paid with before-tax dollars.
   b. Dividends on common and preferred stock are not deductible. Thus, dividends are paid with after-tax dollars.
4. Ordinary operating losses may be carried back 3 years and forward 15 years and used to offset taxable income in those years. This procedure has the effect of averaging income and is particularly helpful to firms with widely fluctuating income.
5. The Internal Revenue Code imposes a penalty on corporations that improperly accumulate earnings. Earnings are considered to be improperly accumulated if the purpose of the accumulation is to enable stockholders to avoid personal income tax on dividends.
6. If a corporation owns 80 percent or more of another corporation's stock, it can aggregate income and file a consolidated tax return. Thus, losses in one area can offset profits in another. Also, if a consolidated subsidiary pays dividends to its parent company, the parent company is not taxed on these dividends.
7. Depreciation, since it affects taxable income, is an important element in federal tax policy.

IV. The investment tax credit (ITC) stimulates business investment by reducing the effective cost of fixed assets.

A. The ITC is a direct reduction of taxes due.

B. It is calculated as a percentage of the cost of new investment in certain categories of assets.

C. Congress varies the ITC over time depending upon economic conditions.

V. The Internal Revenue Code provides that certain small business corporations may elect to be taxed either as proprietorships or as partnerships. These firms are known as S corporations. In order to qualify, a firm must meet certain other restrictions spelled out in the tax code. The S option has several advantages over filing as an ordinary corporation.

   A. Business income is reported by owners on a pro rata basis, which avoids double taxation of dividends.

   B. Operating losses may be claimed on a pro rata basis by stock-holders and deducted against their ordinary income.

   C. The investment tax credit can be passed through to individual stockholders.

VI. Financial markets bring together lenders and borrowers of money.

   A. There are many different financial markets in a developed economy.

   B. Each market deals with a somewhat different type of security, serves a different customer, or operates in a different geo-graphical area.

   C. The following markets are of most interest to financial man-agers.

      1. Money markets are the markets for short-term debt securi-ties, those securities that mature in less than 1 year.
      2. Capital markets are the markets for long-term debt and corporate stocks.
      3. Primary markets are the markets in which newly issued se-curities are sold for the first time.
      4. Secondary markets are the markets in which existing, out-standing securities are bought and sold.

VII. Transfers of capital between savers and borrowers take place in three different ways.

   A. Direct transfer occurs when money passes directly from the investor to the firm issuing the security.

   B. Transfer through an investment banking house occurs when a brokerage firm, such as Merrill Lynch, Pierce, Fenner & Smith, Inc., serves as a middleman.

   C. Transfer through a financial intermediary occurs when a bank or mutual fund obtains funds from savers, issues its own securities in exchange, and then uses these funds to purchase other securities.

VIII. The stock market is one of the most important markets to finan-cial managers since it is here that the price of each stock, hence the value of the firm, is established.

   A. There are two basic types of stock markets:

    1. The organized exchanges, which are typified by the New York Stock Exchange (NYSE) and the American Stock Exchange (AMEX), are tangible, physical entities.

    2. The over-the-counter (OTC) market is, basically, all the dealers, brokers, and communications facilities that provide for security transactions not conducted on the organized exchanges.

  B. Information on the transactions conducted on the organized exchanges and in the OTC market are reported in daily newspapers.

IX. Corporate bonds are traded less frequently than stocks.

  A. Over 95 percent of the bond trading which does occur takes place in the OTC market.

  B. Information on OTC market bond trades is not published, but a representative group of bonds is listed on the NYSE, and these trades are often reported in daily newspapers.

X. The interest rate is the price paid for borrowed capital.

  A. The level of interest rates is determined by the supply of, and demand for, investment capital.

    1. The demand for investment capital depends on the rate of return producers can expect to earn on invested capital.

    2. The supply of investment capital depends on consumers' time preferences for current versus future consumption.

  B. The real rate of interest (k*) is the equilibrium level of interest on a totally riskless debt security if there is zero inflation.

  C. The actual, or nominal, rate of interest is the real rate of interest plus premiums to compensate investors for inflation and risk.

    1. The inflation premium (IP), which is the average inflation rate expected over the life of the security, compensates the investor for the expected loss of purchasing power.

    2. The default risk premium (DP) compensates investors for the risk that a borrower will default, or not pay the interest or principal on a loan.

    3. A security which can be sold and quickly converted into cash at a fair price is said to be liquid. A liquidity premium (LP) is added to the real rate for securities that are not liquid.

    4. Long-term securities are more price sensitive to interest rate changes than are short-term securities. Therefore,

a maturity risk premium (MP) is added to longer-term securities to compensate investors for interest rate risk.

D. The nominal rate of interest can be expressed as $k = k^* + IP + DP + LP + MP$, where the values of the risk premiums vary among debt securities.

E. For very short-term U.S. Treasury securities, the default, liquidity, and maturity risk premiums are all zero. The interest rate on these securities, $k = k^* + IP$, is called the risk-free rate and is often referred to as R_F.

XI. The term structure of interest rates is the relationship between yield to maturity and term to maturity for bonds of a given default risk class.

A. This relationship when plotted produces a yield curve.

B. Yield curves have different shapes depending on expected inflation rates and supply and demand conditions.

1. If inflation, hence interest rates, are expected to remain constant or increase in the future, the yield curve will be upward sloping.
2. The yield curve will be downward sloping if investors expect inflation to decrease.
3. However, the shape of the yield curve is affected by supply and demand conditions, which are influenced by Federal Reserve actions in the short-term market, as well as by inflation expectations.

Definitional Questions

1. Sole proprietorships are easily formed, but they often have difficulty raising _____, subject proprietors to unlimited _____, and have a limited _____.

2. Partnership profits are taxed as _____ income in proportion to each partner's ownership.

3. A partnership is dissolved upon the _____ or _____ of any one of the partners. In addition, the difficulty of _____ _____ is a major disadvantage of the partnership form of business organization.

4. A corporation is a legal _____ created by a state, and it is separate from its _____ and managers.

5. The concept of _____ _____ means that a firm's stockholders are not personally liable for the debts of the business.

6. Capital is raised by a firm in two basic forms, _____ and _____.

7. _____ have first claim against a firm's income.

8. Common equity funds are obtained by a firm through the _____ of common stock, and by _____ earnings within the firm.

9. A _____ tax system is one in which tax rates are higher at higher levels of income.

10. In order to offset _____ _____, the first $_____ of an individual's dividend income is excluded from personal income taxes.

11. Interest received on _____ bonds is not subject to federal income taxes. This feature makes them particularly attractive to investors in _____ tax brackets.

12. In order to qualify as a long-term capital gain or loss, an asset must be held for more than _____ months.

13. Gains or losses on assets held less than 6 months are referred to as _____ transactions and are taxed as _____ _____.

14. Interest income received by a corporation is taxed as _____ income. However, only _____ percent of dividends received from another corporation is subject to taxation.

15. Another important distinction is that between interest and dividends paid by a corporation. Interest payments are _____, while dividend payments are made with _____ dollars.

16. Ordinary corporate operating losses can be carried back _____ years and forward _____ years.

17. A firm that refuses to pay dividends in order to help stockholders avoid personal income taxes may be subject to a penalty for _____ _____ of earnings.

18. A corporation that owns 80 percent or more of another corporation's stock may file _____ tax returns.

19. The _____ _____ credit, which is calculated as a percentage of the cost of _____ _____, reduces the effective cost of fixed assets and thus serves to stimulate _____.

20. The S option permits a corporation to be taxed at the owners' _____ tax rates and also avoids the impact of _____ _____ of dividends. It also permits a pro rata share of the corporation's _____ to be passed through to stockholders as personal deductions.

21. Markets for short-term debt securities are called _____ markets, while markets for long-term debt and equity are called _____ markets.

22. Newly issued securities are initially sold in the _____ market, while existing, outstanding securities are traded in the _____ market.

23. An institution which issues its own securities in exchange for funds and then uses these funds to purchase other securities is called a _____ _____.

24. The two basic types of stock markets are the _____ _____, such as the NYSE, and the _____ market.

25. The risk that a borrower will not pay the interest or principal on a loan is _____ risk.

26. _____ bonds have zero default risk.

27. The _____ premium is added to the real rate to protect investors against loss of purchasing power.

28. The nominal rate of interest is determined by adding the _____ premium plus the _____ risk premium plus the _____ premium plus the _____ risk premium to the real riskless rate of return.

29. The relationship between yield to maturity and term to maturity for bonds in a given default risk class is called the _____ _____ of interest rates, while the resulting plotted curve is the _____ curve.

30. The shape of the yield curve is determined by _____ expectations and _____ policy, plus other factors affecting supply and demand conditions.

Conceptual Questions

31. The fact that 85 percent of the dividends received by a corporation is excluded from taxable income has encouraged debt financing over equity financing.

    a. True   b. False

32. An individual with substantial personal wealth and income is considering the possibility of opening a new business. The business will have a relatively high degree of risk and losses may be incurred for the first several years. Which legal form of business organization would probably be best?

    a. Proprietorship
    b. Corporation
    c. Partnership
    d. S corporation
    e. Limited partnership

33. If the economy is about to enter a recession, and a firm needs to borrow money, it should probably use short-term rather than long-term debt.

    a. True   b. False

34. Long-term interest rates reflect expectations about future inflation. Inflation has varied greatly from year to year over the last 10 years, and, as a result, long-term rates have fluctuated more than short-term rates.

    a. True   b. False

Problems

35. In 1984, Wayne Corporation had income from operations of $385,000, received interest payments of $15,000, paid interest of $20,000, received dividends from another corporation of $10,000, and paid $40,000 in dividends to its common stockholders. What is Wayne's 1984 federal income tax?

    a. $122,760
    b. $141,700
    c. $155,240
    d. $163,500
    e. $175,490

36. A firm purchases corporate bonds having a before-tax interest yield of 16 percent. If the firm's marginal tax rate is 46 percent, what is the after-tax interest yield?

    a. 7.36%
    b. 8.64%
    c. 13.61%
    d. 14.90%
    e. 16.00%

37. Refer to Problem 36. The firm also invests in the common stock of another company having a 16 percent before-tax dividend yield. What is the after-tax dividend yield?

    a. 7.36%
    b. 8.64%
    c. 13.61%
    d. 14.90%
    e. 16.00%

38. The Berwyn Company's taxable income and income tax payments are shown below for 1980 through 1983:

Year	Taxable Income	Tax Payment
1980	$10,000	$1,700
1981	5,000	850
1982	10,000	1,700
1983	5,000	850

    Assume that Berwyn's tax rate for all 4 years was a flat 17 percent; that is, each dollar of taxable income was taxed at 17 percent. In 1984, Berwyn incurred a loss of $17,000. Using corporate loss carry-back, what is Berwyn's adjusted tax payment for 1983?

a. $850
b. $750
c. $610
d. $550
e. $510

39. Prime Company has taxable income of $100,000 in 1984, thus the calculated tax payment is $25,750. However, Prime purchased a capital asset that cost $10,000 and which qualifies for a 10 percent investment tax credit. What is Prime's total tax payment?

a. $0
b. $23,175
c. $24,750
d. $25,000
e. $25,250

40. Assume that a 3 year Treasury note has no maturity risk premium or liquidity premium and that the real rate of interest (real riskless rate) is 2 percent. The T-note carries a yield to maturity of 12 percent. If the expected inflation rate is 12 percent next year and 10 percent the year after, what is the implied expected inflation rate for the third year?

a. 8%
b. 9%
c. 10%
d. 11%
e. 12%

Answers and Solutions

1. capital; liability; life

2. personal

3. withdrawal; death; transferring ownership

4. entity; owners

5. limited liability

6. debt; equity

7. Creditors

8. sale; retaining

9. progressive

10. double taxation; 100

11. municipal; high

12. 6

13. short-term; ordinary income

14. ordinary; 15

15. tax-deductible; after-tax

16. 3; 15

17. improper accumulation

18. consolidated

19. investment tax; new assets; investment

20. personal; double taxation; losses

21. money; capital

22. primary; secondary

23. financial intermediary

24. organized exchanges; over-the-counter (OTC)

25. default

26. U.S. Treasury

27. inflation

28. inflation; default; liquidity; maturity

29. term structure; yield

30. inflation; Federal Reserve

31. b. Debt financing is encouraged by the fact that interest payments are tax deductible while dividend payments are not.

32. d. The S option limits the liability of the individual, but permits losses to be deducted against personal income.

33. a. The firm should borrow short-term until interest rates drop due to the recession, then go long-term.

34. b. Fluctuations in long-term rates are dampened because the long-term inflation premium is an average of inflation expectations over many years.

35. c. The first step is to determine taxable income:

Income from operations	$385,000
Interest income (fully taxable)	15,000
Interest expense (fully deductible)	(20,000)
Dividend income (15% taxable)	1,500
Total	$381,500

(Note that dividends are paid from after-tax income and do not affect taxable income.)

Based on the 1983 corporate tax table, the tax calculation is as follows:

15% of first $25,000	$ 3,750
18% of next $25,000	4,500
30% of next $25,000	7,500
40% of next $25,000	10,000
46% of $281,500	129,490
Total tax	$155,240

36. b. The after-tax yield (or dollar return) equals the before-tax yield (or dollar return) multiplied by one minus the effective tax rate, or

$$AT = BT(1 - \text{Effective } T).$$

Therefore,

$$AT = 16\%(1 - 46\%) = 16\%(1 - 0.46) = 16\%(0.54)$$
$$= 8.64\%.$$

37. d. Since the dividends are received by a corporation, only 15 percent are taxable, and the Effective T = tax rate x 15 percent:

$$AT = BT(1 - \text{Effective } T) = 16\%(1 - 46\% \times 15\%)$$
$$= 16\%(1 - 0.46 \times 0.15) = 16\%(1 - 0.069)$$
$$= 16\%(0.931) = 14.90\%.$$

38. e.

Year	Taxable Income	Tax Payment	Adjusted Taxable Income	Adjusted Tax Payment
1980	$10,000	$1,700	$10,000	$1,700
1981	5,000	850	0	0
1982	10,000	1,700	0	0
1983	5,000	850	3,000	510

The carry-back can only go back 3 years. Thus, there was no adjustment made in 1978. After $5,000 of adjustment in 1979 and $10,000 in 1980, there was $2,000 loss remaining to apply to 1981. The 1981 adjusted tax payment is $3,000(0.17) = $510. Thus, Berwyn received a total of $2,890 in tax refunds after the adjustment.

39. c. The investment tax credit (ITC) is a direct reduction of taxes by the ITC percentage multiplied by the cost of the qualifying asset. Therefore, direct reduction = $10,000(0.10) = $1,000; tax payment = $25,750 - $1,000 = $24,750.

40. a. $k = k* + IP$
     $12\% = 2\% + IP$
     $IP = 10\%.$

Thus, investors expect inflation to average 10 percent over the next 3 years. Therefore, $10\% = (12\% + 10\% + X)/3$; $X = 8\%$.

CHAPTER 3

FINANCIAL RATIO ANALYSIS

Overview

This chapter describes the basic financial statements and discusses the techniques used by investors and managers to analyze these statements. Financial analysis is designed to determine the relative strengths and weaknesses of a company. Investors need this information to estimate both future cash flows from the firm and the riskiness of these flows. Financial managers need this information to evaluate their own performance and map future plans. The study of financial analysis is concentrated on a set of ratios designed to highlight the key aspects of a firm's operation. The ratios for a given firm are calculated, then compared with those of other firms in the same industry to judge the relative strength of the firm being analyzed. Trends in ratios are also considered in the analysis. Although ratio analysis has limitations, when used with care and judgment, it can be most helpful.

Outline

I. The firm's financial statements provide the data needed to calculate the financial ratios of the firm and to analyze its position.

   A. The balance sheet shows the firm's assets and claims on assets and represents its financial condition at a point in time.

      1. Assets, found on the left-hand side of the balance sheet, are typically shown in the order of their liquidity. Claims, found on the right-hand side, are generally listed in the order in which they are to be paid.
      2. Assets expected to be converted to cash within one year are defined as current assets. Assets not expected to be converted to cash within one year are called fixed assets.
      3. Claims against assets are made up of liabilities and the stockholders' ownership positions.

   B. The income statement reports the income and expenses of operations during an interval of time. Earnings per share is generally considered to be the most important item shown on this statement.

C. The statement of retained earnings shows the amount of net income reinvested in the business.

    1. Retained earnings represent funds reinvested in the business over a period of years.

    2. Retained earnings are usually not held as cash, and therefore, are not available for the payment of dividends or anything else.

II. Financial statements can be analyzed from different points of view. Investors are interested in past events primarily as an aid in predicting future success or failure. Management analyzes the data in order to anticipate future events and to improve operations. Financial ratios are a useful tool in the analysis of financial statements.

A. Liquidity ratios measure the firm's ability to meet its current obligations as they come due.

    1. The current ratio (current assets divided by current liabilities) is a measure of the extent to which short-term creditors are covered by short-term assets.

        a. Current assets include cash, marketable securities, accounts receivable, and inventories.

        b. Current liabilities consist of accounts payable, short-term notes payable, current maturities of long-term debt, accrued income taxes, and other accrued expenses.

    2. The quick ratio, or acid test, is calculated by deducting inventories from current assets and dividing the remainder by current liabilities. This ratio measures short-term solvency but removes inventories from the calculation because inventories are the least liquid of a firm's current assets, and their liquidation frequently results in losses.

B. Leverage ratios measure the extent to which the firm has been financed by debt. Creditors look to the equity to provide a margin of safety, but by raising funds through debt, owners gain the benefits of maintaining control of the firm with a limited investment. If a firm earns more on borrowed funds than it pays in interest, the return to the owners is magnified.

    1. The debt to total assets ratio, or the debt ratio, measures the percentage of total funds that have been provided by creditors.

      a. The lower the ratio, the greater the protection against creditors' losses in the event of liquidation.

      b. Owners may seek high leverage either to magnify earnings or because raising new equity means giving up some degree of control.

2. The times-interest-earned ratio is calculated by dividing net income before interest and taxes by the interest charges. It measures the extent to which earnings can decline yet still be sufficient to meet fixed interest costs.

3. The fixed charge coverage ratio--net income before interest, taxes, and lease obligations divided by interest charges plus lease obligations--generalizes the preceding ratio by adding fixed charges such as long-term lease payments to recognize the increasing use of lease arrangements.

4. Cash flow coverage is calculated as cash inflows divided by the sum of fixed charges plus preferred stock dividends and debt principal repayment on a before-tax basis and measures a firm's ability to meet cash obligations. Depreciation, a noncash expense, is added to the numerator, and the nontax-deductible expenses in the denominator are adjusted by dividing by 1 minus the tax rate (1 - T).

C. Activity ratios measure how effectively a firm is using its resources and whether or not the level of the firm's assets is properly related to sales.

1. Inventory turnover, defined as sales or cost of goods sold divided by average inventory, measures the efficiency of inventory utilization.

      a. A high inventory turnover demonstrates that a company does not hold excessive stocks of inventory.

      b. The average figure should be adjusted if the firm's business is highly seasonal or if there has been a strong upward or downward sales trend during the year.

2. The average collection period represents the average length of time that a firm must wait after making a sale before receiving cash. Annual sales are divided by 360 to get average daily sales, which are then divided into accounts receivable to find the number of days' sales are tied up in receivables.

      a. The average collection period is compared to the terms on which the firm sells its goods to determine the firm's efficiency in collecting accounts receivable.

  b. The average collection period should be supplemented with the aging schedule. This groups accounts receivable according to how long they have been outstanding.

 3. Fixed asset turnover (sales divided by fixed assets) measures the utilization or the efficiency of fixed assets; a low ratio indicates idle capacity of assets.

 4. Total asset turnover is the ratio of sales to total assets. It measures the overall utilization of assets. A low ratio indicates that the company is not generating an adequate volume of business for the size of its asset investment.

D. Profitability ratios measure management's overall effectiveness as shown by the returns generated on sales and investment.

 1. The profit margin is calculated by dividing net profit after taxes by sales. A profit margin somewhat below the industry average indicates that the firm's sales prices are relatively low or that its costs are relatively high, or both.

 2. The basic earning power of assets ratio is calculated by dividing the earnings before interest and taxes (EBIT) by total assets.

 3. Net profit to total assets measures the return on the firm's total investment, or the ROI. A low ratio can result from a low profit margin on sales, or from a low turnover of total assets, or both.

 4. Net income to shareholders' equity or net worth indicates the rate of return on the stockholders' investment.

E. Growth ratios measure how well the firm is maintaining its economic position in the general economy and within its own industry.

 1. Growth rate analysis must separate real growth from nominal growth which includes the influence of inflation.

 2. To find the growth rate over a period of time, divide the last period figure by the first period figure to obtain a compound sum interest factor. The percent growth rate can then be determined from the compound interest tables.

F. Valuation ratios reflect the combined influence of risk ratios and return ratios.

 1. The price/earnings ratio, or price per share divided by earnings per share, shows the amount that investors are currently willing to pay per dollar of reported earnings. It is positively related to a firm's growth prospects and inversely related to risk.

2. Another indicator of investors' feelings is the market to book value ratio, defined as market value per share divided by book value per share. Higher ratios are generally associated with firms that have a high rate of return on common equity.

III. Ratio analysis of financial statements can provide meaningful information; however, care must be taken in performing the analysis and in interpreting the results.

A. Individual ratios based on one year's data are not very useful. The trend of a particular ratio over a period of time, or this relationship to some meaningful average, is a better indicator of the firm's actual financial condition.

B. Comparative ratio analysis can be performed using information from financial sources such as Dun & Bradstreet, Robert Morris Associates, and the Federal Trade Commission.

C. The emphasis of financial ratio analysis varies with the requirements of the analysis.

1. The emphasis in credit analysis is on the ability to repay short-term debts.
2. Among the qualitative factors considered by the credit manager are the economic position of the customer firm and its managerial qualities, as well as his own firm's profit margin.
3. The principal emphasis in security analysis is on the long-run profit potential of the firm. The focus is on activity, profitability, and leverage ratios.

D. When a company's ratios depart from the industry norm, there is a need to question and analyze further to determine whether there is a sound explanation for the variance or whether changes in policies or correction of management practices is required.

E. There are a number of limitations to ratio analysis.

1. Ratios may be distorted by seasonal factors or manipulated by management to give the impression of a sound financial condition.
2. The use of industry averages may not provide a very challenging target for high-level performance.
3. Different operating policies, such as the decision to lease rather than buy equipment, may have an impact of financial ratios.
4. Many ratios can be interpreted in different ways. Whether a particular result is good or bad will depend on the outcome of a complete financial analysis rather than the level of a single ratio.

Definitional Questions

1. The _____ _____ lists the firm's assets as well as _____ against those assets.

2. Typically, assets are listed in order of their _____, while _____ are listed in order of payment.

3. The _____ statement reports the results of operations during the past year, the most important item being _____ _____ _____.

4. _____ _____ represent income earned by the firm in past years that has not been paid out in _____.

5. Retained earnings are generally reinvested in _____ _____ and are not held in the form of _____.

6. The current ratio and acid test ratio are examples of _____ ratios. They measure a firm's ability to meet its _____ obligations.

7. Current _____ include cash, marketable securities, accounts _____, and inventories.

8. Current liabilities consist of _____ payable, notes payable, _____ income taxes, and accrued expenses.

9. Leverage ratios are used to evaluate the firm's use of _____.

10. The debt ratio, which is the ratio of _____ to _____ _____, measures the proportion of funds supplied by _____.

11. The _____ ratio is calculated by dividing earnings before interest and taxes by the amount of _____ charges.

12. _____ _____ _____ measures a firm's ability to meet cash obligations.

13. The average collection period is found by dividing _____ _____ by _____, and then dividing average sales per day into accounts _____. The average collection period is the length of time that a firm must wait after making a sale before it receives _____.

14. _____ ratios measure management's overall effectiveness as shown by the returns generated on _____ and investments.

15. Dividing net profit after tax by sales gives the _____ _____ on sales.

16. The _____ ratio measures how much investors are willing to pay for each dollar of a firm's reported profits.

17. Firms with high rates of return on stockholder's equity tend to sell at relatively high ratios of _____ _____ to _____ _____.

18. Individual ratios are of little value in analyzing a company's financial condition. More important are the _____ of a ratio over time and the comparison of the company's ratios to _____ _____ ratios.

19. The emphasis in credit analysis is on the ability to repay _____ _____, while _____ analysis emphasizes long-run profitability.

Conceptual_Questions

20. Southwest Industries, Inc., has a current ratio of 0.5. Which of the following actions would improve (increase) this ratio?

    a. Use cash to pay off current liabilities.
    b. Collect some of the current accounts receivable.
    c. Use cash to pay off some long-term debt.
    d. Purchase additional inventory on credit.
    e. Sell some of the existing inventory at cost.

21. A high quick ratio is always a good indicator of a well-managed liquidity position.

    a. True   b. False

22. An average collection period of 42 days in an industry where the norm is 35 days indicates poor receivables management.

    a. True   b. False

23. Credit analysts are concerned primarily with:

    a. Profitability ratios.
    b. Growth ratios.
    c. Valuation ratios.
    d. Leverage ratios.
    e. Activity ratios.

Problems

(The following financial statements apply to the next five problems).

Regal Lighting Corporation
Balance Sheet
December 31, 1984
(Thousands of Dollars)

Assets		Liabilities	
Cash	$ 70	Accounts payable	$150
Accounts receivable	425	Notes payable	250
Inventories	325	Other current liabilities	75
Total current assets	$820	Total current liabilities	$475
Net fixed assets	180	Long-term debt	200
		Shareholder's equity	325
Total assets	$1,000	Total claims on assets	$1,000

Regal Lighting Corporation
Income Statement
for Year Ended December 31, 1984
(Thousands of Dollars)

Sales	$1,800
Cost of goods sold	1,220
Gross profit	$ 580
Operating expenses	490
Net operating income	$ 90
Interest expense	53
Earnings before tax	$ 37
Tax at 40%	15
Net income	$ 22

24. Calculate the liquidity ratios, that is, the current ratio and the quick ratio.

    a. 1.73; 1,04
    b. 1.73; 0.90
    c. 1.85; 1.04
    d. 1.85; 0.90
    e. 1.67; 1.09

25. Calculate the debt ratio and the times-interest-earned ratio.

    a. 0.75; 1.70
    b. 0.48; 1.52
    c. 0.68; 0.70
    d. 0.75; 1.52
    e. 0.68; 1.70

26. Calculate the activity ratios, that is, the inventory turnover ratio, the fixed asset turnover ratio, the total asset turnover ratio, and the average collection period.

    a. 5.54; 10.00; 1.60; 78.50 days
    b. 5.34; 10.00; 1.95; 90.30 days
    c. 5.54; 10.10; 1.80; 85.00 days
    d. 5.34; 10.10; 1.60; 90.30 days
    e. 5.54; 10.00; 1.80; 85.00 days

27. Calculate the profitability ratios, that is, the profit margin on sales, the basic earnings power of assets, the return on total assets, and the return on common equity.

    a. 1.22%; 9.50%; 2.20%; 6.77%
    b. 1.18%; 9.00%; 2.45%; 7.35%
    c. 1.22%; 9.00%; 2.20%; 6.77%
    d. 1.35%; 9.50%; 2.45%; 6.40%
    e. 1.35%; 9.00%; 2.45%; 7.35%

28. Calculate the price/earnings ratio and the market to book value ratio. Regal had an average of 4,000 shares outstanding during 1984, and the stock price on December 31, 1984, was $27.50.

    a. 5.52; 1.48
    b. 5.00; 0.34
    c. 4.68; 1.48
    d. 5.00; 1.48
    e. 4.68; 0.34

29. The Gamble Company has sales of $1,187,000 per year, all of which are credit sales. Their average collection period is 21 days. What is their average accounts receivable?

    a. $79,242
    b. $169,000
    c. $100,000
    d. $69,242
    e. $87,359

30. If a firm has total interest charges of $20,000 per year, sales of $1,800,000, a tax rate of 40 percent, and a profit margin of 4 percent, what is the firm's times-interest-earned ratio?

    a. 6
    b. 7
    c. 8
    d. 9
    e. 10

Answers and Solutions

1. balance sheet; claims

2. liquidity; liabilities

3. income; earnings per share

4. Retained earnings; dividends

5. operating assets; cash

6. liquidity; short-term

7. assets; receivable

8. accounts; accrued

9. debt

10. debt; total assets; creditors

11. times-interest-earned; interest

12. Cash flow coverage

13. annual sales; 360; receivable; cash

14. Profitability; sales

15. profit margin

16. price/earnings

17. market price; book value

18. trend; industry average

19. short-term debts; security

20. d.   This question is best analyzed using numbers.   For example, assume current assets = $50 and current liabilities = $100; thus, the current ratio = 0.5.   For answer a, assume $5 in cash is used to pay off $5 in current liabilities.   The new current ratio would be $45/$95 = 0.47.   For answer d, assume a $10 purchase of inventory on credit.   The new current ratio would be $60/$110 = 0.55, which is an increase over the old current ratio of 0.50.

21. b.   Excess cash, a result of poor management, would produce a high quick ratio.

22. b.   The average collection period must be compared to the firm's credit terms before a judgment can be made concerning the firm's efficiency in collecting accounts receivable.   The firm may not be managing its receivables well, or it may sell on terms that are lenient as compared to the industry norm.

23. d.   Credit analysts are not primarily interested in the long-term growth prospects or the valuation of a firm.   They are concerned with how much of the firm's assets are financed with debt, and the extent to which the firm's earnings are capable of covering interest charges.

24. a.   Current ratio = Current assets/Current liabilities
                    = $820/$475
                    = 1.73.

    Quick ratio = (Current assets - Inventory)/Current liabilities
                = $495/$475
                = 1.04.

25. e.   Debt ratio = Total debt/Total assets
                   = $675/$1,000
                   = 0.68.

    TIE ratio = Net Income/Interest
              = $90/$53
              = 1.70.

26. e.   Inventory turnover = Sales/Inventories
                           = $1,800/$325
                           = 5.54.

    Fixed asset turnover = Sales/Fixed assets
                         = $1,800/$180
                         = 10.00.

    Total asset turnover = Sales/Total assets
                         = $1,800/$1,000
                         = 1.80.

    Average collection period = (Accounts receivable)/(Sales/360)
                              = ($425)/($1,800/360)
                              = 85 days.

27. c. Profit margin = Net income/Sales
                       = $22/$1,800
                       = 1.22%.

         Basic earnings power = Net operating income/Total assets
                              = $90/$1,000
                              = 9.00%.

         Return on total assets = Net income/Total assets
                                = $22/$1,000
                                = 2.20%.

         Return on common equity = Net income/Common equity
                                 = $22/$325
                                 = 6.77%.

28. b. EPS = Net income/Number of shares outstanding
             = $22,000/4,000
             = $5.50.

         P/E ratio = Price/EPS
                   = $27.50/$5.50
                   = 5.00.

         Market/book value = Market value/Book value
                           = ($27.50)(4,000)/$325,000
                           = 0.34.

29. d.   ACP = Accounts receivable/(Sales/360)
         21 days = AR/($1,187,000/360)
              AR = $69,242.

30. b.   Net profit = $1,800,000 (0.04) = $72,000.
         Earnings before taxes = $72,000/0.60 = $120,000.
                           NOI = $120,000 + $20,000 = $140,000.
                           TIE = NOI/Interest
                               = $140,000/$20,000 = 7.

CHAPTER 4

FINANCIAL FORECASTING

Overview

Growing firms constantly require new investment in assets to finance sales growth. Some of the capital required to acquire and service assets can be obtained through retained earnings, but if the growth rate is high, even a very profitable firm will need external capital. The cost per dollar of external capital raised declines as the size of the issue increases; therefore, new debt and equity funding is typically raised in large increments at long intervals. To avoid cash flow problems, financial managers must use the forecasting techniques presented in this chapter to estimate the need for funds during the planning period.

Outline

I. Both managers and investors are concerned about the impact of future operations and alternative plans on the future financial condition of the firm. Pro forma, or projected, statements are useful in forecasting the results of different courses of action.

    A. The most important element in financial planning is the sales forecast.

    B. Sales forecasting is a corporate activity, and most large firms have a specialized staff to carry it out.

II. Causality and stability are basic relationships required in any forecasting model.

    A. Sales demand is the causal variable motivating firms to invest in the various asset accounts.

        1. Some asset accounts, such as fixed assets and raw materials inventories, must increase before sales can occur. Investments in these accounts lead sales.

        2. Investments in other asset accounts lag sales. Accounts receivables lag sales because accounts receivables are created after sales are made.

B. Forecasting models require relative stability in the relationships between individual asset items and sales.

C. Two basic methods of forecasting are the percent-of-sales method and the regression method.

III. The percent-of-sales method is widely used to forecast a firm's financial requirements and to measure the impact of financial plans and policies on operations.

A. The first step in the percent-of-sales method of forecasting is to express various balance sheet items as a percentage of sales.

1. Only asset accounts of significant size that vary directly with sales need to be calculated.
2. Cash, receivables, and inventories are items that typically increase with an expansion of sales. Fixed assets may not have to increase with sales if the firm is operating at less than full capacity.
3. Certain liability accounts, such as accounts payable and accruals, will increase spontaneously with sales. Retained earnings will increase but not proportionately with sales.

B. Once the balance sheet percentages have been determined and a forecast of sales and costs has been made, a pro forma financial statement can be constructed.

C. Increases in assets require new financing; liabilities grow spontaneously with sales and provide a spontaneous source of funds. The difference between the required financing for growth in asset accounts and the spontaneously generated funds from liability increases represents the firm's total financing requirements. Financing needs are normally first met by internally generated increases in retained earnings. Under normal conditions, a significant increase in sales will require additional long-term financing. If a need for long-term financing is indicated, management must evaluate the various possible external sources of funds, such as borrowing or selling new common stock.

1. Restrictions in existing debt contracts may limit a firm's ability to borrow.
2. Equity capital, in addition to retained earnings, may be necessary to finance the increase in sales.

D. Although the forecast of capital requirements can be made by constructing pro forma financial statements, it is often easier to use a simple forecasting formula. In addition, the formula can be used to clearly show the relationship between sales growth and financing requirements.

1. The formula for calculating financing requirements is as follows:

$$\text{External funds required} = \text{EFR} = \frac{A}{S}(\Delta S) - \frac{D_s}{S}(\Delta S) - mb(S_1),$$

where

$\frac{A}{S}$ = Assets that increase spontaneously with sales as a percentage of sales.

S_1 = Total sales projected for next year.

$\frac{D_s}{S}$ = Liabilities that increase spontaneously with sales as a percentage of sales.

ΔS = Change in sales = $(S_1 - S)$.

m = Profit margin on sales.

b = Earnings retention ratio = (1.0 - Dividend payout ratio).

2. The equation must be used with caution if excess capacity exists in any of the asset accounts.
3. The equation can also be used to calculate the maximum growth rate that can be financed without external funds. This is done by setting the additional funds requirement equal to zero and solving for the growth rate in sales.
4. If management cannot (or does not wish to) use external financing, it may have to limit potential growth and turn away sales beyond some specific amount.

E. The forecasting process is greatly complicated if the ratios of balance sheet items to sales are not constant at all levels of sales.

1. The "lumpiness" of additions to fixed assets makes the ratio of fixed assets to sales relatively unstable.
2. Excess operating capacity will also influence the stability of other ratios. Such excess capacity is often related to movements in the overall business cycle.

F. The percent-of-sales method of forecasting is neither simple nor mechanical.

1. It is important to understand the basic technology of the firm and the logic of the relationship between its sales and assets.
2. The percent-of-sales method is best used to forecast relatively short-term changes in financing needs.

IV. The regression method calculates average relationships over a period of time. It is more general than the percent-of-sales method and more accurate if a large growth rate is projected or if the forecast is for a period of several years.

   A. Regression analysis develops relationships based on sales as the independent variable and on the asset item as the dependent variable. A scatter diagram plots sales on the horizontal scale and the asset item on the vertical scale.

   B. Regression analysis involves several steps.

      1. First, the firm's sales are projected for the time period under consideration.
      2. Next, the relationships between sales and major asset, liability, and equity accounts are plotted on a scatter diagram. A regression line is fit to the scatter diagram by free-hand or numerical calculation.
      3. Finally, the projected regression equations are used to determine the level of each balance sheet category for the forecast value of sales.
      4. The difference between total asset requirements and financing sources directly related to sales indicates financial requirements.

V. Both forecasting techniques offer the advantage of being simple and easy to apply and both supply a good basis for quick review of more complicated methodologies. However, there are significant differences between the two methods.

   A. The percent-of-sales method assumes that certain balance sheet items vary directly with sales; it implicitly assumes a linear relationship that passes through the origin. The scatter diagram method does not assume that the line of relationship passes through the origin.

   B. For short-term forecasts, such as month-to-month, either the percent-of-sales method or the regression method may be employed. For longer term forecasts, it is best to use the regression method to avoid major errors that might result from systematic shifts in the ratios.

   C. The following are some guidelines for use of the percentage method versus the regression method:

      1. When the regression line has a nonzero intercept, the use of the percent-of-sales method for forecasting would involve error.
      2. In general, the regression method is more dependable as a method for forecasting.
      3. Either method provides about the same results under three circumstances:

          a. The regression line has a small intercept (close to zero).

          b. For monthly forecasts or other circumstances in which sales do not vary greatly, the percent-of-sales method will provide reasonably dependable control estimates.

          c. The rate of inflation is so high that the changes in the numbers dominate the base stock (or intercept) figure.

      4. The costs of using more refined techniques (such as multiple regression) must be weighed against the benefits of increased forecast accuracy.

VI. The statement of changes in financial position, called the sources and uses of funds statement, reports how funds were obtained by the firm, how they were used, and how the firm's liquidity position changed during the year.

    A. Financial forecasting is used to plan for financing requirements, such as a bank loan.

    B. The statement of changes in financial position, or sources and uses of funds statement, can help answer three questions of interest to potential lenders as well as to management and other parties:

      1. What has the firm done with its funds in the past?
      2. What does the firm plan to do with the new funds?
      3. How will it repay the loan?

    C. In financial analysis, depreciation is often considered an important source of funds.

      1. Depreciation is a non-cash charge against income to allocate the cost of long-term assets used in the production process.

      2. Depreciation may be considered a source of funds only so long as there are actual sales revenues against which the charge can be made.

    D. The statement is constructed by analyzing changes in balance sheet items from one year to the next.

      1. A source of funds is either a decrease in an asset account or an increase in a liability account.

      2. A use of funds is either an increase in an asset account or a decrease in a liability account.

      3. In the sources and uses of funds statement, net income is considered a source of funds, while dividends are a use. These items are not netted out as retained earnings.

      4. Changes in net working capital, or current assets minus current liabilities, are used to measure changes in a firm's liquidity position.

E. The sources and uses of funds statement can show how funds
were acquired and used in the past; and on a pro forma basis,
it can show how a firm plans to acquire and use funds in the
future.

Definitional Questions

1. The most important element in financial planning is the forecast
of _____.

2. _____ _____ is the variable which motivates firms to invest in
various asset accounts.

3. Forecasting models require that the relationships between individual asset items and sales be relatively _____.

4. Two widely used methods of forecasting _____ _____ are the
percent-of- sales method and the _____ method.

5. Those asset items that typically increase proportionately with
higher sales are _____, _____, and _____.

6. Typically, certain liabilities will rise _____ with sales.
These include accounts _____ and _____.

7. A significant increase in sales may require additional _____
_____, which will be met by borrowing or selling _____ _____.

8. The equation for external funds required can be used to calculate
the maximum _____ rate that can be financed without _____
funds.

9. The percent-of-sales method assumes that the _____ of balance
sheet items to _____ is _____ at all levels of sales.

10. The assumption of constant percentage of sales ratios may not be
accurate due to the _____ of increments in _____ assets.

11. The regression method calculates _____ relationships over time.

12. A _____ _____ plots sales against asset items.

13. The statement of _____ _____ _____ _____ shows how funds were
acquired and used in the past.

14. An _____ in a claim against assets or a decrease in an _____

account is a source of funds.

15. A decrease in a _____ account or an _____ in an asset account is a use of funds.

16. _____ _____, or projected sources and uses of funds statements show how a firm _____ to acquire and use funds in the future.

17. As the dividend _____ _____ is increased, the amount of earnings available to finance a new asset is _____.

Conceptual Questions

18. An increase in a firm's inventories will call for additional financing unless the increase is matched by an equal or larger increase in some other asset account.

    a. True   b. False

19. If the dividend payout ratio is 100 percent, the financial ratios are held constant, and the firm is operating at full capacity, any increase in sales will require additional financing.

    a. True   b. False

20. Which of the following would reduce the additional funds required if all other things are held constant?

    a. An increase in the dividend payout ratio
    b. A decrease in the profit margin
    c. An increase in the expected sales growth rate
    d. A decrease in the firm's tax rate
    e. An increase in the amount of assets required per dollar of sales

21. Which of the following account changes would be classified as a use of funds?

    a. A decrease in accounts receivable
    b. An increase in retained earnings
    c. A decrease in long-term debt
    d. A decrease in cash
    e. An increase in accounts payable

Problems

22. Tandon, Inc., had the following balance sheet for the year ended December 31, 1984.

Assets		Liabilities	
Current assets	$60,000	Accounts payable	$18,000
Fixed assets	40,000	Notes payable	10,000
		Long-term debt	9,000
		Common equity	63,000
Total assets	$100,000	Total claims	$100,000

Business has been booming, and the firm is growing rapidly. The sales manager believes that 1985 sales will be 50 percent greater than the 1984 level of $200,000. Since the firm is operating at full capacity, additional fixed assets will be required to meet the increase sales demand. The company's treasurer predicts that net income before taxes will be 15 percent; the firm's tax rate is 40 percent. The firm will retain all earnings in 1985. What is next year's external funding requirement?

a. $0
b. $4,000
c. $9,000
d. $14,000
e. $18,000

23. The 1984 balance sheet for Blue Sky Tractors is shown below (dollars in millions):

Assets		Liabilities	
Cash	$ 3.0	Accounts payable	$ 3.0
Accounts receivable	4.0	Accruals	1.0
Inventory	3.0	Notes payable	1.0
Current assets	$10.0	Long-term debt	5.0
Fixed assets	5.0	Common equity	5.0
Total assets	$15.0	Total claims	$15.0

Management believes that sales will increase in 1985 by 20 percent to a total of $24 million. The profit margin is expected to be 8 percent, and the dividend payout ratio is targeted at 20 percent. The firm has excess capacity and no increase in fixed assets will be required. What is the additional funding requirement for 1985?

a. -$0.34 million
b. -$0.16 million
c. $0 million
d. $0.16 million
e. $0.34 million

24. Refer to Problem 23. Assume all of the above except that there had been no excess capacity in plant and equipment; therefore, the assets must increase spontaneously with sales. How much in additional funds will be required?

    a. -$0.66 million
    b. -$0.34 million
    c. $0 million
    d. $0.34 million
    e. $0.66 million

25. Refer to Problem 23. Assume no excess capacity exists. How much can sales grow without requiring any external funding?

    a. 12.38%
    b. 13.17%
    c. 14.65%
    d. 15.22%
    e. 16.81%

26. Leisure Crafts, Inc., has a net income this year of $500 on sales of $2,000 and is operating its fixed assets at full capacity. Management expects sales to increase by 20 percent next year and is forecasting a dividend payout ratio of 30 percent. The profit margin is not expected to change. If spontaneous liabilities are $500 this year, and no excess funds are expected next year, what is Leisure Crafts' total assets this year?

    a. $1,000
    b. $1,500
    c. $2,250
    d. $3,000
    e. $3,500

(The following balance sheets apply to the next two problems.)

Ameritronics Corporation
Balance Sheets
(Millions of Dollars)

	December 31, 1983	December 31, 1984
Cash	$ 45	$ 21
Marketable securities	33	0
Net receivables	66	90
Inventories	159	225
Total current assets	$303	$336
Gross fixed assets	225	450
Less: Accumulated depreciation	(78)	(123)
Net fixed assets	147	327
Total assets	$450	$663
Accounts payable	$ 45	$ 54
Notes payable	45	9
Other current liabilities	21	45
Long-term debt	24	78
Common stock	114	192
Retained earnings	201	285
Total claims on assets	$450	$663

During 1984, the company earned $114 million after taxes, of which $30 million were paid out as dividends.

27. Looking only at the balance sheet accounts, what are the total sources of funds (which must equal the total uses of funds) for 1984?

    a. $213 million
    b. $286 million
    c. $351 million
    d. $428 million
    e. $531 million

28. What are the total sources and total uses of working capital for 1984?

    a. $351 million; $351 million
    b. $351 million; $291 million
    c. $291 million; $255 million
    d. $255 million; $291 million
    e. $291 million; $351 million

Answers_and_Solutions

1. sales

2. Sales demand

3. stable

4. financial requirements; regression

5. cash; receivables; inventories

6. spontaneously; payable; accruals

7. long-term financing; common stock

8. growth; external

9. ratio; sales; constant

10. "lumpiness"; fixed

11. average

12. scatter diagram

13. changes in financial position

14. increase; asset

15. liability; increase

16. Pro forma; plans

17. payout ratio; retained; decreased

18. a.   When an increase in an asset account is not offset by an equivalent decrease in an asset account, then financing is needed to re-establish equilibrium on the balance sheet.

19. a.   With no retained earnings, to avoid external financing, any growth in assets must be matched by a growth in spontaneous liabilities. When operating at full capacity, all assets are spontaneous, but all liabilities cannot be spontaneous since a firm must have common equity. Thus, the growth in assets cannot be matched by a growth in spontaneous liabilities and additional financing will be required.

20. d.

21. c. A use of funds is a decrease in a liability or equity account or an increase in an asset account. Therefore, only a decrease in long-term debt qualifies as a use of funds.

22. d. Look at next year's balance sheet.

Assets		Liabilities	
Current assets	$ 90,000	Accounts payable	$ 27,000
Net fixed assets	60,000	Notes payable	10,000
		Long-term debt	9,000
		Common equity	90,000
Total assets	$150,000	Total claims	$136,000

Increase in common equity = (0.60)(0.15)($200,000 X 1.5)
                          = (0.60)(0.15)($300,000)
                          = $27,000.

With no dividends paid out, the common equity account increases to $90,000. Thus, the additional financing requirement is $150,000 - $136,000 = $14,000.

23. a. Since fixed assets are sufficient to absorb the increase in sales, this item is not included in the computation. Therefore, only $10 million of the $15 million in total assets will increase spontaneously with sales. On the right side of the balance sheet, only accounts payable and accruals increase spontaneously with sales. Therefore,

$$EFR = (A/S)(\Delta S) - (B/S)(\Delta S) - mb(S_1)$$

$$= (\$10/\$20)(\$4) - (\$4/\$20)(\$4) - (0.08)(0.80)(\$24)$$

$$= \$2.0 - 0.8 - 1.54$$

$$= - \$0.34 \text{ million.}$$

This means that the increased profits and spontaneously generated liabilities are sufficient to support the additional assets required. Thus, no additional funds will be required. In fact, there will be an internally generated surplus of funds of $340,000.

24. e. $EFR = (A/S)(\Delta S) - (B/S)(\Delta S) - mb(S_1)$

$$= (\$15/\$20)(\$4) - (\$4/\$20)(\$4) - (0.08)(0.80)(\$24)$$

$$= \$3.0 - \$0.8 - \$1.54$$

$$= \$0.66 \text{ million.}$$

25. b. Note that g = sales growth = $\Delta S/S$, and

$S_1 = S_0(1 + g)$. Then,

EFR = $(A)(g) - (B)(g) - mb(S_0)(1 + g) = 0$

$\$15g - \$4g - (0.08)(0.80)(\$20)(1 + g) = 0$

$\$9.72\ g = \$1.28$

$g = 0.1317 = 13.17\%$.

26. c. $0 = (A/S)(\Delta S) - (B/S)(\Delta S) - mb(S_1)$

$= (A/\$2,000)(\$500) - (\$500/\$2,000)(\$500)$

$-(\$500/\$2,000)(0.70)(\$2,500)$

$= 0.25A - \$125 - \$437.50$

$= 0.25A - \$562.50$

$\$562.50 = 0.25A$

$A = \$2,250.$

27. c.

	Sources	Uses
Cash	$ 24	
Marketable securities	33	
Net receivables		$ 24
Inventories		66
Gross fixed assets		225
Accumulated depreciation	45	
Accounts payable	9	
Notes payable		36
Other current liabilities	24	
Long-term debt	54	
Common stock	78	
Retained earnings	84	
	$351	$351

Note that accumulated depreciation is a contra-asset account, and an increase is a source of funds. Also note that no total lines such as total current assets can be used to determine sources and uses since to do so would be "double counting."

28. c.   Sources of Working Capital:

Net income after taxes	$114
Depreciation	45
Increase in common stock	78
Increase in long-term debt	54
Total sources	$291

Uses of Working Capital:

Increase in gross fixed assets	$225
Dividends paid out	30
Total uses	$255
Net increase in working capital	$ 36

CHAPTER 5

FINANCIAL PLANNING AND CONTROL

Overview

In Chapter 4, we discussed methods of forecasting financial requirements. This chapter expands the planning framework. It begins by examining the relationship between sales volume and profitability under different operating conditions. Breakeven analysis and operating analysis are emphasized here. Next, cash budgeting is discussed as a tool to aid managers in planning to meet forecasted needs for funds. Finally, the chapter examines the control processes, particularly DuPont analysis, used by firms to insure that plans are executed properly and modified when needed.

Outline

I. Financial planning and control processes are needed to insure that financial needs are met and that plans are executed properly.

   A. Financial planning involves the use of projections based on standards of performance and marketing strategies.

   B. The development of a mechanism for feedback and adjustment to plans is the basis of financial control.

   C. A budget system encompasses planning and control aspects, by comparing projections with results.

      1. Budgets analyze costs for every major area of a firm's activities.
      2. Projections in pro forma budgets for each department lead to forecasted income statements, balance sheets, and other financial statements for the firm.
      3. Projections of financing requirements give a firm the lead time necessary to arrange for such financing with greater flexibility.
      4. Comparisons of projected and actual financial statements help the firm to pinpoint reasons for deviations from the plan and to correct problems. Thus, the planning and control process helps a firm improve its performance and profitability.

II. Breakeven analysis is an important tool for profit planning.

    A. The relationships among fixed costs, variable costs, and profits can be studied using an analytical technique called cost-volume-profit planning, or breakeven analysis.

        1. Breakeven analysis provides information on the volume of sales at which total revenues begin to cover total costs fully.

        2. The practical significance of breakeven analysis is that it guides the manager in the comparison of prices, expected volume, and the required volume to cover total costs.

    B. A firm's breakeven point can be calculated algebraically as a breakeven quantity or a breakeven sales volume.

        1. The breakeven quantity is defined as that volume of output at which revenue are just equal to total costs (fixed costs plus variable costs).

           a. Let:

P = Sales price per unit.
F = Total fixed costs.
v = Variable costs per unit.
c = Contribution margin per unit = $P - v$.

The breakeven quantity, $Q*$, is that quantity which solves the following equation for total revenues equal to total costs:

$$PQ* = vQ* + F.$$

           b. The revenue-cost equation can be simplified and solved for $Q*$:

$$Q* = \frac{F}{c}.$$

        2. The breakeven sales volume, $S*$, can be calculated as $Q*(P)$.

    C. Although breakeven analysis is useful in studying cost-volume-profit relationships, it does have limitations.

        1. Any linear breakeven chart is based on the assumption of constant sales price. Profit possibilities under different prices require a whole series of breakeven charts.

        2. Breakeven analysis assumes that total fixed costs and variable cost per unit are constant for all quantities of output. Variable costs per unit may rise as capacity limits are approached. Increasing levels of output may require additional fixed investments in plant and equipment.

3. Product mix changes over time may influence the level and slope of the cost function, which will affect the break-even quantity and sales volume.

D. Used appropriately, breakeven analysis is applicable to three important types of business decisions.

1. New product decisions. Breakeven analysis helps determine the sales volume required on a new product to realize a profit.
2. General expansion of operations. Breakeven points are calculated on the basis of total sales (in dollar amounts rather than in units of output) and total costs.
3. Automation and modernization decisions. Breakeven analysis helps determine the consequences of substituting fixed costs for variable costs, and the effects of volume changes on profitability at varying relationships of fixed and variable costs.

III. Operating leverage is defined as the extent to which fixed costs are used in operations. High fixed costs arise from employing larger amounts of capital, thus permitting the firm to operate with reduced labor and smaller variable costs.

A. A high degree of operating leverage implies that a relatively small change in sales results in a large change in net operating income.

1. The breakeven point is higher with higher operating leverage because fixed costs are greater.
2. Once sales exceed the breakeven point, profits rise at a faster rate with higher operating leverage.

B. The degree of operating leverage (DOL) is defined as the percentage change in operating income that results from a percentage change in units sold.

1. The degree of operating leverage can be expressed as:

$$DOL = \frac{\text{Percentage change in net operating income}}{\text{Percentage change in units sold}}$$

$$= \frac{\frac{\Delta X}{X}}{\frac{\Delta Q}{Q}} .$$

2. The degree of operating leverage of a firm has a number of important implications:
   a. A high degree of operating leverage suggests that a firm could make gains from increasing its sales volume even if it had to lower its price to do so.

        b. On the other hand, a high degree of operating lever-
age indicates that a firm is subject to large swings
in profit as its volume fluctuates.

IV. Cash breakeven analysis can be used to analyze the firm's situation on a <u>cash</u> basis. It allows the firm to calculate a breakeven point considering only cash inflows and outflows.

    A. The formulas for breakeven quantity and sales level must be
adjusted for noncash outlays:

$$Q* = \frac{F - \text{Noncash outlays}}{\text{Contribution margin per unit}}$$

$$S* = \frac{F - \text{Noncash outlays}}{\text{Contribution ratio}} .$$

    B. Cash breakeven analysis provides a picture of the flow of
funds from operations.

        1. A firm may utilize a higher degree of operating leverage
(high fixed costs) to achieve higher profits if its risk
of insolvency (in the sense of being unable to meet cash
obligations) is low.

        2. If cash outlays are low, such a firm will be able to con-
tinue to operate during periods of loss, as long as it
remains above the cash breakeven point.

V. The cash budget is an important aspect of financial planning.

    A. A cash budget reflects the effects of future operations on
the firm's cash flow.

    B. It indicates not only the total amount of financing required
but its timing as well.

    C. The methodology is quite logical.

        1. If a firm sells on credit, there is a lag between sales
and cash collections.

        2. Similarly, a firm buying on credit benefits from a
waiting period before having to disburse cash.

        3. In expenditures, some cash payments are made in "lumps"
at uneven intervals, while some expenses may be assigned
on a uniform monthly basis.

        4. It is important to take into account interest and princi-
pal repayment as outward cash flows.

    D. The cash budget projects cash inflows and outflows over some
specified period of time.

        1. The cash budget is useful to determine when cash sur-
pluses or shortages will occur.

        2. Improved forecasts of cash inflows and outflows permit
the firm to hold a smaller cash balance.

VI. The DuPont system of financial analysis is a form of control in multidivisional companies.

    A. The DuPont system reveals how activity ratios and profit margins on sales interact to determine the profitability of assets.

    B. A modified DuPont control chart illustrates, among other things, that profits and return on investment depend upon control of costs and investment. If investment is not controlled, the asset turnover ratio (sales to net operating assets) declines.

    C. Profit planning depends to a great extent upon control of costs and utilization of assets.

        1. Cost control requires detailed study of the operations of the individual business firm to determine the nature of the costs inherent to the firm's industry.

        2. Firms which have low asset turnover ratios must have correspondingly higher profit margins than firms with high turnover ratios.

        3. The profit margin times the total asset turnover, which gives the return on investment (ROI), is called the DuPont equation:

$$ROI = \frac{Profit}{Sales} \times \frac{Sales}{Investment}.$$

    D. When the DuPont system is used for divisional control, it is often called ROI control.

        1. Each division is defined as a profit center with its own investments and is expected to earn an appropriate return on them.

        2. Profits are measured by operating earnings, and total gross assets are measured before deduction of depreciation reserve.

        3. If a division's ROI falls below a target figure, the centralized corporate staff traces back through the DuPont system to locate the cause.

        4. Division managers are judged by their division's ROI, and therefore are motivated to keep the ROI up to target level.

        5. ROI may be influenced by factors other than managerial competence. These factors include:

           a. Depreciation policy.

           b. Book value versus current value of assets.

           c. Transfer pricing methods.

           d. Short-term versus long-term perspectives.

           e. Industry conditions.

6. These factors necessitate supplementing the performance evaluation with other criteria, including the following:
   a. The division's growth rate in sales.
   b. The division's equipment modernization and replacement policies.
   c. The division's market share as compared with other firms in the industry.

Definitional Questions

1. _____ _____ involves the use of projections based on _____ of performance and marketing _____.

2. A _____ _____ compares projected financial statements with actual statements and allows the firm to pinpoint reasons for _____.

3. Breakeven analysis, or _____ _____, allows managers to study the relationships among fixed costs, _____ _____, and profits.

4. The _____ _____ is that volume of output at which _____ just equal total costs.

5. The breakeven sales volume can be expressed as the ratio of total fixed costs to the _____ _____.

6. Breakeven analysis assumes that _____ _____ and costs are _____ for all quantities of output.

7. _____ _____ is defined as the extent to which fixed costs are used in the firm's operations.

8. The _____ of operating leverage is defined as the percentage change in _____ _____ that result from a _____ change in units sold.

9. A high degree of operating leverage subjects the firm to _____ changes in net income in response to relatively small changes in _____.

10. Cash breakeven analysis allows a firm to calculate a _____ _____ for _____ inflows and outflows.

11. The cash breakeven volume is equal to fixed _____ outlays divided by the _____ _____ per unit.

12. A cash budget reflects the effects of _____ operations on the firm's cash _____ .

13. Cash budgeting improves _____ of cash inflows and outflows and permits firms to hold _____ cash balances.

14. The _____ _____ reveals how activity ratios and profit margins on sales interact to determine the _____ of assets.

15. The Du Pont equation is equal to the _____ _____ on sales times the _____ _____ turnover.

Conceptual Questions

16. The goal of financial planning and control is to:

    a. Project financial statements.
    b. Analyze costs in each of the firm's divisions.
    c. Help the firm improve its performance and profitability.
    d. Project costs based on standards of performance.
    e. Reward managers for adhering to budgets.

17. A high degree of operating leverage lowers risk by stabilizing a firm's earnings stream.

    a. True   b. False

18. Which of the following assumptions is not a limitation of breakeven analysis?

    a. Constant price for all levels of sales.
    b. Constant variable cost per unit for all levels of output.
    c. Constant total fixed costs over the range of output being evaluated.
    d. Constant product mix over time.
    e. Constant sales volume over time.

19. A low ROI is an indicator of managerial incompetence.

    a. True   b. False

Problems

20. Aquarium Suppliers, Inc., produces 10-gallon aquariums. The firm's variable costs equal 40 percent of dollar sales, while fixed costs total $150,000. The firm plans to sell the aquariums for $10 each. What is Aquarium Suppliers' breakeven quantity of sales.

   a. 22,000
   b. 25,000
   c. 28,000
   d. 30,000
   e. 40,000

21. Refer to Problem 20. What is the firm's breakeven sales volume?

   a. $100,000
   b. $150,000
   c. $200,000
   d. $250,000
   e. $300,000

22. Refer to Problem 20. What price must Aquarium Suppliers charge to breakeven at sales of 40,000 units.

   a. $5.28
   b. $5.60
   c. $5.95
   d. $6.25
   e. $7.00

23. The Spade Company has identified two methods of producing playing cards. One method involves using a machine having a fixed cost of $20,000 and variable costs of $1.00 per deck. The other method would use a less expensive machine having a fixed cost of $5,000, but it would require variable costs of $2.00 per deck. If the selling price will be the same under each method, at what level of output would the two methods produce the same net operating income (EBIT)?

   a. 5,000
   b. 10,000
   c. 15,000
   d. 20,000
   e. 25,000

24. Outfitters, Inc., is a new firm just starting operations. The firm will produce backpacks which will sell for $22.00 apiece. Fixed costs are $500,000 per year, and variable costs are $2.00 per unit of production. The company expects to sell 50,000 backpacks per year, and its effective tax rate is 40 percent. What is Outfitters' degree of operating leverage at the expected level of sales?

    a.   1.00
    b.   1.08
    c.   2.00
    d.   2.16
    e.   3.00

25. Refer to Problem 24. What is Outfitters' breakeven sales volume?

    a.   5,000
    b.   10,000
    c.   15,000
    d.   20,000
    e.   25,000

26. Refer to Problem 25. If Outfitters has $120,000 in noncash expenses, what is the firm's cash breakeven volume?

    a.   27,000
    b.   25,000
    c.   23,000
    d.   21,000
    e.   19,000

27. Robinson and Company has a total asset utilization of 0.30 and a profit margin of 10 percent. The president is unhappy with the current return on investment, and he thinks it could be doubled. This could be accomplished (1) by increasing the profit margin to 15 percent and (2) by increasing the total asset utilization. What new total asset turnover ratio, along with the 15 percent profit margin, is required to double the return on investment?

    a.   30%
    b.   35%
    c.   40%
    d.   45%
    e.   50%

Answers and Solutions

1. Financial planning; standards; strategies

2. budget system; deviations

3. cost-volume-profit planning; variable costs

4. breakeven quantity; revenues

5. contribution ratio

6. sales price; constant

7. Operating leverage

8. degree; operating income; percentage

9. large; sales

10. breakeven point; cash

11. cash; contribution margin

12. future; flow

13. forecasts; smaller

14. Du Pont system; profitability

15. profit margin; total asset

16 c.

17. b.

18. e.

19. b.   A division's ROI is influenced by factors other than managerial competence, such as the firm's depreciation policy, transfer pricing methods, and industry conditions.

20. b.
$$c = P - v$$
$$= \$10.00 - (0.40)(\$10.00)$$
$$= \$10.00 - \$4.00$$
$$= \$6.00.$$

$$Q* = \frac{F}{c}$$

$$= \$150,000/\$6.00$$
$$= 25,000.$$

21. d.
$$S* = (P)(Q*)$$
$$= (\$10)(25,000)$$
$$= \$250,000.$$

or $\qquad S* = \dfrac{F}{CR}$

$$= \dfrac{\$150,000}{1.00 - 0.40}$$

$$= \dfrac{\$150,000}{0.60}$$

$$= \$250,000.$$

22. d. $\qquad\qquad Q* = \dfrac{F}{c}$

$$40,000 = \dfrac{\$150,000}{c}$$

$$c = \$3.75 = P - v.$$

$$v = 0.40P$$
$$P - 0.40P = \$3.75$$
$$0.60P = \$3.75$$
$$P = \$6.25.$$

23. c. $\qquad\qquad NOI = PQ - vQ - F$

First method: $NOI = PQ - \$1.00Q - \$20,000.$
Second method: $NOI = PQ - \$2.00Q - \$5,000.$

Now, equate the NOIs:
$$PQ - \$1.00Q - \$20,000 = PQ - \$2.00Q - \$5,000$$
$$\$1.00Q = \$15,000$$
$$Q = 15,000.$$

24. c. To calculate the DOL at 50,000 units, we must first calculate the net operating income resulting from a sales level of 50,000 units and from some higher sales volume, say 60,000 units.

$$NOI_{50,000} = \$22(50,000) - \$2(50,000) - \$500,000$$

$$= \$1,100,000 - \$100,000 - \$500,000$$
$$= \$500,000.$$

$$NOI_{60,000} = \$22(60,000) - \$2(60,000) - \$500,000$$

$$= \$1,320,000 - \$120,000 - \$500,000$$
$$= \$700,000.$$

$$DOL_{50,000} = \frac{\dfrac{\Delta Income}{Income}}{\dfrac{\Delta Q}{Q}}$$

$$= \frac{\dfrac{\$200,000}{\$500,000}}{\dfrac{10,000}{50,000}}$$

$$= \frac{0.40}{0.20}$$

$$= 2.00.$$

25. e.

$$Q* = \frac{F}{c}$$

$$= \frac{\$500,000}{\$22 - \$2}$$

$$= \frac{\$500,000}{\$20}$$

$$= 25,000.$$

26. e.

$$Q* = \frac{F - noncash\ outlays}{c}$$

$$= \frac{\$500,000 - \$120,000}{\$22 - \$2}$$

$$= \frac{\$380,000}{\$20}$$

$$= 19,000.$$

27. c.   ROI = (Profit margin)(Total asset utilization)

Before: ROI = (10%)(0.30) = 3.00%.
After: 6% = (15%)(Total asset utilization)
         Total asset utilization = 0.40
                                 = 40%.

CHAPTER 6

WORKING CAPITAL POLICY

Overview

Working capital refers to a firm's investment in short-term assets. Working capital management involves a large portion of the firm's total assets; more than half the typical firm's total investment is in current assets. Thus, proper working capital management is crucial to the survival of the firm. This chapter focuses on principles and techniques used for effective control of overall working capital management.

Outline

I. Working capital management is concerned with decisions involving current assets.

   A. Working capital is defined as total current assets, while net working capital is current assets minus current liabilities.

   B. Working capital management refers to the administration of both current assets and current liabilities.

   C. Working capital management is important for several reasons:

   1. A large proportion of the financial manager's time is allocated to working capital management.
   2. More than half of the total assets are typically invested in current assets.
   3. The relationship between sales growth and the need to invest in current assets is close and direct. For example, if a firm's average collection period is 30 days and its credit sales are $2,000 per day, it has an investment of $60,000 in accounts receivable. If sales rise to $3,000 per day, the investment in accounts receivable will rise to $90,000.
   4. For the small firm, working capital management is particularly important.
      a. Investment in fixed assets can be reduced by renting or leasing, but current asset investment in receivables and inventory is unavoidable.

b. Because they may have limited access to capital markets, small firms must rely more heavily on short-term credit, increasing current liabilities and reducing net working capital.

II. The cash flow cycle of a firm will influence the amount of growth which can be financed without causing cash flow problems.

A. Working capital management seeks to provide financing for increases in current asset requirements caused by growth, cyclical and seasonal variations in sales levels, and random fluctuations in sales.

B. Firms need assets in order to make sales, and if sales increase, assets must also grow.

C. The cash flow cycle shows the process of converting cash into inventories, then into receivables, and then back into cash.

1. The original cash investment is used to pay rent and buy equipment.

2. Raw material purchases are financed by trade credit, giving rise to accounts payable.

3. Funds are paid to labor to begin processing the raw materials.

4. Before goods are completed, they represent work-in-process inventories. The firm's cash has declined, and current liabilities in the form of accounts payable and accrued wages payable are in existence.

5. Goods are finished and go from work-in-process inventories to finished goods inventories. The firm is more liquid at this point because finished goods can be sold to raise cash, while work-in-process inventories cannot be sold.

6. When goods are sold on credit, accounts receivable are created.

7. The collection of accounts receivable generates cash to complete a cycle.

8. The firm buys raw materials, and the cash cycle is repeated.

III. Managing the cash flow cycle is the crux of working capital management.

A. Working capital management requires a consideration of two separate factors, the operating cycle and the payments cycle, which combine to form the cash conversion cycle.

1. The operating cycle takes into account two determinants of liquidity:

a. The inventory conversion period is an indicator of the average time it takes a firm to convert its inventories into finished goods.

        b. The receivables conversion period is an indicator of the average time it takes a firm to convert its accounts receivables into cash.

    2. The payments cycle measures the average time that a firm can delay cash payments for raw materials by purchasing goods on credit.

    3. The cash conversion cycle is the net time interval between cash expenditures for raw materials and cash receipts on accounts receivables.

B. The cash flow financing period will be influenced by expansion or contraction on any of the three liquidity flow measures just discussed.

    1. The length of the cash conversion period is equal to the inventory conversion period plus the receivables conversion period, minus the payables deferral period.

    2. An increase in the operating cycle without an offsetting increase in the payables deferral period leads to an increase in the cash conversion period.

    3. A decline in the cash conversion cycle indicates a reduction in required non-spontaneous financing.

C. The cash conversion cycle concept gives a more accurate picture of a firm's liquidity position over time than do conventional liquidity ratios.

IV. Working capital decisions require a knowledge of the term structure of interest rates.

A. The term structure of interest rates describes the relationship between interest rates and loan maturity.

    1. Yields on government securities are generally used to avoid the influence of the risk of default.

    2. The yield curve is typically upward sloping.

        a. An upward sloping yield curve depicts a period of easing monetary conditions.

        b. A downward sloping yield curve represents a period of tight monetary conditions.

B. Another dimension of term structure compares the historical patterns of short-term interest rates versus long-term interest rates.

    1. Short-term rates are generally below long-term rates.

    2. Short-term rates fluctuate much more widely than long-term rates.

    3. During periods of tight monetary conditions, short-term rates generally are above long-term rates and it may be difficult for a firm to obtain financing.

V. Several theories have been advanced to explain the term structure of interest rates.

   A. The expectations theory states that, in equilibrium, the long-term rate is an average of today's short-term rate and expected short-term rates in the future. If future interest rates are expected to rise, long-term rates will be above short-term rates and the yield curve will be upward sloping. The yield curve will be downward sloping if future rates are expected to fall, and flat if investors think an increase is just as likely as a decrease.

   B. The liquidity preference theory holds that long-term bonds will yield more than short-term securities for two reasons:

      1. Investors will accept lower yields on short-term securities because they are more liquid in the sense that they can be converted to cash with less danger of loss of principal.
      2. Borrowers may be willing to pay more for longer-term securities to be assured of a known interest rate and the continued availability of funds.

   C. The market segmentation theory states that different groups prefer to hold securities of differing maturities and that this segmentation can lead to a situation in which the equilibrium rates of interest in the long-term and short-term markets can differ.

      1. If demand for short-term credit is relatively high when the supply of short-term credit is weak and if the situation is reversed in the long-term market, then short-term rates will be above long-term rates and the yield curve will be downward sloping.
      2. Market conditions could also lead to an upward sloping yield curve if there was an excess supply of short-term credit and a shortage of long-term funds.

   D. Empirical studies suggest that there is some validity to each of the three theories.

      1. If investors have no reason to expect a change in the general level of interest rates, the yield curve will be upward sloping due to liquidity preferences.
      2. During periods of extremely high interest rates, the yield curve is downward sloping indicating that the expectations theory also operates.
      3. Tests of the segmentation theory have yielded largely inconclusive results.

E. The <u>interest rates futures market</u> has arisen largely due to the fluctuations in interest rates.

    1. A futures contract is one in which two parties agree to exchange an asset for cash on a specified future date at a specified price, called the <u>futures price</u>.

    2. The futures price reflects the market expectations regarding the cash price of the security which will prevail on the given dates.

    3. Financial futures are used by investors to provide a measure of protection against changes in futures rates and by speculators to make a profit from changes in interest rates.

VI. Working capital management is concerned with decisions regarding the level and financing of current assets.

    A. The level of current assets held by a firm will be influenced by the firm's attitude toward risk.

        1. For a given level of production and sales, a higher current asset level reduces risk, but also reduces the overall return on assets.

        2. Expected sales influence both fixed and current assets, but only current asset levels can be adjusted to short-run fluctuations in sales.

        3. Alternative current asset policies are:
            a. Conservative--high current asset level. Sales may be stimulated, but return on assets may be lower.
            b. Average--moderate level of current assets.
            c. Aggressive--low current asset level. Sales may be reduced, but return on assets may be improved.

    B. All firms maintain some level of current assets on a permanent basis. A firm's risk position will influence its decision to finance permanent assets with long-term or short-term debt.

        1. As sales increase, funding is needed to acquire new assets.
            a. A steadily rising sales level over a period of years results in a permanent increase in current assets.
            b. Permanent assets--both fixed and current--should be financed from long-term sources.
            c. Fluctuating asset requirements, or temporary increases in assets, may be financed from short-term sources.

        2. Working capital financing policies parallel current asset level policies.
            a. Conservative--greater use of long-term funds for financing current assets.

     b. Average--use of long-term debt for permanent assets (current and fixed) and short-term debt for fluctuating current assets.

     c. Aggressive--greater use of short-term funds for financing current assets.

  3. Analyses of decisions in working capital management require an understanding of the relative costs and risks of short-term and long-term financing.

VII. The decision to use short-term debt versus long-term debt involves an analysis of the flexibility, costs, and risks of each.

  A. Short-term debt provides greater flexibility in meeting fluctuating financing needs.

  B. Short-term debt is used because it is often cheaper than long-term debt.

    1. Long-term is usually more expensive because the longer the loan is outstanding, the larger the risks involved, such as inflation, adverse economic trends, and possible government legislation.

    2. Short-term rates, however, are more volatile than long-term rates.

  C. Short-term debt is more risky to use than long-term debt.

    1. Although a firm using short-term financing may pay less interest than a firm financing with long-term debt, it is more risky since short-term rates fluctuate widely and the firm using short-term debt does not know what its interest expense will be.

    2. The short-term loan may not be renewed.

     a. If a firm's financial ratios deteriorate, the firm will have to pay higher interest rates and creditors may refuse to provide financing.

     b. If monetary conditions become tight, the firm may be excluded from financing by the credit rationing policies of lenders.

  D. Thus, the use of short-term debt involved a risk/return tradeoff.

    1. The interest expense of a conservative firm using no short-term credit is unaffected by temporary changes in the term structure of interest rates.

    2. An aggressive policy, using a substantial amount of short-term financing, can result in a higher rate of return.

    3. The final result depends on the patterns of short-term and long-term interest rates.

4. If the unbiased expectations theory of the term structure is correct, on average, there should be no advantage to either short-term or long-term debt.

5. If, on average, liquidity preferences cause long-term rates to be higher than short-term rates, the cost of short-term debt is lower, but its use is riskier.

Definitional_Questions

1. Working capital management involves decisions relating to _____ assets.

2. _____ working capital is defined as current _____ minus current _____.

3. There is a direct relationship between sales _____ and investments in _____ assets.

4. A firm's _____ _____ cycle will influence the amount of growth the firm can _____ without incurring cash flow problems.

5. Firms need _____ to make sales, and if _____ increase, assets must grow also.

6. The cash flow cycle illustrates the process of converting cash into _____, then into _____, and, finally, back to cash.

7. Raw material purchases are financed by _____ _____, giving rise to accounts _____.

8. The operating cycle and the _____ cycle combine to form the _____ _____ cycle.

9. The _____ cycle takes into account the _____ _____ period and the receivables conversion period, two determinants of _____.

10. The cash conversion cycle is the _____ time interval between cash _____ for raw materials and cash receipts on _____ _____.

11. A _____ in the cash conversion cycle reduces the need for _____ financing.

12. The _____ _____ of interest rates describes the relationship between _____ _____ and the time to maturity of loans.

13. The _____ _____ is upward sloping during periods of easy monetary conditions.

14. The _____ theory states that the long-term interest rate is the average of today's _____ and rates expected in the future.

15. If investors believe that future rates will _____, the yield curve will be downward sloping.

16. The slope of the yield curve depends on three factors: investors' expectations about future interest rates, investors' preference for _____ securities, and supply and demand conditions in long-term versus _____ markets resulting from market _____.

17. A _____ contract is one in which two parties agree to exchange an _____ for cash on a specified future date at a specified _____.

18. Working capital management is concerned with decisions regarding the _____ and financing of _____ assets.

19. A firm which holds a high level of current assets has a _____ attitude concerning current assets.

20. A firm which is aggressive in financing current assets will use more _____ funds than a conservative firm.

21. Short-term debt provides greater _____ in meeting _____ financing needs than long-term debt, but short-term debt is more _____.

22. If the unbiased expectations theory of the _____ _____ is correct, on average, there should be no _____ to either short-term or long-term debt.

Conceptual Problems

23. Working capital management is not as important for small firms as it is for large firms because small firms' need for working capital funds is less.

    a. True   b. False

24. Other things held constant, an increase in the payables deferral period will lead to a reduction in the need for nonspontaneous funding.

    a. True   b. False

25. Which of the following will cause the yield curve to slope downward?

    a. Investors feel that the inflation rate, hence the level of interest rates, will increase next year.
    b. Investors feel that the inflation rate, hence the level of interest rates, will decrease next year.
    c. Investors expect no change in the level of interest rates.
    d. An excess supply of short-term credit exists, while there is a shortage of funds in the long-term market.
    e. Statements b and d above are both correct.

26. A firm should always use short-term debt, rather than long-term financing, to minimize its interest expense.

    a. True   b. False

Problems

27. Schnell Industries, Inc., has an inventory conversion period of 60 days, a receivables conversion period of 35 days, and a payments cycle of 28 days. What is the length of the firm's operating cycle?

    a. 67 days
    b. 82 days
    c. 95 days
    d. 104 days
    e. 117 days

28. Refer to Problem 27. What is the length of the firm's cash conversion cycle?

    a. 67 days
    b. 82 days
    c. 95 days
    d. 104 days
    e. 117 days

29. Refer to Problem 27.   If Schnell's sales are $972,000   annually,
    what is the firm's investment in accounts receivable?

    a. $72,450
    b. $79,600
    c. $85,300
    d. $94,500
    e. $100,000

30. Suppose the current annual yield on a two-year bond is 10
    percent, while the yield on a one-year bond of comparable risk is
    12 percent.   According to the expectations theory, what interest
    rate do investors expect to earn on a one-year bond during the
    second year?

    a.   9.67%
    b.   9.23%
    c.   8.60%
    d.   8.43%
    e.   8.04%

Answers and Solutions

1. current

2. Net; assets; liabilities

3. growth; current

4. cash flow; finance

5. assets; sales

6. inventories; receivables

7. trade credit; payable

8. payments; cash conversion

9. operating; inventory conversion; liquidity

10. net; expenditures; accounts receivable

11. decline; nonspontaneous

12. term structure; interest rates

13. yield curve

14. expectations; short-term

15. decline

16. liquid; short-term; segmentation

17. futures; asset; price

18. level; current

19. conservative

20. short-term

21. flexibility; fluctuating; risky

22. term structure; advantage

23. b.   Working capital management is more important for small firms because they have limited access to capital markets and must rely heavily on short-term credit.

24. a.

25. b.

26. b.   If interest rates rise, the firm which financed with short-term debt may pay more interest than a firm which obtained long-term funds when rates were lower.

27. c.   Operating cycle = Inventory conversion period
                            + Receivables conversion period
                          = 60 days + 35 days
                          = 95 days.

28. a.   Cash conversion cycle = Operating cycle - Payments cycle
                                = 95 days - 28 days
                                = 67 days.

29. d.   Average sales per day = $972,000/360
                                = $2,700.

    Average investment in receivables = $2,700(35)
                                      = $94,500.

30. e.   Ending value of a two-year bond:

            $1(1.10)(1.10) = $1.21.

         $1.21 = $1(1.12)(1 + r)
         1 + r = 1.0804
             r = 8.04%.

CHAPTER 7

INVENTORY MANAGEMENT

Overview

Inventory is the first current asset account discussed. Inventory management centers around the balancing of a set of costs that increase with larger inventory holdings, such as storage costs, and a set of costs that decline with larger holdings, such as ordering costs. The economic ordering quantity (EOQ) model was developed to control investment in inventory and is useful in the analysis of investments in other current assets.

Outline

I. Inventories are essential to the operation of most businesses, and the typical manufacturing firm has about 25 percent of its assets tied up in inventories.

    A.   Inventories are commonly classified into the following categories:

        1. Raw materials.
        2. Work-in-process.
        3. Finished goods.

    B.   The level of the raw materials inventory is influenced by:

        1. Anticipated production levels.
        2. Seasonality of production.
        3. Reliability of materials suppliers.
        4. Nature of the production process.

    C.   Work-in-process inventory is strongly influenced by the length of the production period.

    D.   The level of finished goods inventory is influenced directly by production and sales levels and indirectly by credit terms and standards.

    E.   The major determinants of the size of inventories are:

        1. Level of sales.
        2. Length and technical nature of the production processes.
        3. Durability and perishability of the end product.

      4.   Ease of replenishing stocks.
      5.   Consequences of running short of an item.

F.   Managing all types of assets is basically an inventory problem.

      1.   A working stock must be on hand to balance inflows and outflows of the items.
      2.   Safety stocks are necessary to meet unexpected needs.
      3.   Anticipation stocks may be required to meet future growth needs.
      4.   The optimum purchase size is called the economic ordering quantity (EOQ).

G.   As inventory size increases, some costs decrease while other costs increase. These costs, when added together, comprise the total cost curve for inventory. The minimum point on the total cost curve designates the optimal inventory position.

II. The first step in building an inventory model is to specify those costs which rise and those which decline with higher levels of inventory.

A.   Three categories of costs are typically associated with investments in inventory:

      1.   Carrying costs--those associated with holding inventories.
      2.   Stock-out costs--those associated with running short of inventories.
      3.   Ordering costs--those associated with ordering and receiving inventories.

B.   Carrying costs generally rise with higher inventory levels. These costs include:

      1.   Interest forgone on funds tied up in inventories.
      2.   Storage costs.
      3.   Insurance costs.
      4.   Property taxes.
      5.   Depreciation and obsolescence.

C.   Costs of running short generally decline with higher levels of inventory due to lost sales, loss of customer goodwill, and disruption of production schedules·

D.   Ordering costs will vary according to the number of orders placed, but are fixed per order. The ordering costs include the costs of placing an order, including production set-up costs, and shipping and handling costs.

E.   Rising inventory levels at first cause total inventory costs to decline, until the carrying costs (which rise with inventory levels) offset the declining ordering costs (which decline with the <u>number</u> of orders). The point at which total inventory costs are at a minimum is the economic ordering quantity.

III. The economic ordering quantity (EOQ) model is a commonly used approach to determine the optimal level of inventory.

A. The EOQ model is: $\sqrt{2VU/CP}$,

where

EOQ = the economic ordering quantity, or the optimal quantity to be ordered each time an order is placed.

V = costs of placing and receiving an order.

U = annual usage in units.

C = carrying cost expressed as a percentage of inventory value.

P = purchase price per unit of inventory.

1. The optimal average inventory, A, is found as $A = EOQ/2$.
2. The total costs of ordering and carrying inventories, T, is found as

$$T = CP\left(\frac{EOQ}{2}\right) + V\left(\frac{U}{EOQ}\right).$$

B. The relationship between sales and inventory can be expressed by the following:

1. The larger the sales per period or processing costs per order, the larger the EOQ.
2. The larger the inventory carrying charge, the smaller the EOQ.
3. An increase in sales calls for a less than proportionate increase in the EOQ.

C. The assumptions of the EOQ model include the following:

1. Demand is known with certainty.
2. Sales are uniformly distributed over time.
3. Orders are received instantaneously.

D. Under conditions of certainty, the instantaneous order and delivery assumption may be relaxed to find the inventory level at which an order should be placed. (With instantaneous order and delivery, the order point is zero.)

1. Find the daily rate of usage.
2. The lead time is the number of days required to place an order and receive delivery.
3. <u>Order point</u> = (Daily usage)(Lead time).

E.   Demand, rate of usage, and order lead time cannot always be known with certainty. Therefore, firms add a <u>safety stock</u> to their inventories to avoid running out of inventory and suffering sales losses.

   1.   At the optimal level of safety stock, the probable cost of running out of inventory is just offset by the cost of carrying the additional inventory.
   2.   The costs of a <u>stock-out</u> include the following:
       a.   Customer ill-will.
       b.   Production delays.
       c.   Lost sales.
   3.   The probability of a stock-out is influenced by fluctuations in usage rate and delivery time.
   4.   Inclusion of a safety stock does not affect the EOQ.
       a.   The average inventory with safety stock is

       $$A = EOQ/2 + Safety\ stock.$$

       b.   The order point is increased by the amount of safety stock.
       c.   Total inventory costs are increased by the carrying costs of the safety stock, so that minimal total costs will be to the right of the intersection of rising (carrying) and declining (ordering) costs.

V.   During inflation, the EOQ must be updated frequently.

   A.   Values used in the EOQ equation may not remain constant for an appreciable length of time.

   B.   A firm needs more flexible inventory management so it can take advantage of bargains and provide for future contingencies.

   C.   The basic logic for inventory models is still valid, only finding the optimal becomes more difficult.

Definitional Questions

1. Inventories are usually classified as _____ _____, _____, and _____ _____.

2. Major determinants of the size of inventories are sales _____, length of _____ processes, and the durability and _____ of the end products.

3. A _____ stock is needed to balance inflows and outflows, while _____ stocks are held to meet unexpected needs.

4. Storage costs, obsolescence, and other costs that _____ with larger inventories are known as _____ costs.

5. The _____ _____ quantity minimizes the total costs of ordering and holding inventories.

6. When the level of inventories reaches the _____, the EOQ amount should be ordered.

7. _____ _____ must be maintained in order to allow for shipping delays and changes in the rate of _____.

Conceptual Questions

8. Among the carrying costs associated with inventories are:

    a. Disruption of production schedules.
    b. Loss of customer goodwill.
    c. Depreciation and obsolescence.
    d. Shipping and handling costs.
    e. Production set-up costs.

9. The economic ordering quantity is the order quantity that provides the minimum total cost; that is, both the ordering and carrying cost components are minimized.

    a. True   b. False

10. If a firm's fixed ordering costs double, the economic ordering quantity will also double.

    a. True   b. False

11. The addition of a safety stock to the EOQ model:

    a.   Increases the EOQ proportionately.
    b.   Raises the reorder point.
    c.   Lowers the reorder point.
    d.   Does not change the total inventory costs.
    e.   Results in greater variability in the time required to receive deliveries.

Problems

(The following information applies to the next three problems.)

The South Florida Lawn Supply Company is reviewing its inventory policy regarding lawn seed. The following relationships and conditions are known by management to exist:

1. Orders must be placed in multiples of 100 bags.
2. Requirements for the year are 16,200 bags.
3. The purchase price per bag is $5.00.
4. The carrying cost is 20 percent of the purchase price of the seed.
5. The variable cost per order is $25.
6. The desired safety stock is 300 units; this amount is on hand initially.
7. Five days are required for delivery.

12. What is the economic ordering quantity?

    a.   600 bags
    b.   700 bags
    c.   800 bags
    d.   900 bags
    e.   1,000 bags

13. How many orders should South Florida Lawn Supply place each year?

    a.   22
    b.   20
    c.   18
    d.   16
    e.   14

14. At what level of inventory should these orders be placed?

    a.   525
    b.   425
    c.   345
    d.   300
    e.   225

(The following information applies to the next 5 problems.)

The Magnuson Company is trying to determine its optimal inventory policy. The following relationships and conditions exist for the firm:

1. Annual sales are 120,000 units.
2. The purchase price per unit is $500.
3. The carrying cost is 20 percent of the purchase price.
4. The variable cost per order is $600.
5. The optimal safety stock is 500 units.

15. What is the economic ordering quantity?

   a. 600 units
   b. 800 units
   c. 1,000 units
   d. 1,200 units
   e. 1,400 units

16. What is the maximum inventory the company will hold?

   a. 1,300 units
   b. 1,400 units
   c. 1,500 units
   d. 1,600 units
   e. 1,700 units

17. What is the average inventory the company will hold?

   a. 600 units
   b. 850 units
   c. 1,100 units
   d. 1,200 units
   e. 1,700 units

18. How often will the company order?

   a. 2.0 days
   b. 3.65 days
   c. 5.25 days
   d. 2 weeks
   e. Continually

19. What is the firm's annual total inventory costs?

   a. $50,000
   b. $100,000
   c. $150,000
   d. $170,000
   e. $200,000

Answers and Solutions

1. raw materials; work-in-process, finished goods

2. level; production; perishability

3. working; safety

4. increase; carrying

5. economic ordering

6. ordering point

7. Safety stocks; sales

8. c.

9. b.   The total cost, or sum of ordering and carrying costs, is minimized, but neither of the component costs is minimized. For example, to minimize carrying costs, no inventory would be kept on hand at all.

10. b.   Since the optimal ordering quantity is equal to $\sqrt{2VU/CP}$, a doubling of S will increase the optimal ordering quantity by $\sqrt{2}$.

11. b.

12. d. $EOQ = \sqrt{\dfrac{2VU}{CP}} = \sqrt{\dfrac{(2)(\$25)(16,200)}{(0.20)(\$5)}} = \sqrt{\dfrac{\$810,000}{\$1.00}} = 900$ bags.

13. c. $\dfrac{16,200 \text{ units per year}}{900 \text{ units per order}} = 18$ orders per year.

14. a.   Daily rate of use = 16,200/360 = 45 bags.
            Reorder point = 300 + 5(45)
                          = 525 bags.

Thus, South Florida Lawn Supply Company will have 1,200 bags on hand immediately after a shipment is received, will use 45 bags per day, will reorder when the stock is down to 525 bags (which is 5 days' requirements, plus the safety stock), and will be down to 300 bags just before a shipment arrives.

15. d. $EOQ = \sqrt{\dfrac{2VU}{CP}} = \sqrt{\dfrac{(2)(\$600)(120,000)}{(0.20)(\$500)}} = \sqrt{\dfrac{\$144,000,000}{\$100}}$

$= 1,200$ units.

16. e.   Maximum inventory = EOQ + Safety stock
$= 1,200 + 500$
$= 1,700$ units.

17. c.   Average inventory = EOQ/2 + Safety stock
$= 600 + 500$
$= 1,100$ units.

18. b. $\dfrac{120,000 \text{ units per year}}{1,200 \text{ units per order}} = 100$ orders per year.

$\dfrac{365 \text{ days per year}}{100 \text{ orders per year}} = 3.65$ days.

The firm must place one order every 3.65 days.

19. d. $T = CP(\dfrac{EOQ}{2} + \text{Safety stock}) + V(\dfrac{U}{EOQ})$.

$= 0.2(\$500) + (\dfrac{1,200}{2} + 500) + \$600(\dfrac{120,000}{1,200})$.

$= \$110,000 + 60,000$.

$= \$170,000$.

CHAPTER 8

CREDIT MANAGEMENT

Overview

Chapter 8 looks at a firm's investment in receivables. The investment in receivables is dependent on the firm's credit policy, which is based on four variables. The four credit policy variables are (1) credit standards, (2) credit period, (3) cash discounts, and (4) collection policy. Credit policy has an important impact on sales volume, and the optimal credit policy involves the trade-off between the costs inherent in various credit policies and the profits generated by these policies. Credit policy changes are covered in detail.

Outline

I. Effective management of accounts receivables is important to the profitability and risk level of the firm.

    A. Accounts receivable are created when a firm sells goods or performs services on credit rather than a cash basis. When cash is received, accounts receivable are reduced by the same amount.

    B. The total amount of accounts receivable outstanding is determined by (1) the volume of credit sales and (2) the average length of time between sales and collections.

II. Sales and collections are influenced by economic conditions and by the firm's credit policy which includes four variables.

    A. Credit standards relate to decisions about who will be granted credit. If the firm extended credit to only the strongest of customers, it would never have bad debt losses. On the other hand, it would probably be losing sales.

        1. The optimal credit standard involves relating the marginal costs of credit to the incremental profits on increased sales.

           a. Marginal costs include production and selling expenses.

           b. Other marginal costs relate to credit quality. These credit costs include:

      (1) Bad debt losses or defaults.
      (2) Credit investigation and collection expenses.
      (3) Cost of capital tied up in accounts receivable.

2. A key element in setting credit standards is the evaluation of credit risk. To evaluate credit risk, credit managers consider the five C's of credit.

   a. <u>Character</u>--the probability that the customer will try to honor his obligation.

   b. <u>Capacity</u>--subjective judgment or evaluation of the ability of the customer to pay.

   c. <u>Capital</u>--measured by the general financial position of the firm as indicated by financial ratio analysis.

   d. <u>Collateral</u>--represented by assets the customer may offer as security to obtain credit.

   e. <u>Conditions</u>--the impact of general or specific economic trends on the firm.

3. Modern credit managers classify customers into five to eight categories according to degree of risk. Then, the credit manager concentrates his time and attention on the weakest customers.

B. The terms of credit specify the period for which credit is extended, and the discount, if any, for early payment.

   1. The credit term "2/10, net 30" means that a 2 percent discount is allowed if the purchase is paid within 10 days; otherwise the entire amount is due in 30 days.

      a. The credit term "net 30" indicates that no discount is offered, and the full amount is due in 30 days.

      b. A credit term "2/10, net 30, May 1 dating" means that the effective invoice date is May 1. The 2 percent discount may be taken until May 10, and the net is due May 30. Seasonal dating on invoices is used when sales are seasonal.

   2. The credit period is the length of time for which credit is granted.

      a. Lengthening the credit period stimulates sales.

      b. The higher level of receivables caused by both the higher sales and longer credit terms increases the cost of carrying receivables.

   3. Cash discounts attract customers and encourage early payment but reduce the dollar amount received on each discount sale.

      a. Increasing the size of the discount will increase sales, decrease the average collection period, and increase the cost of the discount.

      b. The optimal discount point should be established at the point where costs and benefits are exactly offsetting.

C. Collection policy refers to the procedures the firm follows to collect past-due accounts. The collection process can be expensive in terms of both direct costs and lost goodwill, but at least some of the firmness is needed to prevent an undue lengthening of the collection period and to minimize outright losses.

III. The credit manager's basic objective is to build an increasing base of profitable sales and to increase the value of the firm by extending credit to worthy customers.

A. A credit manager can play an active role in increasing sales by learning the business of his or her customers and by counseling customers.

1. Credit analysis may reveal problems or deterioration of a firm's financial condition which reduce its credit worthiness.
2. The credit manager can alert the customer to the problems and may assist in correcting them.
3. Sales may increase as the customer's business expands profitably.

B. The credit manager will be able to perform effectively only if he or she can obtain and analyze information on customers and their industries. The credit manager can obtain credit information from a number of sources.

1. Financial statements submitted by credit applicants are analyzed with special emphasis on liquidity, leverage, and profitability ratios.
2. Credit information exchanges involve periodic meetings of credit managers of firms selling to firms in a particular industry for the purpose of exchanging credit experiences.
3. Credit interchange bureaus are formal networks that compile data from local credit bureaus and member firms; they provide credit reports to clients for a fee. Examples include the following:
   a. The National Credit Interchange System.
   b. TRW, a private firm which compiles credit bureau information.
4. Credit reporting agencies, such as Dun & Bradstreet, Inc., publish reference books giving credit ratings and measures of overall strength for 3 million firms. Clients can purchase more detailed business information reports including discussion of business operations and payment experience.
5. Banks can provide general background information useful to credit managers.

C. After the manager collects credit information, the information must be analyzed before credit is extended or denied.

    1. The credit manager compares the firm's financial ratios to industry norms.
       a. Trend analysis of liquidity, leverage, and profitability ratios is emphasized.
       b. Multiple discriminant analysis may be used to develop a formal system for credit scoring.
    2. Information on a firm's payment pattern is compared to two standards: the credit terms of the selling firm and the average payment pattern for the customer's industry.
    3. Qualitative and quantitative analysis go into the development of the firm's credit policy.

IV. Firms use incremental analysis to analyze increases or decreases in sales and in costs associated with changes in one or more of the credit policy variables.

A. The incremental returns resulting from a change in credit policy are related to the incremental costs in a two-step analysis.

    1. First, the incremental investment in receivables is determined.
       a. When the change causes the collection period on existing sales to change, the change in receivables investment is measured at sales value because this is the amount that otherwise would have been received earlier or later.
       b. The receivables resulting from a change in sales due to a change in credit policy are measured at the variable cost outlays.
       c. When sales are changed by a credit policy change, the other net working capital requirements related to sales levels should also be taken into account in calculating the amount of investment in receivables.
    2. Second, the incremental profitability resulting from the change is calculated.
       a. Cash flows are increased by the contribution margin on the incremental sales.
       b. Cash flows are decreased by any increase in discounts in bad debt and losses and by the cost of capital tied up in the incremental investment in receivables.

B. Any change in credit policy requires estimates of its future effects.

    1. The percentage of credit customers who will take the discount as well as the length of the new average collection period must be projected.

2. Firms tend to move toward optimal credit policies slowly by observing the effects of small changes in credit policy variables in an environment of fluctuating economic conditions.

V. Accounts receivable must be monitored to determine if the firm's credit policy is effective.

A. The average Days' Sales Outstanding (DSO) is one control method for accounts receivable management.

$$DSO_t = \frac{\text{Total accounts receivable}_t}{\text{Daily sales}}.$$

B. The Aging Schedule (AS) shows the percentage of accounts receivable in different age groups representing the length of time the receivables have been outstanding.

C. Both DSO and AS can give false signals to the financial manager.

1. Sales patterns such as seasonal variations can distort the results.
2. DSO figures will vary greatly depending on the averaging period used to calculate daily sales.

D. The Payment Pattern Approach analyzes the key issue of payment behavior.

1. A payment pattern is characterized by the proportions of credit sales in a given month that are paid in that month and in subsequent months.
   a. The payment proportion is the percentage of a month's credit sales which is paid in each of the months following the month of sale.
   b. The balance fraction is the percentage of a month's credit sales remaining in accounts receivable in each of the months following the month of sale.
2. A constant payment pattern (payment proportions remain the same) makes any change in payment behavior immediately noticeable.
3. The payment pattern approach is independent of sales levels or changing sales patterns.

VI. Credit management lends itself to the use of computer controls.

A. The collection, analysis, compilation, storage, and retrieval of data involved in credit management make it well-suited to computerization.

B. Computer capabilities can enhance the effectiveness of the credit department staff.

1. Analytical reports may be drawn on individual companies, groups of companies, or on the status of accounts receivable as a whole.
2. Computers can monitor delinquency.
3. Accounts approaching credit limits can be flagged.
4. Accounts exhibiting abnormal payment behavior may be detected early enough to avoid serious credit problems.
5. Selected credit decisions can be made on the basis of quantitative guidelines.

Definitional Questions

1. _____ _____ are created when goods are sold or services are performed on credit.

2. A firm's outstanding accounts receivables will be determined by the _____ of credit sales and the length of time between _____ and _____.

3. Sales volume and the collection period will be affected by a firm's _____ _____.

4. Extremely strict credit sales will result in lost _____.

5. Effective credit standards require a balance between the _____ costs of credit and marginal _____ on increased sales.

6. The five Cs of credit refer to _____, _____, _____, _____, and _____.

7. Credit terms generally specify the _____ for which credit is granted and any _____ _____ that is offered for early payment.

8. The optimal credit terms involve a trade-off between increased _____ and the cost of carrying additional _____ _____.

9. _____ policy refers to the manner in which a firm tries to obtain payment from past-due accounts.

10. The basic objective of the credit manager is to build _____ _____.

11. The credit manager must obtain and _____ information on customers and their _____ .

12. The credit manager compares the firm's liquidity, _____, and _____ ratios to industry _____ .

13. A firm's payment pattern is compared to the _____ _____ of the selling firm and the average _____ _____ for the customer's industry.

14. Firms use _____ _____ to analyze the effects of changes in credit policy variables.

15. Incremental cash flows are increased by the _____ _____ on incremental sales and are decreased by any increase in _____ and bad debt losses.

16. The _____ _____ shows the percentage of accounts receivable in different age groups.

17. The Payments Pattern Approach is _____ of sales levels or changing sales patterns.

Conceptual Questions

18. A firm changes its credit policy from 2/10, net 30, to 3/10, net 30. The change is to meet competition, so no increase in sales is expected. The firm's average investment in accounts receivable will probably increase as a result of this change.

    a. True   b. False

19. An aging schedule is constructed by a firm to keep track of when its various accounts payable are due.

    a. True   b. False

20. In credit analysis, particular emphasis is placed on:

    a. Valuation and growth ratios.
    b. Liquidity, activity, and growth ratios.
    c. Leverage, profitability, and liquidity ratios.
    d. Profitability and activity ratios.
    e. Leverage and valuation ratios.

21. A good credit manager tries to:

    a. Reduce bad debt losses to an absolute minimum.
    b. Reduce the average days' sales in accounts receivable.
    c. Collect all accounts regardless of the expense.
    d. Minimize collection expenses.
    e. Extend credit to the point where marginal profits equal marginal costs.

Problems

(The following information applies to the next three problems.)

The Coleman Stove Company sells on terms of 3/10, net 30. Gross sales for the year are $3 million, and the collections department estimates that 30 percent of the customers pay on the tenth day and take discounts; 40 percent pay on the thirtieth day; and the remaining 30 percent pay, on average, 40 days after the purchase.

22. What is the average collection period?

    a. 10 days
    b. 13 days
    c. 20 days
    d. 27 days
    e. 40 days

23. What is the average investment in receivables?

    a. $200,000
    b. $225,000
    c. $300,000
    d. $350,000
    e. $440,000

24. What would be the new average investment if Coleman toughened up on its collection policy, with the result that all non-discount customers paid on the thirtieth day?

    a. $200,000
    b. $225,000
    c. $300,000
    d. $350,000
    e. $440,000

25. The Winthrop Company, a major retail firm, currently has sales of $72 million per year. Its average collection period is 50 days, and 2 percent of its sales end up as bad debts. Winthrop's credit manager estimates that if the firm extends credit to 75 days, sales will increase by $3,600,000, but its bad debts on new sales will be 4 percent. Variable costs equal 60 percent of sales, and the cost of carrying receivables, k, is 15 percent. The new sales will require an investment in net working capital of 30 percent of the incremental sales. What would be the incremental pre-tax profits if the credit period is extended to 75 days?

    a. $192,000
    b. $235,500
    c. $264,000
    d. $316,500
    e. $382,000

26. Walker Furniture Company has annual sales of $4,000,000. Its average collection period is 40 days, and bad debts are 5 percent of sales. The credit and collection manager is considering instituting a stricter collection policy, whereby bad debts would be reduced to 2 percent of all sales, and the average collection period would fall to 30 days. However, sales will also fall by an estimated $500,000 annually. What would be the incremental pre-tax profits associated with such a change in collection policy, if variable costs are 60 percent of sales and the cost of carrying receivables is 12 percent?

    a. -$54,330
    b. -$23,450
    c.   0
    d. $23,450
    e. $54,330

Answers and Solutions

1. Accounts receivable

2. Volume; sales; collection

3. credit policy

4. sales

5. marginal; profits

6. character; capacity; capital; collateral; conditions

7. period; cash discount

8. sales; accounts receivable

9. Collection

10. profitable sales

11. analyze; industries

12. leverage; profitability; norms

13. credit terms; payment pattern

14. incremental analysis

15. contribution margin; discounts

16. Aging Schedule

17. independent

18. b. No new customers are being generated. The current customers pay either on Day 10 or Day 30. The increase in trade discount will induce some customers who are now paying on Day 30 to pay on Day 10. Thus, the average collection period is shortened which, in turn, will cause a decline in accounts receivable.

19. b. The aging schedule breaks down accounts receivable according to how long they have been outstanding.

20. c.

21. e.

22. d. $(0.3)(10 \text{ days}) + (0.4)(30 \text{ days}) + (0.3)(40 \text{ days}) = 27$ days.

23. b. Average receivables = (ACP)(Sales/360)
    $$= (27)(\$3,000,000/360)$$
    $$= \$225,000.$$

24. a. New average collection period = $(0.3)(10) + (0.7)(30)$
    $$= 24 \text{ days.}$$
    Average receivables = $(24)(\$3,000,000/360)$
    $$= \$200,000.$$

25. d. $\Delta I = (ACP_N - ACP_O)(S_O/360) + v[ACP_N(\Delta S/360)] + (0.3)(\Delta S)$

    $$= (75 - 50)(\$72,000,000/360) +$$
    $$(0.6)[75(\$3,600,000/360)] + (0.3)(\$3,600,000)$$

    $$= \$5,000,000 + \$450,000 + \$1,080,000$$
    $$= \$6,530,000.$$

$$\Delta P = (\Delta S)(1 - v) - (B_N)(\Delta S) - k(\Delta I)$$

$$= (\$3,600,000)(0.4) - (0.04)(\$3,600,000)$$
$$- 0.15(\$6,530,000)$$

$$= \$316,500.$$

26. a. $\Delta I = (ACP_N - ACP_O)[(S_O + \Delta S)/360] + v[ACP_O(\Delta S/360)]$

$$= (30 - 40)[(\$4,000,000 - \$500,000)/360)]$$
$$+ 0.60[40(\$500,000/360)]$$

$$= -\$97,222 - \$33,333$$

$$= -\$130,555.$$

$$\Delta P = (\Delta S)(1 - v) - k(\Delta I) + [B_O(S_O) - B_N(S_O + \Delta S)]$$

$$= (-\$500,000)(0.4) - 0.12(-\$130,555)$$
$$+ [0.05(\$4,000,000) - 0.02(\$4,000,000 - \$500,000)]$$

$$= -\$54,330.$$

CHAPTER 9

CASH AND MARKETABLE SECURITIES MANAGEMENT

Overview

Cash management has begun receiving increased emphasis due to inflation and higher interest rates that reduce the real value of idle cash and provide incentives for the development of improved cash management techniques. This chapter begins with a discussion of cash management. Next, the Baumol model, one of several models designed to determine the optimal cash balance, is examined. The chapter concludes with a description of the various types of marketable securities. Generally, safety is the watchword, and rarely will a financial manager sacrifice safety for higher yields.

Outline

I. The cash management function involves decisions related to the level and allocation of liquid assets.

A. A risk/return trade-off is involved in determining a firm's level of liquid assets (cash and marketable securities), since liquid assets reduce risk, but generally yield less than the average return to the firm.

B. The distribution of liquid assets between cash and marketable securities must also be determined.

C. Firms hold cash for four primary reasons.

1. The transactions motive enables the firm to conduct its ordinary business operations--making purchases and sales. This provides liquidity to the firm and might also be called the liquidity motive.
2. The precautionary motive refers to the need to meet fluctuating demands for cash or unexpected cash drains. These needs depend on two factors:
    a. The predictability of cash inflows and outflows.
    b. The firm's ability to borrow on short notice.
3. The speculative motive is to enable a firm to take advantage of profit-making opportunities that may arise.
    a. Large accumulations of cash for speculative purposes are rarely found.

b. Both the precautionary and speculative motives are largely satisfied by holdings of marketable securities, which may be regarded as "near-cash" assets.

4. <u>Compensating balance requirements</u> of commercial banks represent minimum levels of cash that the firm agrees to maintain in its checking account, for example, during the duration of a loan, or to pay for "free" bank services.

D. Most firms do not segregate funds for each of these motives but do consider them in setting their overall cash positions.

E. Adequate cash provides several kinds of benefits.

1. Sufficient cash permits the firm to take trade discounts.
   a. When firms offer cash discounts for early payment, an implicit cost is involved if discounts are not (or cannot) be taken.
   b. The annualized cost of not taking discounts can be calculated as follows:

$$\text{Cost} = \left(\frac{\text{Discount percent}}{100 - \begin{array}{c}\text{Discount}\\ \text{percent}\end{array}}\right)\left(\frac{360}{\begin{array}{c}\text{Final due}\\ \text{date}\end{array} - \begin{array}{c}\text{Discount}\\ \text{period}\end{array}}\right).$$

For example, the implicit cost involved in credit terms of 2/15, net 40 is computed as follows:

$$\text{Cost} = \left(\frac{2}{100 - 2}\right)\left(\frac{360}{40 - 15}\right)$$

$$= 29.4\%.$$

2. Adequate cash is required to strengthen the current and quick ratios, which are key items in the appraisal of the firm's credit position.
3. Ample cash also is desirable to take advantage of favorable business opportunities.
4. Adequate cash is necessary to provide the firm with sufficient liquidity to meet unexpected developments.

F. Synchronization of cash flows is an important element of cash management.

1. Frequent requisitioning of funds by division offices from the central office enables funds to remain in the central interest-earning pool for a longer period.
2. Effective forecasting reduces the precautionary need for cash.
3. Effective forecasting allows a firm to minimize the cash it must borrow, keeping interest expense to a minimum.

II. Float is an important factor in the management of cash flows.

A. Float time refers to the interval between when a check is written and the point at which the payee has use of the funds; float refers to the amount of funds involved and is measured as the difference between the firm's balance on its own books and its balance on the bank's books.

    1. Mail-time float is the result of the time which elapses between the mailing of a check by a customer and its receipt by the seller.

    2. Processing float arises due to the time required to credit the customer's account and to deposit the check.

    3. Transit float results from the clearing time in the banking system.

B. Float is an advantage to the firm as a buyer of goods and a disadvantage to the firm as a seller. To maximize its advantage, the firm should strive to accelerate the cash-gathering process and decelerate cash disbursements.

III. A firm can accelerate the cash-gathering process by decentralizing collections, utilizing a cash-gathering system, and monitoring cash flows.

A. Decentralized collection points can reduce mail-time float and processing float. One important decentralized collection method is a lockbox system.

    1. In a lockbox system, customers mail checks to a post office box in a specified city. A local bank collects the checks, deposits them, and starts the clearing process before notifying the selling firm that payment has been received.

    2. Processing time is further reduced because it takes less time for the bank to collect local checks.

B. A cash-gathering system consists of a network of banks to channel funds efficiently.

    1. Local depository banks operate lockboxes.

    2. Funds are channeled to regional concentration banks to be available for disbursement.

        a. A concentration bank should be in a Federal Reserve Bank city.

        b. It should have access to the bank wire fund transfer system.

        c. It should be located so as to receive 80 percent or more customer checks within one day of mailing.

        d. It should be competitive with respect to its fees.

    3. The primary bank is the overall control bank for the firm's cash-gathering network. The main advantages of centralizing the firm's pool of cash include:

        a. Better control is achieved.

        b. Unused cash in minimized. Cash in excess of local needs is regularly transferred to the central bank.

        c. Marketable securities investment is facilitated.

IV. A transfer mechanism is a means of moving funds among accounts at different banks.

   A. <u>Depository transfer checks</u> (DTCs) are checks for deposit only to a firm's account at a particular bank. Electronic depository transfer checks (EDTCs) eliminate mail-time float.

   B. Wire transfers make possible immediate availability of funds transferred from one bank to another.

      1. The Federal Reserve Wire System is available to all member banks.
      2. A private bank wire system is used by approximately 300 U.S. banks for transfer of funds, securities, and credit information.

   C. The cost of a transfer mechanism is related to its speed.

      1. Wire transfers are instantaneous, but cost $6 to $8.
      2. Mail DTCs cost $0.40 to $0.50, but may take 2 to 7 days.
      3. By relating the cost of a faster mechanism to the value of the extra interest which could be earned by the funds after transfer, the breakeven transfer size can be found:

$$S* = \frac{\Delta C}{I \Delta T} \, ,$$

where

   $S*$ = the breakeven size of transfer above which the faster, higher cost mechanism should be used.

   ΔC = the incremental cost of the faster mechanism.

   I = the applicable daily interest rate.

   ΔT = the difference in transfer time in days.

      4. This methodology has been criticized on several counts.
         a. Funds in the depository bank are assumed to have no value when in fact they earn service credits which may reduce bank service charges.
         b. Timing of transfer alternatives may eliminate the advantage of a faster mechanism.

V. The goal of managing disbursements is to keep cash on hand longer.

   A. Payments can be delayed, but this creates other difficulties.

   B. Some firms maintain funds in distant or remote banks to legitimately lengthen the collection period on their checks. A wide range of methods exists to accomplish this goal.

      1. Use of drafts. Only when a draft must be submitted to the issuer for payment must the issuer deposit funds to cover the draft.

2. Use of floats. Banks have taken steps to reduce the gain from float, but companies that use float still have an advantage over those that do not.

VI. Cash management models have been developed to help determine optimal cash balances.

A. Cash management may be considered as an inventory problem.

B. The Baumol model is an application of EOQ inventory analysis to cash management.

1. Ordering costs are represented by the clerical and transactions costs of making transfers between the marketable securities portfolio and the cash account.
2. The carrying cost is the interest foregone on cash balances held.
3. The optimal size of transfer (C*) from marketable securities to cash is calculated as

$$C^* = \sqrt{\frac{2bT}{i}} \, ,$$

where

T = the total cash required for the time period involved.

b = the fixed cost of the transaction to purchase or sell marketable securities.

i = the applicable interest rate on marketable securities.

4. Assuming no precautionary balance, the optimal average cash balance is C*/2.
5. The total costs per year of maintaining cash balances, TC, is found as

$$TC = b(T/C^*) + i(C^*/2).$$

6. Baumol makes two major assumptions regarding the behavior of cash balances.
   a. Expenditures occur continuously.
   b. Receipts, or cash inflows, come in lump sums at periodic intervals.

VII. A firm's liquidity policies are affected by both individual and industry-wide circumstances and needs.

A. Uncertainty increases the need for liquidity to protect against a number of contingencies.

B. A forecasted cash drain calls for building up liquidity in advance of need.

C. An abundance of investment opportunities requires higher liquidity levels to be able to take advantage of them.

VIII. Management of the marketable securities portfolio involves choices among alternative financial assets.

    A. Criteria used in selecting portfolios.

        1. Default risk refers to the risk that the issuer cannot meet interest or principal as they come due.

        2. Interest rate risk refers to changes in the price of a security caused by changes in the general level of interest rates.

            a. Interest rate fluctuations generally cause substantial price changes in longer term maturities.

            b. Because the marketable securities portfolio is used to supply current cash requirements, it is generally advisable to confine security selection to the shorter maturities.

        3. Liquidity or marketability risk refers to whether an asset can be sold at or near its quoted market price.

        4. Taxability considerations arise because of differential tax treatment of:

            a. Dividend and interest income.

            b. Capital and ordinary gains.

            c. Certain types of government and municipal securities.

        5. Generally, higher relative yields can only be achieved at the cost of higher levels of risk.

    B. The financial manager must select securities with maturities and risks which are appropriate to the financial situation of the firm.

    C. Many types of securities are available for investment of surplus cash. Among those most suitable for holding as near-cash reserves are U.S. Treasury bills, commercial paper, negotiable certificates of deposit, money market funds, and Eurodollar time deposits.

    D. Inflation increases the need to invest cash balances appropriately.

        1. During periods of tight money, no firm can be confident of receiving bank loans to meet cash shortages, so it must keep cash reserves for future contingencies.

        2. Funds must be invested aggressively in order to protect them against inflation.

        3. Certificates of deposit, municipal securities, and commercial paper offer higher rates of return than Treasury bills and are thus increasing in popularity.

Definitional Questions

1. The funds needed to carry on the everyday business activities of the firm are referred to as _____ balances.

2. _____ balances are maintained in order to allow for random, unforeseen fluctuations in cash _____ and _____.

3. Cash balances held to enable the firm to take advantage of bargain purchases are known as _____ balances.

4. _____ balances are maintained to pay banks for services they perform.

5. Adequate cash balances are necessary to allow firms to take advantage of _____ _____ and favorable _____ _____.

6. _____ of cash flows and effective forecasting allows a firm to minimize cash borrowing, and hence to minimize _____ expense.

7. The difference between a firm's balance on its own books and its balance as carried on the bank's books in known as _____.

8. Firms try to maximize the advantages of float by accelerating the _____ _____ and _____ cash disbursements.

9. A firm can accelerate the cash-gathering process by using a _____ system to decentralize collections.

10. In a cash-gathering system, local depository banks channel funds to a _____ _____ _____ to be available for disbursement.

11. Three mechanisms by which firms transfer funds between accounts at different banks are _____ _____ _____, _____ depository transfer checks, and _____ _____.

12. Many firms try to delay the actual payment of bills by the use of _____ rather than checks.

13. A firm's need for liquidity is increased by _____, forecasted cash _____, and an _____ of investment opportunities.

14. _____ risk refers to an issuer's inability to make interest payments and to repay _____ at maturity.

15. Generally, higher _____ can only be achieved at the cost of higher levels of risk.

Conceptual Questions

16. Money market funds are suitable vehicles for investment of surplus cash.

    a. True   b. False

17. Which of the following actions would <u>not</u> be consistent with good management of the cash account?

    a. Increased synchronization of cash flows
    b. Use of drafts in disbursing funds
    c. Use of lockboxes in funds collection
    d. Maintaining an average cash balance equal to that required as a compensating balance or that which minimizes total cost, whichever is lower
    e. Maximum use of float

18. Which of the following investments is not likely to be a proper investment for temporary idle cash?

    a. Commercial paper
    b. Treasury bills
    c. Recently issued long-term AAA corporate bonds
    d. Treasury bonds due within one year
    e. AAA corporate bonds due within one year

19. The term "interest rate risk" refers to the probability that a firm will be unable to continue making interest payments on its debt.

    a. True   b. False

Problems

20. The Morgan Supply Company has a daily average collection of $150,000. It takes the company four days to convert the checks to cash. Assume a lockbox system could be employed which would reduce the cash conversion procedure to three days. The lockbox system would have a net cost of $20,000 per year, but any additional funds made available could be invested to net 10 percent per year. Should Morgan adopt the lockbox system?

    a. Yes; the system would free $150,000 in funds.
    b. Yes; the benefits of the lockbox system exceed the costs.
    c. No; the benefit is only $10,000.
    d. No; the firm would lose $5,000 per year if the system were used.
    e. The benefits and costs are equal, hence the firm is indifferent toward the system.

21. The Northrup Corporation needs to transfer $30,000 in excess cash from its field office in Miami to its regional concentration bank in Dallas. A mail depository transfer check will cost $0.50 and take two days to arrive in Dallas, while a wire transfer will cost $8.00 and will be immediately available. Northrup earns 12 percent annual interest on funds in its concentration bank. Which transfer method should be used?

   a. DTC; it will save Northrup $7.50 over using the wire transfer.
   b. DTC; the breakeven transfer volume is $12,500, indicating that the DTC should be used.
   c. The breakeven transfer size is $30,000, hence the firm is indifferent between the two methods.
   d. wire; the breakeven transfer volume is $12,500, indicating that the wire transfer should be used.
   e. wire; the breakeven volume is $25,000, indicating that the wire transfer should be used.

(The following information applies to the next two problems.)

The Bryer Company uses the Baumol model to determine its optimal cash balances. Recently, when the interest rate on marketable securities was 10 percent, the model called for an average cash balance of $600. A rapid increase in interest rates has driven this rate up to 15 percent. Bryer does not carry any precautionary balances.

22. What is the appropriate cash balance now?

   a. $489.90
   b. $475.00
   c. $433.40
   d. $385.50
   e. $350.00

23. If the cost per transaction of converting marketable securities to cash is $10, what will be Bryer's total cost of maintaining cash balances?

   a. $100.00
   b. $121.75
   c. $135.22
   d. $146.96
   e. $172.81

Answers and Solutions

1. transactions

2. Precautionary; inflows; outflows

3. speculative

4. Compensating

5. trade discounts; business opportunities

6. Synchronization; interest

7. float

8. cash-gathering system; decelerating

9. lockbox

10.ʻ regional concentration bank

11. depository transfer checks; electronic; wire transfers

12. drafts

13. uncertainty; drains; abundance

14. Default; principal

15. yields

16. a. Money market funds are highly liquid investments and, therefore, are suitable for holding as near-cash assets.

17 d. Management should maintain whichever balance is higher. The firm must maintain an average cash balance which is at least as great as its compensating balance requirement, and if the balance which minimizes total cost is greater than the compensating balance, it would be to the firm's best interest to choose the higher.

18. c. The long-term bonds would not be a proper investment for idle cash because they have significant interest rate risk.

19. b. Interest rate risk is the loss of value to a security if interest rates rise. The probability that a firm will fail to make interest payments is known as default risk.

20. d. Currently, Morgan has 4($150,000) = $600,000 in unavailable collections. If lockboxes were used, this could be reduced to $450,000. Thus, $150,000 would be available to invest at 10 percent, resulting in net income of 0.10($150,000) = $15,000. Since the lockbox system would cost $20,000, Morgan would lose $5,000 per year by adopting the system.

21. d. The breakeven transfer size is found as

$$S* = \frac{\Delta C}{I \Delta T} \ .$$

For the Northrup Company

$$S* = \frac{\$8.00 - \$0.50}{(0.12/360)(2)} = \frac{\$7.50}{0.0003(2)} = \$12,500.$$

The breakeven transfer volume, above which the wire transfer is preferred, is \$12,500. Since Northrup needs to transfer \$30,000, it should use a wire transfer.

22. a. The Baumol model is $C* = \sqrt{2bT/i}$. Initially, the average cash balance, $C*/2$, was \$600; thus, $C* = 2(\$600) = \$1,200$. Therefore,

$$\$1,200 = \sqrt{\frac{2bT}{0.10}} \ ,$$

and we can solve this equation for 2bT. Squaring both sides, we obtain

$$1,440,000 = \frac{2bT}{0.10} \ ,$$

so 2bT = 144,000.

We can now solve the model to find the new average cash balance, using the model

$$C* = \sqrt{\frac{\$144,000}{k}} \ .$$

If k is now 15 percent, $C* = \sqrt{\$144,000/0.15} = \$979.80$. Therefore, the average cash balance, $C*/2$, is now \$489.90.

23. d. The total cost is found using the equation, $TC = b(T/C*) + i(C*/2)$.

First, we must determine the value of T, given b = \$10, by solving 2bT = \$144,000 for T.

$$2bT = 2(10)T = 144,000$$
$$T = 144,000/20$$
$$T = 7,200.$$

$$TC = \$10(\$7,200/\$979.80) + 0.15(\$979.80/2)$$
$$= \$73.48 + \$73.49$$
$$= \$146.96.$$

CHAPTER 10

SHORT-TERM FINANCING

Overview

Short-term credit is defined as debt originally scheduled for repayment within one year. This chapter describes the four major sources of short-term financing: (1) accruals, (2) accounts payable, or trade credit, (3) loans from commercial banks, and (4) commercial paper. Companies use accruals on a regular basis, but this usage is not discretionary. Trade credit, bank loans, and commercial paper are controllable, at least within limits. In many situations, lenders require security, in the form of accounts receivable and inventories, when furnishing short-term credit. This chapter concludes with a discussion of the use of security in short-term loans.

Outline

I. Accrued wages and taxes increase and decrease spontaneously as a firm's operations expand and contract.

   A. This type of debt is "free" in the sense that no interest is paid on funds raised through accruals.

   B. The amount of accruals is determined by economic forces, industry custom, and payment dates established by the law. Thus, firms have no control over the supply of capital from this source.

II. Accounts payable, or trade credit, is the largest single category of short-term debt.

   A. The purchase of materials or supplies on credit from other firms is recorded as accounts payable.

   B. Trade credit is a "spontaneous" source of financing in that it arises from ordinary business transactions.

   C. The length of the credit period is determined by the:

      1. Economic nature of the product. Products with higher turnover and higher perishability have shorter credit terms.

2. Seller's circumstances. Longer terms correspond to greater financial strength of the seller, larger size of the seller, greater use of credit terms in sales promotion, and higher degree of excess capacity of the seller.
3. Buyer's circumstances. A higher degree of financial strength of the buyer and higher risks associated with the product lead to longer credit terms.
4. Cash discounts given to induce early payment.
    a. Savings from the discount frequently exceed the rate of interest on borrowed funds; therefore, trade credit can be expensive.
    b. The length of the credit period is influenced by the size of the discounts offered.

D. The cost of trade credit is made up of discounts lost by not paying invoices within the discount period.

1. Trade credit can be divided into two components.
    a. Free trade credit is that credit received during the discount period.
    b. Costly trade credit is obtained by forgoing discounts. This costly component should be used only when it is less expensive than funds obtained from other sources.
2. The following equation may be used to calculate the approximate annual percentage cost of not taking discounts:

$$\% \text{ cost} = \frac{\text{Discount \%}}{100 - \text{Discount \%}} \times \frac{360}{\text{Days credit is} - \text{Discount}}$$
$$\text{outstanding} \qquad \text{period}$$

3. Competitive conditions may permit firms to do better than the stated credit terms by taking discounts beyond the discount period or by simply paying late. Such practices reduce the cost of trade credit, but they also result in poor relationships with suppliers.

E. Trade credit is both a source and a use of funds for the firm.

1. Trade credit is a source of credit for financing purchases.
2. Trade credit is a use of funds to the extent that the firm finances credit sales to customers.
3. Net credit extended is the difference between accounts receivable and accounts payable.

F. Trade credit is an important source of financing.

1. The use of trade credit is convenient and informal.
2. Its wise use promotes sound customer relations.

    3. A firm that does not qualify for credit from a financial institution may receive credit from the seller because of his greater experience and knowledge of the firm.

    4. The cost of trade credit may be higher or lower than bank loans.

       a. The cost is commensurate with risks to the seller.

       b. The buyer may use the more expensive trade credit because he does not have better alternatives.

       c. Sometimes the buyer has not calculated the cost of trade credit and does not realize that trade credit may be more costly than bank loans.

G. Good supplier relations are important during inflationary periods.

    1. Suppliers become more selective when extending trade credit during periods of tight money.

    2. A firm must earn the confidence of its suppliers by:

       a. Maintaining strong financial ratios.

       b. Paying promptly.

       c. Offering realistic plans for improving its situation when necessary.

III. Commercial bank loans appear on a firm's balance sheet as notes payable.

A. Bank loans are second in importance to trade credit as a source of short-term financing.

    1. Banks occupy a pivotal position in the short-term money market, because they provide non-spontaneous funds.

    2. Banks often provide the marginal credit that allows firms to expand.

B. The main features of bank loans include the following:

    1. When a firm obtains a bank loan, a promissory note specifying the following items is signed:

       a. The amount borrowed.

       b. The percentage interest rate.

       c. The repayment schedule.

       d. Any collateral offered as security.

       e. Other terms of the loan.

    2. A line of credit is a formal or informal understanding between the bank and the borrower concerning the maximum loan balance the bank will allow. Normally, the borrower will pay the bank a commitment fee to compensate the bank for guaranteeing that the funds will be available. This fee is paid in addition to the regular interest charge.

    3. Small firms account for more than 50 percent of the number of all bank loans, but large firms account for the bulk of the dollar amount of all loans.

4. About two-thirds of all bank loans mature in a year or less, although banks do make longer term loans.
5. Banks may require security for loans made to borrowers of questionable risks and to firms whose borrowings exceed that which the bank feels is prudent. More than two-thirds of bank loans are secured or guaranteed by a third party.
6. Banks normally require regular borrowers to maintain compensating balances equal to 10 to 20 percent of the face value of loans. Such required balances increase the effective interest rate on the loan.
7. Banks often require borrowers to "clean up" their short-term loans for at least one month each year to insure that bank credit is not being used as a source of permanent financing.

C. The interest cost of loans will vary for different types of borrowers and for all borrowers over time. Rates charged will vary depending on economic conditions, the risk of the borrower, and the size of the loan.

1. The prime rate is the interest rate charged to a bank's most creditworthy customers.
2. Smaller, financially weaker firms must pay higher rates and may be required to provide collateral.
3. Interest rates are calculated in three ways.
   a. Regular, or simple, interest. The interest payment is determined by multiplying the loan balance, or principal, by the stated interest rate. Principal and interest are then paid at the end of the loan period.
   b. Discount interest. Under this method, the bank deducts interest in advance. The effective rate of interest is higher than the stated rate.

$$\text{Effective rate} = \frac{\text{Interest}}{\text{Amount borrowed} - \text{Interest}}.$$

   c. Installment loans: add-on interest. Interest charges are calculated and added-on to the funds received to determine the face amount of the note. The borrower has use of the full amount of the loan only until the first installment is paid. The effective rate is approximately double the stated rate since the average amount of the loan outstanding is about half the face amount borrowed.

$$\text{Approximate effective rate} = \frac{\text{Average annual interest}}{\text{Loan amount}/2}.$$

4. Compensating balances tend to raise the effective interest rate on bank loans.

  a. In general, the following formula is used to find the effective interest rate when compensating balances apply:

  $$\text{Effective rate} = \frac{\text{Stated interest rate (\%)}}{1.0 - \text{Compensating balance fraction}}.$$

  b. The analysis can be extended to the case where compensating balances are required and the loan is based on discount interest:

  $$\text{Effective rate} = \frac{\text{Stated interest rate (\%)}}{1.0 - \left(\begin{array}{c}\text{Compensating}\\\text{balance}\\\text{fraction}\end{array}\right) - \left(\begin{array}{c}\text{Stated}\\\text{interest}\\\text{rate}\end{array}\right)}.$$

  c. It should be noted that when compensating balance or discount interest or both apply, the borrower must borrow an amount greater than that actually required. For a discount loan with a compensating balance, the loan amount is calculated as

  $$\text{Amount of Loan} = \frac{\text{Funds needed}}{1.0 - \left(\begin{array}{c}\text{Compensating}\\\text{balance}\\\text{fraction}\end{array}\right) - \left(\begin{array}{c}\text{Stated}\\\text{interest}\\\text{rate}\end{array}\right)}$$

D. In choosing a bank, the financial manager should analyze the following variables:

1. The bank's policy toward risk.
2. The availability of management counseling services.
3. The loyalty of the bank when the firm encounters difficulties.
4. The stability of the bank's deposits as a measure of possible repayment pressure.
5. The degree to which the loan areas in which the bank specializes match the borrower's area of operations.
6. The maximum size loan a bank can make.
7. The range of financial and business services offered by the bank.

IV. Commercial paper consists of the unsecured promissory notes of large, stable firms. It is sold primarily to other business firms, insurance companies, investment funds, pension funds, and banks.

A. Maturities vary from a few days to nine months, but the great majority mature in two to six months.

B. Interest rates on commercial paper are generally 1 1/4 to 1 1/2 percent below the prime rate. Since no compensating balance is required, the effective rate differential is even wider in comparison to bank loans.

C. The open market for commercial paper is limited to firms which are good credit risks.

1. The commercial paper market has some significant advantages.
   a. It provides funds to the borrower at relatively low rates.
   b. The borrower avoids the inconvenience and expense of financing arrangements.
   c. Publicity and prestige are enhanced.
2. There are some disadvantages associated with borrowing in the commercial paper market.
   a. The amount of funds available is limited to the excess liquidity of the main suppliers of funds at a particular time.
   b. A commercial paper borrower who is in temporary financial difficulty receives little consideration because of the impersonal nature of the commercial paper market.

V. Borrowing on an unsecured basis is generally cheaper and simpler than on a secured loan basis because of the administrative costs associated with the use of security. However, lenders will demand some form of collateral if a borrower's credit standing is questionable.

A. Most secured short-term business loans involve the pledge of short-term assets such as accounts receivable or inventories.

B. The legal procedures for establishing loan security have been standardized and simplified in the Uniform Commercial Code.

VI. Accounts receivable financing involves either the pledging of receivables or the selling (factoring) of receivables.

A. In pledging accounts receivable as security for financing, no notification is made to the buyer of the goods, and the lender has recourse to the holder of the account receivable in case of default. The receivable is not sold to the lender; it is merely used as a security for a loan.

B. In factoring, the buyer of the goods makes payment directly to the factor who has no recourse to the seller of the goods in case of default. The receivable is sold outright to the factoring firm.

C. The cost of receivables financing can be quite high.

1. Interest rates on borrowed funds under receivables financing are usually above the prevailing prime rate.
   a. The credit rating of the borrower is usually below that of firms qualifying for prime rate loans.
   b. The processing of the invoices (receivables) involves additional expenses.
2. Factoring charges consist of two elements.
   a. A fee for credit checking of 1 to 3 percent.
   b. An interest charge (somewhat above the prevailing prime rate) on the funds provided by the factor.
   c. Also, if the risk is high, the factor may purchase the invoices at a discount from face value.

D. There are several advantages of receivables financing.

1. It is a flexible method.
2. The security provided may allow the firm to receive financing that would otherwise be unobtainable.
3. Factoring may provide the services of a credit department.

E. The disadvantages of accounts receivable financing are:

1. When invoices are numerous, administrative costs may be high.
2. The firm is using a highly liquid asset as security.

F. In the future, accounts receivable financing will increase in relative importance as automation reduces the costs and increases the convenience of employing receivables financing. Credit card use is a prime example of a type of automated accounts receivable financing.

VII. A large volume of credit is secured by business inventories.

A. The blanket inventory lien gives the lending institution a lien against all inventories of the borrowing firm. However, the firm is free to sell the inventories. This reduces the value of the collateral.

B. A trust receipt is an instrument acknowledging that the borrower holds goods in trust for the lender. The borrower may keep the goods in his possession, but he must remit the proceeds of the sale of the specific goods to the lender at the end of each day.

C. A third means of inventory financing is warehouse financing. In warehouse financing, a third party acts as a supervisory agent for the lender.

Definitional Questions

1. _____ wages and taxes are common sources of short-term credit. However, most firms have little control over the _____ of these accounts.

2. Accounts payable, or _____ _____, is the largest single source of short-term credit for business.

3. Trade credit is a _____ source of funds in the sense that it automatically increases if sales increase.

4. The length of the credit period is influenced by the nature of the product, _____ circumstances, seller _____, and the _____ _____ policy.

5. Trade credit can be divided into two components: _____ trade credit and _____ trade credit.

6. _____ trade credit is that credit received during the _____ period.

7. _____ trade credit extended is the difference between accounts receivable and accounts payable.

8. The majority of all short-term bank loans mature in _____ year(s) or less.

9. Bank loans are an important source of short-term financing because banks provide _____ funds.

10. The instrument signed when bank credit is obtained is called a _____ _____.

11. Most banks require borrowers to keep _____ _____ equal to 10 or 20 percent of the face value of a loan on deposit with the bank.

12. The rate charged to a bank's most creditworthy loan customers is known as the _____ _____.

13. If interest charges are deducted in advance, this is known as _____ interest, and the effective rate is higher than the _____ interest rate.

14. With an _____ loan, the average amount of the loan outstanding during the loan period is equal to approximately _____ of the face amount of the loan.

15. Maturities on commercial paper generally range from _____ to _____ months, with interest rates set 1 1/4 to 1 1/2 percent _____ the _____ rate.

16. A _____ _____ _____ is an understanding between a bank and a borrower as to the maximum loan that will be permitted.

17. The fee paid to the bank to make a line of credit available is known as a _____ fee.

18. A _____ loan is one where collateral such as _____ or _____ have been pledged in support of the loan.

19. Accounts receivable financing involves either _____ or _____ receivables.

20. The four forms of inventory financing are the _____ _____ lien, trust receipt, _____ _____, and _____ certificate.

21. A _____ _____ acknowledges that the borrower holds goods in trust for the lender.

22. A _____ _____ guarantees the existence of the amount of _____ pledged as loan collateral.

Conceptual Questions

23. Accruals are "free" in the sense that no interest must be paid on these funds.

    a.   True   b.   False

24. The effect of compensating balances is to decrease the effective interest rate of a loan.

    a.   True   b.   False

25. Spontaneous sources of financing include all of the following except

    a.   Trade credit.
    b.   Accrued interest.
    c.   Accrued wages.
    d.   Notes payable.
    e.   Deferred income taxes.

26. Net credit extended refers to

    a. The date for final payment in credit terms, as 2/10 net 30.
    b. The difference between accounts receivable and accounts payable.
    c. The difference between cash sales and credit sales.
    d. Bank loans to commercial fishermen.
    e. The difference between credit sales and cash received after discounts have been taken.

27. Which of the following statements concerning commercial paper is correct?

    a. Commercial paper is secured debt of large, financially strong firms.
    b. Commercial paper is sold primarily to individual investors.
    c. Maturities of commercial paper generally exceed nine months.
    d. Commercial paper interest rates are typically 1.25 to 1.5 percentage points above the stated prime rate.
    e. None of the above statements are correct.

Problems

28. A firm buys on terms of 2/10, net 30, but generally does not pay until 40 days after the invoice date. Its purchases total $1,080,000 per year. How much "non-free" trade credit does the firm use on average each year?

    a. $120,000
    b. $90,000
    c. $60,000
    d. $30,000
    e. $20,000

29. Refer to Problem 28. What is the approximate cost of the "non-free" trade credit?

    a. 16.2%
    b. 19.4%
    c. 21.9%
    d. 24.5%
    e. 33.3%

30. Beckett Pumps, Inc., has developed plans for a revolutionary pump that will allow more efficient and economical operation in the company's oil pumps. Management estimates that $2,400,000 will be required to put this new pump into operation. Funds can be obtained from a bank at 10 percent <u>discount</u> interest, or Beckett can finance the expansion by delaying payment to its suppliers. Presently, Beckett purchases under terms of 2/10, net 40, but management believes payment could be delayed 30 additional days without penalty; that is, payment could be made in 70 days. Which means of financing should Beckett use?

   a. Trade credit, since the cost is approximately 12.24 percent.
   b. Trade credit, since the cost is approximately 3.13 percentage points less than the bank loan.
   c. Bank loan, since the cost is approximately 1.13 percentage points less than trade credit.
   d. Bank loan, since the cost is approximately 3.13 percentage points less than trade credit.
   e. The firm could use either since the costs are the same.

(The following information applies to the next four problems.)

You plan to borrow $10,000 from you bank, which offers to lend you the money at a 10 percent stated rate on a 1 year loan.

31. What is the effective interest rate if the loan is a discount loan?

   a. 11.1%
   b. 13.3%
   c. 15.0%
   d. 17.5%
   e. 20.0%

32. What is the approximate effective interest rate if the loan is an installment loan with 12 monthly payments?

   a. 11.1%
   b. 13.3%
   c. 15.0%
   d. 17.5%
   e. 20.0%

33. What is the effective interest rate if the loan is a discount loan with a 15 percent compensating balance.

   a. 11.1%
   b. 13.3%
   c. 15.0%
   d. 17.5%
   e. 20.0%

34. Under the terms of Problem 33, how much would you have to borrow to have the use of $10,000?

    a. $10,000
    b. $11,111
    c. $12,000
    d. $13,333
    e. $15,000

Answers and Solutions

1. Accrued; size

2. trade credit

3. spontaneous

4. buyer; circumstances; cash discount

5. free; costly

6. free; discount

7. Net

8. one

9. nonspontaneous

10. promissory note

11. compensating balance

12. prime rate

13. discount; simple

14. installment; half

15. two; six; below; prime

16. line of credit

17. commitment

18. secured; receivables; inventories

19. pledging; factoring

20. blanket inventory; field warehousing; collateral

21. trust receipt

22. collateral certificate; inventory

23. a. Accruals are interest-free sources of financing which arise spontaneously from the normal operations of a firm.

24. b. Compensating balances reduce the amount of usable funds available to firms, thus raising the effective interest rate.

25. d. Spontaneous sources of financing are those balance sheet accounts which increase or decrease as a firm's operations expand or contract. Notes payable, which represents bank loans, do not increase spontaneously. The firm must apply to the bank for increases in notes payable.

26. b. A firm extends credit to its customers to finance their sales, and it uses trade credit extended to it by its suppliers to finance purchases. Net trade credit extended is the difference in credit extended by the firm (accounts receivable) and credit extended to the firm (accounts payable).

27. e. Commercial paper is unsecured debt of large, financially strong firms which is sold primarily to other businesses, insurance companies, investment and pension funds, and banks at rates below the prime rate. Maturities of commercial paper are generally in the range of two to six months.

28. b. $1,080,000/360 = $3,000 in purchases per day. Typically, there will be $3,000(40) = $120,000 of accounts payable on the books at any given time. Of this, $3,000(10) = $30,000 is "free" credit, while $3,000(30) = $90,000 is "non-free" credit.

29. d.

$$\text{Approx. \% cost} = \frac{\text{Discount \%}}{100 - \text{Discount \%}} \times \frac{360}{\text{Days credit} - \text{Discount}}$$
$$\text{is outstanding} \quad \text{period}$$

$$= \frac{2}{100 - 2} \times \frac{360}{40 - 10}$$

$$= \frac{2}{98} \times \frac{360}{30} = 24.5\%.$$

30. c. Effective rate on bank loan $= \dfrac{\text{Interest}}{\text{Borrowed amount} - \text{Interest}}$

$$= \frac{(\$2,400,000)(0.10)}{\$2,400,000 - (\$2,400,000)(0.10)}$$

$$= \frac{\$240,000}{\$2,160,000} = 0.1111 = 11.11\%.$$

Credit terms are 2/10, net 40, but delaying payments 30 additional days is the equivalent of 2/10, net 70. Assuming no penalty, the approximate cost is as follows:

Approximate % cost $= \dfrac{\text{Discount \%}}{100 - \text{Discount \%}} \times \dfrac{360}{\text{Days credit} \quad \_\text{Discount}}$
$\qquad\qquad\qquad\qquad\qquad\qquad\qquad\qquad$ is outstanding period

$$= \frac{2}{100 - 2} \times \frac{360}{70 - 10}$$

$$= \frac{2}{98} \times \frac{360}{60}$$

$$= 0.0204(6) = 12.24\%.$$

Therefore, the loan cost is 12.24 - 11.11 = 1.13 percentage points less than trade credit.

31. a. Effective rate $= \dfrac{\text{Interest}}{\text{Borrowed amount} - \text{Interest}}$

$$= \frac{\$10,000(0.10)}{\$10,000 - \$10,000(1.0)}$$

$$= \frac{\$1,000}{\$9,000} = 11.1\%.$$

32. e. Approximate effective rate $= \dfrac{\text{Interest}}{\text{Borrowed amount}/2}$

$$= \frac{\$10,000(0.10)}{\$10,000/2}$$

$$= \frac{\$1,000}{\$5,000}$$

$$= 20.0\%.$$

33. b.

$$\text{Effective rate} = \frac{\text{Stated interest rate}}{1.0 - \begin{array}{c}\text{Compensating}\\\text{balance}\\\text{fraction}\end{array} - \begin{array}{c}\text{Stated}\\\text{interest}\\\text{rate}\end{array}}$$

$$= \frac{0.10}{1.0 - 0.15 - 0.10}$$

$$= \frac{0.10}{0.75}$$

$$= 13.3\%.$$

34. d.

$$\text{Loan} = \frac{\text{Funds needed}}{1.0 - \begin{array}{c}\text{Compensating}\\\text{balance}\\\text{requirement}\end{array} - \begin{array}{c}\text{Stated}\\\text{interest}\\\text{rate}\end{array}}$$

$$= \frac{\$10,000}{1 - 0.15 - 0.10} = \$13,333,$$

since $0.15(\$13,333) = \$2,000$ is required for the compensating balance, and $0.10(\$13,333) = \$1,333$ is required for the immediate interest payment.

CHAPTER 11

TIME VALUE OF MONEY

Overview

A dollar in the hand today is worth more than a dollar to be received in the future because, if you had it now, you could invest that dollar and earn interest. A knowledge of compound value, or future value, and present value techniques is essential to an understanding of many aspects of finance, such as security valuation and capital budgeting. This chapter begins by describing the time value calculations for lump sums, annuities, perpetuities, and uneven payment series, and concludes by examining compounding periods other than annual and loan amortization. Chapter 11 implicitly assumes that growth occurs at discrete intervals--annually, semiannually, and so forth. For some purposes, it is better to assume instantaneous, or continuous, growth. Appendix 11A discusses continuous compounding and discounting.

Outline

I.   Future value (FV_n) is defined as the value to which a beginning lump sum or present value (PV) will grow in n periods at a specified interest rate, k. The amount of interest earned in each period is designated as I.

A.   The formula for the future value after one period is

$$FV_n = PV + I = PV + PV(k) = PV(1 + k).$$

B.   However, for more than one period the formula is

$$FV_n = PV(1 + k)^n.$$

C.   In the above equation, $(1 + k)^n$ is known as the future value interest factor, or $FVIF_{k,n}$. Therefore,

$$FV_n = PV(FVIF_{k,n}).$$

D.   These factors have been calculated for various interest rates and time periods and organized into tables to simplify future value calculations. FVIFs may be found in text Table A-3.

1.   Select the appropriate $FVIF_{k,n}$ for the specified interest rate and the given number of periods.

2. Multiply the initial PV by the interest factor to determine the future value, or ending amount.

E. For example, the future value of $1,000 at 6 percent for 5 years is $FV_5 = \$1,000(1.3382) = \$1,338.20$.

F. The same calculation can be made using a calculator.

1. Using the exponential function, simply raise 1.06 to the 5th power, $(1.06)^5 = 1.33823$, then multiply by $1,000 to get $1,338.23.

2. When using a financial calculator, you need only enter n = 5, i = 6, and PV = $1,000. Then press the FV key and $1,338.23 is displayed.

3. The differences between the tabular and calculator solutions are caused by rounding errors.

II. The concept of present value is the reverse of compounding and is often referred to as "discounting."

A. Discounting determines the present value of a sum to be received at a future point in time.

B. The formula for present value is

$$PV = \frac{FV_n}{(1 + k)^n} = FV_n \left(\frac{1}{1 + k}\right)^n .$$

C. The amount shown above in brackets is known as the present value interest factor, $PVIF_{k,n}$, and has also been determined for a wide range of interest rates and time periods. PVIFs may be found in text Table A-1. Therefore,

$$PV = FV_n(PVIF_{k,n}).$$

D. The present value of $1,338.20 to be received in 5 years discounted at an interest rate of 6 percent is $1,338.20(0.7473) = $1,000.04. This result can be compared with the future value calculation to confirm that these are reciprocal processes. The slight difference in values is due to the fact that the interest factors are only carried to four places.

E. The present value interest factor is the reciprocal of the future value interest factor:

$$PVIF_{k,n} = \frac{1}{FVIF_{k,n}}$$

$$PVIF_{6\%,5 \text{ years}} = \frac{1}{1.3382} = 0.7473.$$

F. Present value calculations can be made using a calculator.

    1. The exponential function and reciprocal key can be used to calculate the $PVIF_{k,n}$.

    2. Using the financial functions, you need only enter n = 5, i = 6, and FV = $1,338.20. Then hit the PV key and $999.98 is displayed. If you had used FV = $1,338.23-- the future value obtained using the financial function-- the PV would be $1,000.

III. An annuity is defined as a series of payments of a fixed amount for a specified number of periods. If the payments occur at the end of each period, as they typically do, the annuity is an ordinary, or deferred, annuity. If the payments occur at the beginning of each period, the annuity is an annuity due.

    A. The future value of an annuity is the total amount one would have at the end of the annuity period if each payment were invested at a given periodic interest rate and held to the end of the annuity period.

        1. Defining S_n as the compound sum of an ordinary annuity of n years and PMT as the periodic receipt, we can write

$$S_n = PMT(FVIFA_{k,n}).$$

        2. $FVIFA_{k,n}$ is the future value interest factor for an ordinary annuity. FVIFAs may be found in the text Table A-4.

        3. For example, the future value of a 10-year, 7 percent ordinary annuity of $200 per year would be $200(13.8164) = $2,763.28.

        4. The same calculation can be made using the financial functions of a calculator. First, check to insure that the calculator is set for an ordinary annuity. Now, enter n = 10, i = 7, and PMT = $200. Then, hit the FV key and $2,763.29 is displayed.

        5. For an annuity due, the compound sum is

$$S_n(\text{Annuity due}) = PMT(FVIFA_{k,n})(1 + k).$$

        6. The future value of a 10-year, 7 percent annuity due of $200 per year is $200(13.8164)(1.07) = $2,956.71.

        7. Most calculators with financial functions have an annuity due switch. Merely repeat the procedure in Subparagraph 4 above with the calculator in the annuity due mode. Then, $2,956.72 is displayed.

    B. The present value of an annuity is the lump-sum payment required today that would be equivalent to the annuity payments spread over the annuity period. It is the amount today that would permit withdrawals of equal amount (PMT) at the end (or beginning for an annuity due) of each period for n periods.

1. Defining A_n as the present value of an ordinary annuity of n years and PMT as the periodic receipt, we can write

    $$A_n = PMT(PVIFA_{k,n}).$$

2. $PVIFA_{k,n}$ is the present value interest factor for an ordinary annuity. PVIFAs may be found in text Table A-2.

3. For example, an annuity of $1,200 per year for 10 years at 8 percent would have a present value of $1,200(6.7101) = $8,052.12.

4. The $PVIFA_{k,n}$ is always smaller than the number of years the annuity runs, whereas the $FVIFA_{k,n}$ for the sum of an annuity is larger than the number of years, assuming k is greater than zero.

5. The same calculation can be made using the financial functions of a calculator. First, check to insure that the calculator is set for an ordinary annuity. Now, enter n = 10, i = 8, and PMT = $1,200. Then, hit the PV key and $8,052.10 is displayed.

6. The present value for an annuity due is

    $$A_n(\text{Annuity due}) = PMT(PVIFA_{k,n})(1 + k).$$

7. The present value of a 10-year, 8 percent annuity due of $1,200 is $1,200(6.7101)(1.08) = $8,696.29.

8. To use a calculator, repeat the steps in Subparagraph 5 using the annuity due mode. Then, $8,696.27 is displayed.

IV. An annuity that goes on indefinitely is called a perpetuity. The payments of a perpetuity constitute an infinite series.

A. The present value of a perpetuity is

    $$\text{PV of a perpetuity} = \frac{\text{Payment}}{\text{Discount rate}} = \frac{PMT}{k}.$$

B. For example, if the discount rate were 12 percent, a perpetuity of $1,000 a year would have a present value of $1,000/0.12 = $8,333.33.

V. Many financial decisions require the analysis of irregular cash flows rather than a stream of fixed payments such as an annuity. The present value of an uneven stream of income is the sum of the PVs of the individual cash flow components. Similarly, the future value of an uneven stream of income is the sum of the FVs of the individual cash flow components.

VI. If one knows the relevant cash flows, the effective interest rate can be calculated.

A. For example, if one borrows $2,000 today and agrees to repay $2,805.20 at the end of 5 years, what is the interest rate?

$$FV_n = PV(FVIF_{k,n})$$

$$FVIF_{k,n} = \frac{FV_n}{PV} = \frac{\$2,805.20}{\$2,000} = 1.4026.$$

Looking at the Period 5 row of Table A-3, 1.4026 is the FVIF for 7 percent.

B. To solve this problem using a calculator's financial functions, simply enter n = 5, PV = 2,000, and FV = 2,805.20. Then, hit the i key and 7.00 percent is displayed.

C. Similar procedures can be used to solve for the effective interest rate if the cash flow stream is an annuity.

VII. Semiannual, quarterly, and other compounding more frequent than annual compounding are frequently used in financial transactions. This requires an adjustment in the way in which the interest factors are determined.

A. Divide the nominal, or stated, interest rate by the number of times compounding occurs each year.

B. Multiply the years by the number of compounding periods per year.

C. Use these adjusted values for k and n in the computations and when looking up interest factors in the tables.

D. The annual percentage rate (APR), or effective annual percentage rate, is the rate that would have produced the final compound value under annual compounding. The annual percentage rate is given by the following formula:

$$APR = \left(1 + \frac{k_{nom}}{m}\right)^m - 1.0,$$

where k_{nom} is the stated, or nominal, annual rate and m is the number of compounding periods per year.

E. For example, the APR for 12 percent, compounded quarterly, is as follows:

$$APR = (1 + 0.12/4)^4 - 1.0 = 12.55\%.$$

VIII. An amortized loan is a loan that is paid off in equal, periodic installments over time.

A. The amount of each payment, PMT, is found as follows:

Amount of loan = PV of annuity = $PMT(PVIFA_{k,n})$.

$$PMT = \frac{PV \text{ of annuity}}{PVIFA_{k,n}}.$$

B. Each payment consists partly of interest and partly of a repayment of principal. This breakdown is often depicted in a loan amortization schedule.

1. The interest component is largest in the first period and declines subsequently.
2. The repayment of principal is smallest in the first period and increases thereafter.

IX. A special case of semiannual compounding is bond valuation.

A. Most bonds pay interest semiannually, so semiannual compounding procedures are used for determining bond values.

B. The receipts from a bond consists of an annuity (the interest payments) and a lump sum (the principal) which is paid when the bond matures.

1. First, find the PV of the interest payments using the present value of an annuity form with $k/2$ as the discount rate and $2n$ as the number of payments.
2. Next, find the present value of the maturity value using $k/2$ as the discount rate and $2n$ as the number of periods.
3. Finally, sum the two component PVs to determine the value of the bond.

C. For example, the present value of a 100-year bond paying $60 interest every six months and $1,000 at maturity is found as follows, given a discount rate of 10 percent.

1. The present value of the interest payment is

$$PV = \$60(PVIFA_{k/2,\ 2n})$$
$$= \$60\ (PVIFA_{5\%,\ 20})$$
$$= \$60(12.4622)$$
$$= \$747.73.$$

2. The present value of the maturity value is

$$PV = \$1,000(PVIF_{5\%,\ 20})$$
$$= \$1,000(0.3769)$$
$$= \$376.90.$$

3. The present value of the bond is

$$Bond\ value = \$747.73 + \$376.90$$
$$= \$1,124.63.$$

X. Appendix 11A discusses continuous compounding and discounting.

    A. The future value of a present lump sum, when compounded continuously, is given by $FV_n = PV(e^{kn})$ where k is the stated interest rate, and n is the number of years of continuous compounding.

    B. For example, the future value of $100 compounded continuously for 5 years at 10 percent is $FV_5 = \$100\left[e^{0.1(5)}\right] = \$100\left(e^{0.5}\right) = \$100(1.6487) = \$164.87$. The value of $e^{0.5}$ can be obtained by using the antilog (e^x) function on a calculator, or by using the exponential function and the known value of e, 2.7183.

    C. The present value of a future lump sum, when discounted continuously, is given by $PV = FV_n\left(e^{-kn}\right)$.

Definitional Questions

1. The beginning value of an account or investment in a project is known as its _____ _____.

2. Using a savings account as an example, the difference between the account's _____ value and its _____ value at the end of a period is due to _____ earned during the period.

3. The equation $FV_n = PV(1 + k)^n$ determines the future value at the end of n periods. The factor $(1 + k)^n$ is known as the _____ _____ _____ _____.

4. The process of finding present values is often referred to as _____ and is the reverse of the _____ process.

5. The $PVIF_{k,n}$ for a 5 year, 5 percent investment is _____. This value is the _____ of the $FVIF_{k,n}$ for 5 years at 5 percent.

6. For a given number of time periods, the $PVIF_{k,n}$ will decline as the _____ _____ increases.

7. A series of payments of a fixed amount for a specified number of periods is an _____. If the payments occur at the end of each period it is an _____ annuity, while if the payments occur at the beginning of each period it is an annuity _____.

8. The present value of an uneven stream of future payments is the _____ of the PVs of the individual payments.

9. Since different types of investments use different compounding periods, it is important to distinguish between the stated, or _____, rate and the _____ interest rate, often called the annual percentage rate (APR).

10. To use the interest factor tables when compounding occurs more than once a year, divide the _____ _____ by the number of times compounding occurs and multiply the years by the number of _____ _____ per year.

   (The next question refers to Appendix 11A.)

11. When the number of compounding periods becomes _____, we have the special case of _____ compounding.

Conceptual Questions

12. You have determined the profitability of a planned project by finding the present value of all the cash flows from that project. Which of the following would cause the project to look less appealing, that is, have a lower present value?

   a. The discount rate decreases.
   b. The cash flows are extended over a longer period of time.
   c. The discount rate increases.
   d. b and c are both correct.
   e. a and b are both correct.

13. If a bank uses quarterly compounding for savings accounts, the nominal rate will be greater than the annual percentage rate (APR).

   a. True   b. False

14. If money has time value, the future value of some amount of money will always be more than the amount invested. The present value of some amount to be received in the future is always less than the amount to be received.

   a. True   b. False

Problems

15. Assume that you purchase a 6-year, 8 percent savings certificate for $1,000. If interest is compounded annually, what will be the value of the certificate when it matures?

   a. $630.17
   b. $1,469.33
   c. $1,677.10
   d. $1,586.90
   e. $1,766.33

16. A savings certificate similar to that in Problem 15 is available with the exception that interest is compounded semiannually. What is the difference between the ending value of the savings

certificate compounded semiannually and the one compounded annually?

a. The semiannual is worth $14.10 more than the annual.
b. The semiannual is worth $14.10 less than the annual.
c. The semiannual is worth $21.54 more than the annual.
d. The semiannual is worth $21.54 less than the annual.
e. The semiannual is worth the same as the annual.

17. A friend promises to pay you $600 two years from now if you loan him $500 today. What annual interest rate is your friend offering?

a. 7.5%
b. 8.5%
c. 9.5%
d. 10.5%
e. 11.5%

18. You are offered an investment opportunity with the "guarantee" that your investment will double in 5 years. Assuming annual compounding, what annual rate of return would this investment provide?

a. 40.00%
b. 100.00%
c. 14.87%
d. 20.00%
e. 18.74%

19. You decide to begin saving toward the purchase of a new car in 5 years. If you put $1,000 in a savings account paying 6 percent compounded annually at the end of each of the next 5 years, how much will you accumulate after 5 years?

a. $6,691.13
b. $5,637.10
c. $1,338.23
d. $5,975.33
e. $5,731.95

20. Refer to Problem 19. What would be the ending amount if the payments were made at the beginning of each year?

a. $6,691.13
b. $5,637.10
c. $1,338.23
d. $5,975.33
e. $5,731.95

21. Refer to Problem 19. What would be the ending amount if $500 payments were made at the end of each 6 month period for 5 years and the account paid 6 percent compounded semiannually?

    a. $6,691.13
    b. $5,637.10
    c. $1,338.23
    d. $5,975.33
    e. $5,731.95

22. Calculate the present value of $1,000 to be received at the end of 8 years. Assume an interest rate of 7 percent.

    a. $582.00
    b. $1,718.19
    c. $583.49
    d. $5,971.30
    e. $649.37

23. How much would you be willing to pay today for an investment that would return $800 each year at the end of each of the next 6 years? Assume a discount rate of 5 percent.

    a. $5,441.53
    b. $4,800.00
    c. $3,369.89
    d. $4,060.56
    e. $4,632.37

24. You have applied for a mortgage of $44,500 to finance the purchase of a new home. The bank will require you to make annual payments of $4,532.45 at the end of each of the next 20 years. Determine the interest rate in effect on this mortgage.

    a. 8.0%
    b. 9.8%
    c. 10.9%
    d. 51.0%
    e. 11.2%

25. If you would like to accumulate $7,500 over the next 5 years, how much must you deposit each six months, starting six months from now, given a 6 percent interest rate and semiannual compounding?

    a. $1,330.47
    b. $879.23
    c. $654.23
    d. $569.00
    e. $732.67

26. A company is offering bonds which pay $100 per year indefinitely. If you require a 12 percent return on these bonds--that is, the discount rate is 12 percent--what is the value of each bond?

    a. $1,000.00
    b. $962.00
    c. $904.67
    d. $866.67
    e. $833.33

27. What is the present value (t = 0) of the following cash flows if the discount rate is 12 percent?

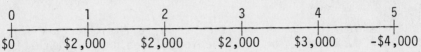

0	1	2	3	4	5
$0	$2,000	$2,000	$2,000	$3,000	-$4,000

    a. $4,782.43
    b. $4,440.50
    c. $4,221.79
    d. $4,041.23
    e. $3,997.98

28. What is the effective annual percentage rate (APR) of 12 percent compounded monthly?

    a. 12.00%
    b. 12.55%
    c. 12.68%
    d. 12.75%
    e. 13.00%

29. Problem 24 refers to a 20-year mortgage of $44,500. This is an amortized loan. How much principal will be repaid in the second year?

    a. $1,050.25
    b. $1,625.76
    c. $2,860.23
    d. $3,622 97
    e. $4,532.45

30. You have $1,000 invested in an account which pays 16 percent com-pounded annually. A commission agent (called a "finder") can lo-cate for you an equally safe deposit which will pay 16 percent, compounded quarterly, for 2 years. What is the maximum amount you should be willing to pay him now as a fee for locating the new account?

    a. $10.92
    b. $13.78
    c. $16.14
    d. $16.79
    e. $21.13

31. The present value (t = 0) of the following cash flow stream is $11,958.20 when discounted at 12 percent annually. What is the value of the missing t = 2 cash flow?

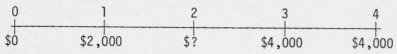

```
    0           1           2           3           4
    +           +           +           +           +
   $0        $2,000        $?        $4,000      $4,000
```

   a. $4,000.00
   b. $4,500.00
   c. $5,000.00
   d. $5,500.00
   e. $6,000.00

32. Today is your birthday and you decide to start saving for your college education. You will begin college on your 18th birthday and will need $4,000 per year at the end of each of the next 4 years. You will make a deposit 1 year from today in an account paying 12 percent annually, and continue to make an identical deposit each year up to and including the year you begin college. If a deposit amount of $2,542.05 will allow you to reach your goal, what birthday are you celebrating today?

   a. 13
   b. 14
   c. 15
   d. 16
   e. 17

(The next two problems relate to Appendix 11A.)

33. You invest $500 for 12 years in an account that pays 9 percent interest, compounded continuously. What is the ending amount?

   a. $1,298.18
   b. $1,376.48
   c. $1,472.35
   d. $1,503.72
   e. $1,591.83

34. A bank that uses continuous compounding claims that a dollar will grow to $1.65 after 5 years. What is the nominal, or stated, rate of interest?

   a. 9%
   b. 10%
   c. 11%
   d. 12%
   e. 13%

Answers and Solutions

1. present value

2. present; future; interest (I)

3. future value interest factor

4. discounting; compounding

5. 0.7835; reciprocal

6. interest rate

7. annuity; ordinary (regular); due

8. sum

9. nominal; effective

10. nominal rate; compounding periods

11. infinite; continuous

12. d. The present value of a project's cash flows will decrease if the discount rate is increased or if the project's cash flows are extended over a longer period of time.

13. b. The APR is always greater than or equal to the nominal rate.

14. a. The future value of an amount of money will always be greater than the present value by the amount of interest earned.

15. d. $FV_n = PV(FVIF_{k,n}) = \$1,000(FVIF_{8\%,6}) = \$1,000(1.5869)$
    $= \$1,586.90$. Calculator solution = $\$1,586.87$.

16. a. $FVIF_{k,n}$ is now $FVIF_{4\%,12}$ or 1.6010. Thus, FV_n
    $= \$1,000(1.6010) = \$1,601.00$. The difference, $\$1,601.00 -$ $\$1,586.90 = \$14.10$, is the additional interest. Calculator solution = $\$14.16$.

17. c. $FV_n = PV(FVIF_{k,n})$
    $\$600 = \$500(FVIF_{k,2})$.

    $FVIF_{k,2} = 1.2000$.

    Looking across the Period 2 row in Table A-3, we see $FVIF_{9\%,2}$ $= 1.1881$ and $FVIF_{10\%,2} = 1.2100$. Therefore, the annual interest rate is between 9% and 10%. Calculator solution = 9.54%.

18. c. Assume any value for the present value and double it:

$$FV_n = PV(FVIF_{k,n})$$
$$\$2 = \$1(FVIF_{k,5})$$

$$FVIF_{k,5} = 2.0000.$$

Looking across the Period 5 row in Table A-3, we see that 2.0000 occurs between 14% and 15%. Calculator solution = 14.87%.

19. b. $S_5 = PMT(FVIFA_{6\%,5}) = \$1,000(5.6371) = \$5,637.10$. Calculator solution = $5,637.09.

20. d. $S_5(\text{Annuity due}) = PMT(FVIFA_{6\%,5})(1 + k)$
$$= \$1,000(5.6371)(1.06) = \$5,975.33.$$
Calculator solution = $5,975.32.

21. e. $S_{10} = PMT(FVIFA_{3\%,10})$
$$= \$500(11.4639) = \$5,731.95.$$

Calculator solution = $5,731.94. (Note that to use the annuity tables the compounding period and payment period must be the same, in this case both are semiannual. If this is not the case, each cash flow must be treated individually.)

22. a. $PV = FV_8(PVIF_{7\%,8})$
$$= \$1,000(0.5820) = \$582.00.$$

Calculator solution = $582.01. (Note that annual compounding is assumed if not otherwise specified.)

23. d. $A_6 = PMT(PVIFA_{5\%,6})$
$$= \$800(5.0757) = \$4060.56.$$
Calculator solution = $4,060.55.

24. a. The amount of the mortgage ($44,500) is the present value of a 20-year ordinary annuity with payments of $4,532.45. Therefore,
$$A_{20} = PMT(PVIFA_{k,20})$$
$$\$44,500 = \$4,532.45(PVIFA_{k,20})$$
$$PVIFA_{k,20} = 9.8181$$
$$k = 8.00\% \text{ exactly.}$$

25. c. $S_{10} = PMT(FVIFA_{3\%,10})$
$$\$7,500 = PMT(11.4639)$$
$$PMT = \$654.23.$$

26. e. $PV = PMT/k = \$100/0.12 = \$833.33.$

27. b. $PV = \$2,000(PVIFA_{12\%,3}) + \$3,000(PVIF_{12\%,4})$
$$- \$4,000(PVIF_{12\%,5})$$
$$= \$2,000(2.4018) + \$3,000(0.6355) - \$4,000(0.5674)$$
$$= \$4,440.50.$$
Calculator solution = $4,440.51.

28. c. $\quad APR = 1 + \left[\dfrac{k_{nom}}{m}\right]^m - 1.0$

$\qquad = 1 + \left[\dfrac{0.12}{12}\right]^{12} - 1.0$

$\qquad = (1.01)^{12} - 1.0$
$\qquad = 1.1268 - 1.0 = 0.1268$
$\qquad = 12.68\%.$

29. a.

Year	Payment	Interest	Principal	Balance
1	$4,532.45	$3,560.00	$ 972.45	$43,527.55
2	4,532.45	3,482.20	1,050.25	42,477.30

30. d. $\quad$ Currently: $\$1,000(FVIF_{16\%,2}) = \$1,000(1.3456) = \$1,345.60$

$\quad$ New account: $\$1,000(FVIF_{4\%,8}) = \$1,000(1.3686) = 1,368.60$

Thus, the new account will be worth $23.00 more after 2 years.

$$PV \text{ of difference} = \$23(PVIF_{4\%,8})$$
$$= \$23(0.7307) = \$16.79.$$

Calculator solution = $16.81.

31. e. $\quad \$11,958.20 = \$2,000(PVIF_{12\%,1}) + x(PVIF_{12\%,2})$
$\qquad\qquad + \$4,000(PVIF_{12\%,3}) + \$4,000(PVIF_{12\%,4})$

$\quad \$11,958.20 = \$2,000(0.8929) + x(0.7972)$
$\qquad\qquad + \$4,000(0.7118) + \$4,000(0.6355)$

$\quad \$11,958.20 = \$7,175.00 + 0.7972x$

$\qquad 0.7972x = \$4,783.20$

$\qquad\qquad x = \$6,000.00$

Calculator solution = $6000.16.

32. b. First, how much must you accumulate on your 18th birthday?

$A_n = \$4,000(PVIFA_{12\%,4}) = \$4,000(3.0373) = \$12,149.20.$

Now, how many payments must you make to accumulate $12,149.20?

$$S_n = \$12,149.20 = \$2,542.05(FVIFA_{12\%,n}).$$
$$FVIFA_{12\%,n} = 4.7793$$
$$n = 4.$$

Therefore, if you make payments at 18, 17, 16, and 15, you are now 14.

33. c. $FV = PV\left(e^{kn}\right)$

$= \$500\left(e^{12(0.09)}\right)$

$= \$500\left(e^{1.08}\right)$

$= \$500(2.9447)$

$= \$1,472.35.$

Calculator solution $= 1,472.34.$

34. b. $FV_n = PV\left(e^{kn}\right)$

$\$1.65 = \$1.00\left(e^{kn}\right)$

or

$e^{5k} = 1.65.$

Now, take the natural logarithm of both sides:

$$\ln(e^{5k}) = \ln(1.65)$$

$$5k = 0.50$$
$$k = 0.10 = 10\%.$$

CHAPTER 12

CAPITAL BUDGETING TECHNIQUES

Overview

This chapter examines the capital budgeting process. Capital budgeting requires that future cash flows be estimated, risks be appraised and reflected in a cost of capital discount rate, and all cash flows be evaluated on a present value basis. Several methods are available to determine which projects should be included in the capital budget. The most commonly used methods are payback, net present value, and internal rate of return. These three methods of capital budgeting analysis are discussed in this chapter.

Outline

I. Capital budgeting is significant for the following reasons:

   A. It represents a decision whose consequences continue over an extended period.

      1. The decision maker must make a commitment into the future and hence gives up some flexibility.
      2. It involves an implicit forecast of future sales. Inaccurate forecasts will result in overinvestment or underinvestment in fixed assets.

   B. Good capital budgeting will improve the timing of asset acquisitions and the quality of assets purchased.

   C. Asset expansion involves substantial expenditures. The requisite financing must be arranged in advance.

II. Capital budgeting is the process of analyzing fixed asset investment proposals and selecting the projects to be included in the capital budget.

   A. It is an application of the classic economic theory that marginal revenue should be equated to marginal cost.

      1. Marginal revenue is the percentage return on an investment.
      2. Marginal cost is the firm's marginal cost of capital.

3. The optimal investment policy can be determined by selecting those projects whose rates of return exceed the firm's percentage cost of capital.

B. Capital budgeting is a complex process.

1. Good investment proposals are the result of hard thinking, planning, and research.
2. It is difficult to accurately forecast the costs and revenues associated with particular projects.
3. Difficult conceptual and empirical problems arise over the methods of calculating cash flows, rates of return, and the cost of capital.

C. Analyzing capital expenditure proposals involves certain costs. Firms may classify projects into different categories to help differentiate the level of analysis required.

1. Replacement--maintenance of business.
2. Replacement--cost reduction.
3. Expansion of existing products or markets.
4. Expansion into new products or markets.
5. Safety and environmental projects.
6. Other, a catchall for miscellaneous projects.

D. Normally, a more detailed analysis is required for expansion and new product decisions than for simple replacement and maintenance decisions. Also, projects requiring larger investments will be analyzed more carefully than smaller projects.

E. Methods must be developed for selecting the projects to be included in the capital budget.

1. Some projects are eliminated because they are mutually exclusive of other projects.
   a. Mutually exclusive projects are alternative invest-ments; if one project is chosen, the other must be rejected. An example of mutually exclusive projects would be the choice between conveyor belts and fork trucks for handling materials.
   b. Independent projects are investments whose costs and revenues are independent of one another, such as the purchase of materials handling equipment versus the purchase of a packaging machine.
2. Since there are often more proposals for projects than the firm is able or willing to finance, the capital budgeting process must distinguish between good or poor projects.
   a. Investment proposals must be ranked according to the estimated benefits to the firm from each investment.
   b. A cutoff point must be selected to determine how far down the ranked list projects should be chosen.

F. Estimating the cash flows associated with a project is the most important and most difficult step in capital budgeting analysis.

1. The firm must estimate both the costs and the cash inflows associated with an investment project.
2. Cash inflows include increased output and sales revenue, as well as cost reductions due to changes in the amount of labor required, in maintenance costs, in scrap rework time, in fuel costs, and so on.
3. Depreciation must be added to after-tax net income to determine the net cash flow from a project; thus, cash flow = net income + depreciation.
4. The most serious errors in capital budgeting are caused by incorrect assumptions about basic operating conditions such as sales levels, production rates, and labor costs.

III. Once cash flow estimates have been made for various projects, different methods can be used to evaluate the proposals and to decide which ones should be accepted for inclusion in the capital budget. The most commonly used methods are (1) payback (or payback period), (2) net present value (NPV), and (3) internal rate of return.

A. The payback period is defined as the number of years it takes to recover the original investment in the project. Its major advantage is that it is easy to calculate and to understand. Its major disadvantages are:

1. It ignores cash flows beyond the payback period. This penalizes long-term projects which may be vital to the firm's long-term success.
2. It ignores the time value of money by assigning equal weight to cash flows in each year during the payback period.

B. The net present value (NPV) method of evaluating investment proposals is a discounted cash flow (DCF) technique that accounts for the time value of all cash flows from a project.

1. The NPV is the present value of future cash flows (CF) discounted at the firm's cost of capital (k), minus the cost of the investment (I):

$$NPV = \left[\frac{CF_1}{(1 + k)^1} + \frac{CF_2}{(1 + k)^2} + \dots + \frac{CF_n}{(1 + k)^n} \right] - I$$

$$= \sum_{t=1}^{n} \frac{CF_t}{(1 + k)^t} - I.$$

2. If the NPV is positive, the project should be accepted; if negative, it should be rejected.

3. If two projects are mutually exclusive, the one with the higher NPV should be chosen.

4. If the costs are spread over several years, the equation can be rewritten as

$$NPV = \sum_{t=0}^{n} \frac{CF_t}{(1 + k)^t},$$

where project costs are treated as outflows when determining the net cash flow for each year.

C. The internal rate of return (IRR) is defined as the discount rate that equates the present value of the expected future cash flows to the initial cost of the project.

1. The IRR formula is the same as the NPV formula, except it sets the NPV equal to zero and solves for the discount rate:

$$\frac{CF_1}{(1 + R)^1} + \frac{CF_2}{(1 + R)^2} + \dots + \frac{CF_n}{(1 + R)^n} - I = 0;$$

or

$$\sum_{t=1}^{n} \frac{CF_t}{(1 = R)^n} - I = 0.$$

This is an equation with one unknown, R, and we can solve for the value of R that will make the equation equal to zero. The solution value of R is defined as the internal rate of return.

2. If the cash flows are equal in each year, then the project is similar to an annuity and the IRR can easily be found using the table of interest factors for an annuity.

3. When uneven cash flows are involved, the IRR can be found by trial and error or through graphical analysis of the net present value profile. Additionally, advanced financial calculators can easily calculate the IRR and NPV.

4. The net present value profile is a plot of the net present value of a project versus the discount rate. The point where the net present value profile crosses the X axis indicates the project's IRR. The net present value profile crosses the Y axis at the undiscounted IRR.

5. If the project's IRR exceeds its cost of capital, taking on the project will increase the value of the firm. If the IRR is less than the cost of capital, the project should be rejected.

D. Firms generally make accept/reject decisions only after analyzing all three criteria: the payback period, the NPV, and the IRR.

1. The NPV focuses on how much the project will add to the value of the firm, while the IRR focuses on a project's rate of return. Firms should try to maximize their value, not their rate of return, if the two methods are in conflict.

2. For independent projects, the NPV and IRR criteria always lead to the same accept/reject decisions.

3. If two mutually exclusive projects are being compared, only one can be accepted. It is possible for the NPV method to rank one project higher while the IRR method gives a higher ranking to the other. Conflicts should be resolved in favor of the project with the higher NPV.

4. Conflicts between NPV and IRR can occur only if one project is larger than the other or if one project has a longer life than the other project.

IV. The NPV of an investment project is calculated using five basic steps.

A. Estimate the net initial cash outlay:

1. If the investment is an expansion project, the initial investment is equal to the purchase price of the new equipment less any investment tax credit, plus the investment in net working capital which must be made to support the higher level of sales.

2. If the investment is a replacement project, the initial investment must be adjusted to reflect the proceeds from the sale of the old machine and any tax effects from a gain or loss on the old machine.

B. Determine the incremental cash flows (ΔF) attributable to the investment using the following equation:

$$\Delta CF = (\Delta S - \Delta OC)(1 - T) + T\Delta Dep,$$

where

ΔS = the change in sales.

ΔOC = the change in operating cost.

T = the marginal corporate income tax rate.

ΔDep = the change in annual depreciation.

C. Using the firm's cost of capital, calculate the present value of the incremental cash flows. Depreciation cash flows using ACRS must be calculated for each year.

D. The present value of the machine's expected salvage value is added as a positive cash inflow. Similarly, the present value of the recovery at the end of the project's life of the incremental working capital investments is an additional positive cash flow.

E. Compare the present value of the cash flows to the present value of cash outlays to determine whether the NPV is positive or negative.

V. Generally, firms accept all independent projects having positive NPVs. However, a firm will occasionally set an absolute limit on the size of its capital budget that is less than the level of investment called for by the NPV criteria. This is called capital rationing.

A. Under capital rationing, the objective should be to select those projects, subject to the capital rationing constraint, that maximize total net present value.

B. Mathematical programming methods are available to help solve the simpler cases.

C. Although the act of forgoing independent projects with positive NPVs seems irrational, there may be cases which give rise to capital rationing that can be rationally handled by increasing the assigned cost of capital as the amount of capital raised increases.

Definitional Questions

1. A firm's _____ _____ outlines its planned expenditures on fixed assets.

2. Good capital budgeting will improve the _____ of asset acquisitions and the _____ of assets purchased.

3. Capital budgeting is an application of the classic economic theory that _____ revenues should equal marginal _____.

4. Investment projects can be classified as _____, _____, safety and environmental, and other.

5. Alternative projects are _____ _____; if one is chosen, then the other must be rejected.

6. The most difficult step in the analysis of capital expenditure proposals involves estimating future _____ _____.

7. The number of years necessary to return the original investment in a project is known as the _____ _____.

8. The primary advantage of payback is its _____.

9. One important weakness of payback analysis is the fact that _____ _____ beyond the payback period are _____.

10. The net present value (NPV) method of evaluating investments is a _____ cash flow (DCF) technique.

11. A capital investment proposal should be accepted if its NPV is _____.

12. If two projects are _____ _____, the one with the _____ NPV should be selected.

13. In the IRR approach, a discount rate is sought which makes the value of the NPV equal to _____.

14. When a project has constant cash flows, it is similar to an _____.

15. The graphical method for determining the IRR involves an analysis of a project's _____ _____ _____ _____.

16. A net present value profile shows the relationship between a project's _____ and the _____ _____ used to calculate the NPV.

17. If a project's _____ is greater than the cost of capital, it should be accepted.

18. If two mutually exclusive projects are being evaluated, and one project has a higher NPV while the other project has a higher IRR, the project with the higher _____ should be preferred.

19. The internal rate of return (IRR) is the _____ rate that equates the present value of future _____ _____ with the _____ of a project.

20. _____ _____ exists if the firm places a limit on the size of the capital budget which precludes acceptance of all projects with positive NPVs.

Conceptual Questions

21. The IRR of a project with cash flows that accrue relatively slowly is more sensitive to changes in the discount rate than is the IRR of a project with cash flows that come in more rapidly.

    a. True   b. False

22. Since the focus of capital budgeting is cash flows, changes in working capital balance sheet accounts such as inventory would not be relevant to the analysis.

    a. True   b. False

23. Other things held constant, a decrease in the cost of capital (discount rate) will cause an increase in a project's IRR.

    a. True   b. False

24. The internal rate of return (IRR) is the interest rate that equates the present value of the expected future receipts to:

    a. The present value of the net returns.
    b. The cost of the investment outlay.
    c. The compound sum of the future receipts.
    d. The depreciate value of the asset.
    e. Zero.

25. The net present value method of capital budgeting assumes that cash flows are reinvested at:

    a. The rate of return on the project.
    b. The treasury bill rate.
    c. The firm's cost of capital.
    d. No rate--they are not reinvested.
    e. The firm's dividend yield.

Problems

26. The management of General Appliances, Inc., is considering the purchase of a new machine which costs $90,120, does not qualify for the investment tax credit, and has an economic life of 5 years. Its ACRS recovery period is also 5 years. It is estimated that the purchase of this machine will increase net after-tax cash flows of $25,000 per year, including depreciation. The machine will have a zero salvage value at the end of its 5-year life. The company has a marginal tax rate of 40 percent and a cost of capital of 10 percent. What is the new machine's IRR?

    a. 18%
    b. 16%
    c. 14%
    d. 12%
    e. 10%

27. The capital budgeting director of National Products, Inc., is evaluating a new project that would decrease operating costs by $30,000 per year without affecting revenues. The project's cost is $50,000, and it does not qualify for an investment tax credit. The project will be depreciated using the ACRS method over its 3-year life. It will have a zero salvage value after 3 years. The marginal tax rate of National Producers is 46 percent, and their cost of capital is 12 percent. What is the project's NPV?

    a. $7,068
    b. $8,324
    c. $9,875
    d. $10,214
    e. $12,387

28. Your firm has a marginal tax rate of 40 percent and a cost of capital of 14 percent. You are performing a capital budgeting analysis on a new project that will cost $500,000. The project is expected to have a useful life of 10 years, although its ACRS class life is only 5 years. The project is expected to increase the firm's net income by $61,257 per year and to have a salvage value of $35,000 at the end of 10 years. The project does not qualify for an investment tax credit. What is the project's NPV?

    a. $48,257
    b. $81,359
    c. $105,000
    d. $132,451
    e. $166,986

29. Your firm is considering the operation of a fast-food concession at the 1988 World's Fair. The cash flow pattern is somewhat unusual since you must build the stands, operate them for 2 years, and then tear the stands down and restore the sites to the original condition. You estimate the net cash flows to be as follows:

Time	Net Cash Flow
0	-$800,000
1	700,000
2	700,000
3	- 400,000

What is the approximate IRR of this venture?

    a. 5%
    b. 15%
    c. 25%
    d. 35%
    e. 45%

30. The Board of Directors of National Brewing, Incorporated, is considering the acquisition of a new still. The still is priced at $600,000 but would require $60,000 in transportation costs and $40,000 for installation. The still and all fixed asset costs related to placing it in operation qualify for a 10 percent investment tax credit. The still has a useful life of 10 years but will be depreciated over its 5-year ACRS life. It is expected to have a salvage value of $10,000 at the end of 10 years. The still would increase revenues by $120,000 per year and have yearly operating costs of $20,000 per year. Additionally, the still would require a $30,000 increase in net working capital. The firm's marginal tax rate is 40 percent, and the cost of capital is 10 percent. What is the NPV of the still?

    a. $60,892
    b. $18,430
    c. ($35,821)
    d. ($150,328)
    e. ($203,450)

31. The capital budgeting director of Giant, Inc., is researching the possibility of purchasing new equipment to expand sales. The equipment under consideration costs $150,000 and is not eligible for an investment tax credit. The production manager estimates that the acquisition will increase operating expenses by $40,000 in each year of its 5-year useful life. The equipment has a zero salvage value. To simplify the preliminary analysis, the capital budgeting director will estimate the project's depreciation by the straight line method. The firm's marginal tax rate is 40 percent and the cost of capital is 15 percent. How much additional sales revenue must the equipment generate for the capital budgeting director to be indifferent to the acquisition?

    a. $24,672
    b. $56,747
    c. $73,994
    d. $94,578
    e. $106,271

(The following information applies to the next two problems.)

Toy Motors needs a new machine for production of its 1988-1990. The financial vice president has appointed you to do the capital budgeting analysis. You have identified two different machines that are capable of performing the job. You have completed the cash flow analysis and estimate the following net cash flows:

	Net Cash Flow	
Year	Machine 1	Machine 2
0	-$5,000	-$5,000
1	2,085	0
2	2,085	0
3	2,085	0
4	2,085	9,677

32. The cost of capital is uncertain at this time, so you construct NPV profiles to assist in the final decision. The profiles for Machines 1 and 2 cross at what cost of capital?

    a. 24%
    b. 18%
    c. 10%
    d. 6%
    e. They do not cross in the northeast quadrant.

33. If the cost of capital is 14 percent at the time the decision is made, which project would you choose?

    a. Project 1; it has the higher positive NPV.
    b. Project 2; it has the higher positive NPV.
    c. Neither; both have negative NPVs.
    d. Either, both have the same NPV.
    e. Project 1; it has the higher IRR.

Answers and Solutions

1. capital budget

2. timing; quality

3. marginal; costs

4. replacement; expansion

5. mutually exclusive

6. cash flows

7. payback period

8. simplicity

9. cash flows; ignored

10. discounted

11. positive

12. mutually exclusive; higher

13. zero

14. annuity

15. net present value profile

16. NPV; discount rate

17. IRR

18. NPV

19. discount; cash flows; cost

20. Capital rationing

21. a. The more the cash flows are spread over time, the greater the effect of a change in discount rate. This is because the compounding process has a greater effect as the number of years (n) increases.

22. b. An increase in an asset account, even though not fixed assets, may require funding similar to capital assets. If the capital investment leads to higher sales, accounts receivables and inventories will probably increase, and the investment required to support this increase must be considered in the capital budgeting analysis.

23. b. A project's IRR is unaffected by the cost of capital. However, a project's NPV will increase if the discount rate decreases.

24. b. The IRR is the interest rate that equates the present value of the expected cash flows to the initial cost of the investment. The IRR is found by setting the NPV equal to zero and solving for the interest rate.

25. c. The NPV method assumes that a project's cash flows are reinvested at the firm's cost of capital, in contrast to the IRR method which assumes reinvestment at the project's rate of return.

26. d. The initial cash flows to consider are cost, investment tax credit, and changes in working capital. In this case only the cost, or $100,000, is applicable. Thus, there is a $90,120 outflow at t = 0. Each year the project will increase net after-tax cash flows by $25,000. These are the only cash flows from the project. Therefore, this is an annuity, and the IRR can be solved as follows:

$$\$90,120 = \$25,000(PVIFA_{IRR,5})$$

$$PVIFA_{IRR,5} = 3.6048; \quad IRR = 12\%.$$

27. a. The only cash outflow is the $50,000 cost of the project. The cash inflows consist of the reduction in operating costs, equal to $30,000(0.54) = $16,200 on an after-tax basis, and depreciation. The value of the depreciation cash flows generated by the project is the amount of tax savings. The after-tax depreciation cash flows are found by multiplying the depreciable basis, $50,000, by the recovery percentages in each year, and then multiplying this product by the tax rate. The allowances in each year are 25 percent, 38 percent, and 37 percent, respectively, and the depreciation cash flows in each year are:

$Dep_1 = \$50,000(0.25)(0.46) = \$5,750.$

$Dep_2 = \$50,000(0.38)(0.46) = \$8,740.$

$Dep_3 = \$50,000(0.37)(0.46) = \$8,510.$

The project's cash flows can be laid out on a time line as follows:

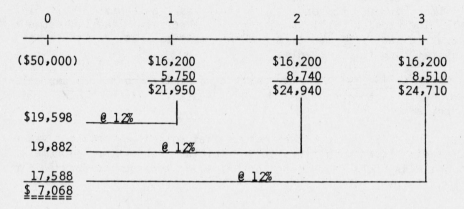

0	1	2	3
($50,000)	$16,200	$16,200	$16,200
	5,750	8,740	8,510
	$21,950	$24,940	$24,710

$19,598   @ 12%

19,882   @ 12%

17,588   @ 12%
$ 7,068

28. e. In this cash the <u>net income</u> of the project is $61,257. Net cash flow = net income + depreciation = $61,257 + depreciation. The depreciation allowed in each year is calculated as:

$Dep_1 = \$500,000(0.15) = \$75,000.$

$Dep_2 = \$500,000(0.22) = \$110,000.$

$Dep_{3-5} = \$500,000(0.21) = \$105,000.$

$Dep_{6-10} = 0.$

In the final year (Year 10), the firm receives the $35,000 from the sale of the machine. The time line is as follows:

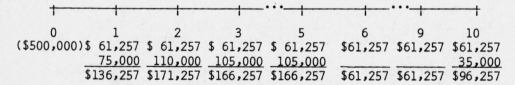

0	1	2	3	5	6	9	10
($500,000)	$ 61,257	$ 61,257	$ 61,257	$ 61,257	$61,257	$61,257	$61,257
	75,000	110,000	105,000	105,000			35,000
	$136,257	$171,257	$166,257	$166,257	$61,257	$61,257	$96,257

The project's NPV can be found by discounting each of the cash flows at the firm's 14 percent cost of capital. Note that the cash flow stream contains two annuities: $166,257 is received in Years 3-5, and $61,257 is received in Years 6-9. The NPV can be found as follows:

$$NPV = -\$500,000 + \$136,257(PVIF_{14\%,1}) + \$171,257(PVIF_{14\%,2}) +$$

$$\$166,257(PVIFA_{14\%,3})(PVIF_{14\%,2}) + \$61,257(PVIFA_{14\%,4})(PVIF_{14\%,5})$$

$$+ \$96,257(PVIF_{14\%,10})$$

$$= -\$500,000 + \$136,257(0.8772) + \$171,257(0.7695) +$$
$$\$166,257(2.3216)(0.7695) + \$61,257(2.9137)(0.5194)$$
$$+ \$96,257(0.2697)$$

$$= -\$500,000 + \$119,525 + \$131,782 + \$297,013 + \$92,705 + \$25,961$$

$$= \$166,986.$$

29.　c.　Unless you have a calculator that performs IRR calculations, the IRR must be obtained by trial and error (or graphically) since the cash flows are not an annuity. (The calculator solution is 25.48 percent.)

30.　d.　The initial net cash flow is as follows:

Price	($600,000)
Transportation	(60,000)
Installation	(40,000)
ITC (0.10 X $700,000)	70,000
Change in net working capital	(30,000)
Initial net outflow	$660,000

The net annual cash flows are equal to the net after-tax increase in revenues, $(0.6)(\$120,000 - \$20,000) = \$60,000$, plus the depreciation tax savings. In Year 10, the firm will recover its investment in net working capital.

The annual depreciation tax savings is calculated as follows:

$$Dep_1 = [\$600,000 - (0.5)(\$70,000)](0.15)(0.4) = \$33,900.$$

$$Dep_2 = (\$565,000)(0.22)(0.4) = \$49,720.$$

$$Dep_3 = (\$565,000)(0.21)(0.4) = \$47,460.$$

Therefore, the time line is as follows:

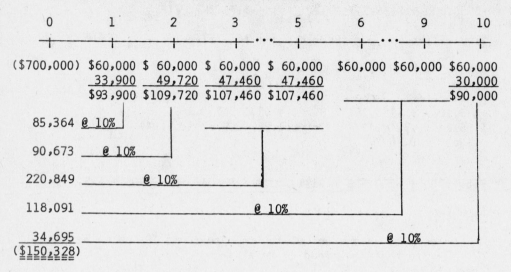

31. d. First, put the data given on a time line as follows:

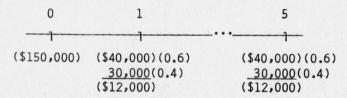

Note that the annual cash flow based on the known data is a $12,000 <u>outflow</u>. To be indifferent on the project, the IRR must be equal to the cost of capital, or 15 percent. We can find the annual net cash flow required to produce an IRR of 15 percent as follows:

$$\$150,000 = PMT(PVIFA_{15\%,5})$$

$$PMT = \$44,747.$$

Thus, the annual net cash flow must be $44,747. However, the known data give a cash outflow of $12,000. Therefore, the revenue component must be $44,747 - (-$12,000) = $56,747. Finally, we must recognize that all data on the time line are after-tax. The sales revenue is before tax. What before-tax revenue produces $56,747 as after-tax revenue? Before-tax revenue = $56,747/0.6 = $94,578.

32. c.   First, construct the NPV profiles as follows:

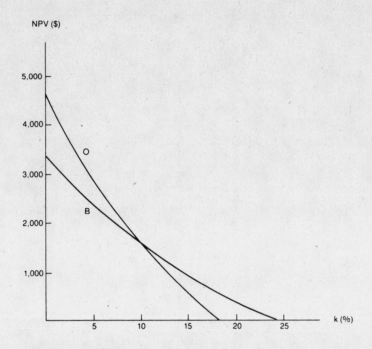

The Y intercept is the NPV when k = 0.   For 1, 4(2,085) - $5,000
= $3,340.   For 2, $9,677 - $5,000 = $4,677. The X intercept is
the discount rate when NPV = 0, or the IRR.   For 1, $5,000 =
$2,085(PVIFA$_{IRR,4}$);   IRR $\simeq$ 24%.   For 2, $5,000 =
$9,677(PVIF$_{IRR,4}$); IRR $\simeq$ 18%.   The graph is an approximation
since we are only using two points to plot lines that are
curvilinear.   However, it shows that there is a crossover point,
and that is occurs somewhere in the vicinity of k = 10%. To find
the exact value, we must find the value of k for which NPV$_1$ =
NPV$_2$.   This is a trial-and-error process, but try the closest
answer listed, 10 percent:

$$NPV_1 = \$2,085(PVIFA_{10\%,4}) - \$5,000 = \$1,609.$$

$$NPV_2 = \$9,677(PVIF_{10\%,4}) - \$5,000 = \$1,610.$$

The NPVs are about equal, so the crossover point is approximately
10 percent.

33. a.   Refer to the NPV profiles. When k = 14%, we are to the right
of the crossover point, and Project 1 has the highest NPV.   You
can verify this fact by calculating the NPVs.   NPV$_1$ = $1,075 and
NPV$_2$ = $730.

CHAPTER 13

RISK ANALYSIS IN CAPITAL BUDGETING

Overview

This chapter covers the very important topics of how risk is measured in financial analysis and how risk affects security prices and rates of return. Risk is related to the variability of expected future returns. However, most rational investors hold portfolios of stocks, and these investors are more concerned with the risks of their portfolios than with the risks of individual stocks. Thus, the most relevant risk is market risk, which is caused by changes in the broad market and which cannot be eliminated by diversification. Company-specific risk, which can be eliminated by diversification, is not relevant to the well-diversified investor. Beta, the measure of market risk, measures the volatility of the stock relative to the market. The chapter incorporates risk into the capital budgeting process by analyzing the effect of a project on the firm's beta coefficient. The major difficulty in determining the beta risk of a given project is to establish the project's beta coefficient. Therefore, in practice, both measuring risk and incorporating risk into capital budgeting decisions involves judgment.

Outline

I. Risk is associated with the variability of future outcomes. The riskiness of an asset is defined in terms of the likely variability of the future returns from the asset. The more variable the expected returns, the riskier the asset.

   A. The probability distribution for an event is the listing of all the possible outcomes surrounding the event, with mathematical probabilities assigned to each.

   1. The probability assigned to each possible outcome of an event represents the relative frequency of occurrence of that outcome.
   2. The sum of the probabilities for a particular event must equal 1.0.

   B. The expected rate of return ($\hat{k}$) is the sum of the products of each possible outcome or rate of return times its associated probability. It is a weighted average of the various possible outcomes, weighted by their probabilities of occurrence. The expected rate of return for a project, Project A, can be found using the equation:

$$\hat{k}_A = \sum_{s=1}^{S} P_s \tilde{k}_A.$$

1. The tighter, or more peaked, a distribution, the more likely it is that the actual outcome will be close to the expected value.

2. One measure for determining the tightness of a distribution is the standard deviation, σ. For Project A, the standard deviations is found as:

$$\sigma_A = \sqrt{\sum_{s=1}^{S} P_s (k_A - \hat{k})^2}$$

3. The smaller the standard deviation, the tighter the distribution and the lower the risk associated with the event.

4. Another measure of the variability of returns is the coefficient of variation, CV. The coefficient of variation is equal to the standard deviation divided by the mean,

$$CV_A = \frac{\sigma_A}{\hat{k}_A},$$

and measures the risk per unit of return.

5. Where the number of possible outcomes is virtually unlimited, continuous probability distributions are used in determining the expected rate of return of the event.

C. Most investors are risk averse. This means that for two alternatives with the same expected rate of return, investors will choose the one with less risk.

1. The mean-variance criterion states that people prefer more return to less return and less risk to more risk.

2. The coefficient of variation helps investors to select the less risky of two investments with different means and different variances.

II. Most institutions and individual investors hold portfolios of securities rather than one stock. Thus, the performance of any one security is less important than the performance of the portfolio as a whole.

A. Diversification can lower a portfolio's risk without changing its overall expected rate of return.

1. This may be accomplished by selecting stocks whose returns do not move together. Such stocks are not perfectly positively correlated.
2. As a rule, as the number of securities in the portfolio increases, the standard deviation of the expected returns decreases, and, hence, portfolio risk decreases.
3. The expected return on a portfolio (k_p) is the weighted average of the expected returns of the individual stocks in the portfolio, with the weights being the fraction of the total dollar value of the portfolio invested in each stock.

$$\hat{k}_p = \sum_{j=1}^{n} w_j \hat{k}_j.$$

4. The standard deviation of a portfolio is not the weighted average of the standard deviations of the individual stocks in the portfolio.

B. Total risk can be separated into two parts, market risk and company-specific risk.

1. Market, or systematic, risk cannot be eliminated by diversification of the portfolio.
2. Company-specific, or diversifiable, risk can be eliminated by proper diversification of securities.

III. With company-specific risk eliminated through proper diversification, the relevant risk to be considered is the market risk associated with general market movements.

A. The relationship of an individual stock's movements to overall market movements is measured by the stock's beta coefficient.

1. The beta coefficient of an individual stock measures the stock's volatility relative to the market. It is an index of the stock's risk relative to that of an average stock.
2. An "average stock" as measured by a market index will have a beta coefficient of 1.0.
3. A stock that is twice as volatile as the market will have a beta of 2.0, while one half as volatile will have a beta coefficient of 0.5.

B. The beta coefficient of an individual stock is estimated using historic market rates of return and historic rates of return on the stock. However, it is impossible to measure the beta of a stock precisely.

C. The beta coefficient of a portfolio of securities is the weighted average of the betas of the individual stocks.

$$b_p = \sum_{i=1}^{n} w_i b_i.$$

1. The weights used to calculate the portfolio beta are the fraction of the total dollar value of the portfolio invested in each stock.
2. The beta of a portfolio may be adjusted by buying and selling stocks within the portfolio to achieve the desired level of risk.

IV. The Capital Asset Pricing Model (CAPM) is a useful concept for analyzing the relationship between risk and return.

A. The expected rate of return is the rate of return investors expect to earn during some future period of time.

1. The expected rate of return is the expected value of a probability distribution of future returns.
2. This return is not a certainty; the actual realized rate of return may be higher or lower than the expected rate of return.

B. The required rate of return is the minimum expected return that will induce investors to buy a particular security.

C. For a stock's price to be in equilibrium, the expected and required rates of return must be equal.

D. The difference between the required rate of return on a risky asset and the risk-free rate (the rate on Treasury securities) is defined as the risky asset's risk premium.

1. The market risk premium is the difference between the required rate of return on the market portfolio and the risk-free rate, $(k_M - R_F)$.

2. The risk premium for an individual investment, for example, Project i, is calculated by multiplying the investment's beta coefficient times the market risk premium, $b_i(k_M - R_F)$.

E. Any investment's required rate of return is equal to the riskless rate of return plus its risk premium. A graph of the equation is called the Security Market Line (SML):

$$k_i = R_F + b_i(k_M - R_F).$$

1. The investment should be accepted if the expected reate of return on the investment exceeds its required return, as calculated by the SML.

      2. The risk-adjusted required rate of return can be used as the discount rate in the fundamental NPV approach to determine the acceptability of risky investments.

   F. The slope of the SML reflects the extent to which investors are averse to risk--the steeper the slope of the line, the greater the risk aversion.

V. In addition to the CAPM approach to measuring risk, a wide range of management science approaches are used and combine quantitative and judgmental analysis.

   A. Sensitivity analysis is one technique used in risk analysis.

      1. This involves changing one of the key variables at a time and observing how sensitive the cash flows (or NPVs) are to those changes.

      2. Sensitivity analysis spotlights the factors that have the greatest effect on cash flows. Then extra effort can be spent to carefully forecast these critical items.

      3. If small changes in relatively uncertain variables will cause a large change in cash flows, the project has a high degree of corporate risk.

   B. Decision trees are useful when the final decision on an investment will be based on a series of decisions made in earlier stages of the investment analysis.

      1. The final decision to accept an investment actually is made in stages, with subsequent decisions depending on the results of the previous ones.

      2. The sequence of decisions can be represented as branches of a tree from a decision point.

      3. The decision tree approach can be used to find the NPV and risk, as measured by the coefficient of variation, of the alternative decisions paths.

   C. Computer simulation of a project's cash flows is a detailed and costly procedure that can best be justified for large projects.

      1. A simulation model requires that a probability distribution be constructed for each of the important variables affecting the project's cash flows.

      2. The computer then randomly selects values of each of these variables and combines them into a cash flow estimate for the project. This process is repeated many times until a new probability distribution for the cash flows has been created.

      3. The expected value of this final distribution as well as its standard deviation can then be used to help make the final decision on the proposal.

Definitional Questions

1. Investment risk is associated with the _____ of low or negative returns; the greater the chance of loss, the _____ the investment.

2. A listing of all possible _____ with a probability assigned to each is known as a _____ _____.

3. Weighting each possible outcome of a distribution by its _____ of occurrence and summing the results give the _____ _____ of the distribution.

4. One measure of the tightness of a probability distribution is the _____ _____.

5. The _____ _____ _____ measures an investment's risk per unit of return.

6. Investors who prefer outcomes with a high degree of certainty to those that are less certain are described as being _____ _____.

7. The _____ _____ states that people prefer more return to less return and less _____ to more risk.

8. Owning a _____ of securities enables investors to benefit from _____.

9. Diversification of a portfolio can result in lower _____ for the same level of _____.

10. Diversification of a portfolio is achieved by selecting securities that are not perfectly _____ correlated with each other.

11. That part of a stock's risk that can be reduced by _____ is known as _____ risk, while the portion that cannot be eliminated is called _____ risk.

12. The _____ _____ measures a stock's relative volatility as compared with a stock market index.

13. A stock that is twice as volatile as the market in general would have a beta coefficient of _____, while a stock with a beta of 0.5 would be only _____ as volatile as the market.

14. The beta coefficient of a portfolio is the _____ _____ of the _____ of the individual stocks.

15. The expected value of a probability distribution of future returns is known as the _____ rate of return. The minimum expected return that will induce investors to buy a particular security is the _____ rate of return.

16. The standard used in defining the risk-free rate is the return available on _____ securities.

17. The difference between the _____ rate of return on a risky asset and the _____ rate is referred to as a _____ _____.

18. The risk premium for a stock may be calculated by multiplying the stock's _____ _____ times the risk premium of the _____.

19. A stock's required rate of return is equal to the _____ rate plus the stock's _____ _____.

20. Changes in investors' _____ _____ alter the _____ of the security market line.

21. The price at which a stock's expected and _____ rates of return are equal is known as the _____ price.

22. Among the factors that may cause a stock's equilibrium price to change are (1) the _____ rate, (2) the stock's _____ coefficient, and (3) the stock's _____ rate of growth.

23. In estimating a project's cash flows, changing one of the key variables at a time is known as _____ _____.

24. The purpose of sensitivity analysis is to determine which of the _____ has the _____ influence on the project's cash flows.

Conceptual Questions

25. The Y axis intercept of the Security Market Line (SML) indicates the required rate of return on an individual stock with a beta of 1.0.

    a. True   b. False

26. If a stock has a beta of zero, it will be riskless when held in isolation.

    a. True   b. False

27. In a portfolio of three different stocks, which of the following could not be true?

    a. The riskiness of the portfolio is less than the riskiness of each stock held in isolation.
    b. The riskiness of the portfolio is greater than the riskiness of one or two of the stocks.
    c. The beta of the portfolio is less than the beta of each of the individual stocks.
    d. The beta of the portfolio is greater than the beta of one or two of the individual stocks.
    e. The beta of the portfolio is equal to the beta of one of the individual stocks.

28. Which is the best measure of risk for an asset held in a well-diversified portfolio?

    a. Variance
    b. Standard deviation
    c. Beta
    d. Semi-variance
    e. Expected value

Problems

29. Stock A has the following probability distribution of expected returns:

Probability	Rate of Return
0.1	-15%
0.2	0
0.4	5
0.2	10
0.1	25

    What is Stock A's expected rate of return and standard deviation?

    a. 8.0%; 9.5%
    b. 8.0%; 6.5%
    c. 5.0%; 3.5%
    d. 5.0%; 6.5%
    e. 5.0%; 9.5%

30. If $R_F = 5\%$, $k_M = 11\%$, and $b = 1.3$ for Stock X, what is k_X, the required rate of return for Stock X?

    a. 18.7%
    b. 16.7%
    c. 14.8%
    d. 12.8%
    e. 11.9%

31. Refer to Problem 30. What would k_X be if investors' risk aversion increased by 3 percentage points?

    a. 18.7%
    b. 16.7%
    c. 14.8%
    d. 12.8%
    e. 11.9%

32. The Apple Investment Fund has a total investment of $450 million in five stocks.

Stock	Investment (millions)	Beta
1	$130	0.4
2	110	1.5
3	70	3.C
4	90	2.0
5	50	1.0

What is the fund's overall, or weighted average, beta?

a. 1.14
b. 1.22
c. 1.35
d. 1.46
e. 1.53

33. Refer to Problem 32. If the risk-free rate is 12 percent, and the market risk premium is 6 percent, what is the required rate of return on the Apple Fund?

a. 20.76%
b. 19.92%
c. 18.81%
d. 17.62%
e. 15.77%

34. You are managing a portfolio of 10 stocks which are held in equal dollar amounts. The current beta of the portfolio is 1.8, and the beta of Stock A is 2.0. If Stock A is sold, and the proceeds are used to purchase a replacement stock, what does the beta of the replacement stock have to be to lower the portfolio beta to 1.7?

a. 1.4
b. 1.3
c. 1.2
d. 1.1
e. 1.0

35. Initially, National Products, an all-equity firm, has a beta of 1.30. The risk-free rate is 12 percent, and the required rate of return on the market is 18 percent. The firm now sells 10 percent of its assets, having a beta of 1.30, and uses the proceeds to purchase a new product line with a beta of 1.00. What is the new overall required rate of return for National Products?

a. 15.11%
b. 16.24%
c. 17.48%
d. 18.00%
e. 19.62%

36. Allied Industries, an all-equity firm, is considering the purchase of a plant that produces plastic products. The plant is expected to generate a rate of return of 20 percent, and the plant's estimated beta is 2.00. If the risk-free rate is 10 percent, and the market risk premium is 6 percent, Allied should make the investment.

    a. True   b. False

37. Diversified Products (DP) is considering the formation of a new division which will double the assets of the firm. DP is an all-equity firm which has a current required rate of return of 20 percent. The risk-free rate is 10 percent, and the market risk premium is 5 percent. If DP wants to reduce its required rate of return to 18 percent, what is the maximum beta the new division could have?

    a. 1.00
    b. 1.10
    c. 1.20
    d. 1.25
    e. 1.30

38. Your company, International Citrus, Inc. (ICI), has two divisions, the orange (O) division and the grapefruit (G) division. The O division, with a beta of 1.0, is the largest, with 80 percent of the firm's assets. ICI is an all-equity firm having a cost of equity of 18 percent, and its stock price is in equilibrium. The current risk-free rate is 12 percent, and the required return on the market is 17 percent. You are considering acquiring an asset with the same beta risk as G division. This asset has an expected return of 21 percent. Should the asset be acquired?

    a. Yes. The asset's expected return is higher than the firm's cost of capital.
    b. No. The beta of the acquisition is higher than the market beta.
    c. No. The asset's required return is greater than the expected return.
    d. Yes. The asset's expected return is higher than the risk-free rate.
    e. Yes. The asset's expected return is greater than the required return on the market.

Answers and Solutions

1. probability; riskier

2. outcomes; probability distribution

3. probability; expected value

4. standard deviation

5. coefficient of variation

6. risk averse

7. mean-variance criterion; risk

8. portfolio; diversification

9. risk; return

10. positively

11. diversification; company-specific; market

12. beta coefficient

13. 2.0; half

14. weighted average; betas

15. expected; required

16. U.S. Treasury

17. required; risk-free; risk premium

18. beta coefficient; market

19. risk-free; risk premium

20. risk aversion; slope

21. required; equilibrium

22. risk-free; beta; expected

23. sensitivity analysis

24. variables; greatest

25. b. The Y axis intercept of the SML is R_F, which is the required rate of return of an individual stock with a beta of zero.

26. b. A zero beta stock is riskless from a market risk viewpoint but still has company-specific risk and will be risky when held in isolation.

27. c.

28. c.

29. e. $\hat{k}_A = 0.1(-15) + 0.2(0) + 0.4(5) + 0.2(10) + 0.1(25) = 5.0\%.$

$$\sigma_A^2 = 0.1(-15 - 5)^2 + 0.2(0 - 5)^2 + 0.4(5 - 5)^2 + 0.2(10 - 5)^2$$
$$+ 0.1(25 - 5)^2 = 90$$

$$\sigma_A = \sqrt{90} = 9.49 \approx 9.5\%.$$

30. d. $k_X = R_F + b(k_M - R_F) = 5\% + 1.3(11\% - 5\%) = 12.8\%.$

31. b. $k_X = R_F + b_X(k_M - R_F) = 5\% + 1.3(14\% - 5\%) = 16.7\%.$

32. d. $b_P = \sum\limits_{i=1}^{5} w_i b_i = (130/450)(0.4) + (110/450)(1.5)$

$$+ (70/450)(3.0) + (90/450)(2.0) + (50/450)(1.0)$$
$$= 1.46.$$

33. a. $k_P = R_F + b_P(k_M - R_F) = 12\% + 1.46(6\%) = 20.76\%.$

34. e. First, find the beta of the remaining 9 stocks:

$$1.8 = 0.9(b_R) + 0.1(b_A) = 0.9(b_R) + 0.1(2.0); \quad b_R = 1.778.$$

Now, what is the beta of the new stock that produces $b_P = 1.7$?

$$1.7 = 0.9(1.778) + 0.1(b_N); \quad b_N = 1.0.$$

35. e. New b = $0.9(1.30) + 0.1(1.00) = 1.27.$

$$k = R_F + b(k_M + R_F) = 12\% + 1.27(6\%) = 19.62\%.$$

36. b. The required rate of return on the plant is

$$k_{plant} = 10\% + 2.0(6\%) = 22\%.$$

37. c. First, find the current beta of the firm:

$$k = 10\% + b(5\%) = 20\%$$
$$b = 2.00.$$

Now, find the beta required to lower the required rate of return to 18 percent:

$$k = 10\% + b(5\%) = 18\%$$
$$b = 1.60.$$

Finally, if the firm doubles, 50 percent of the expanded firm's assets will be old, while 50 percent will be the new division. Thus, $0.5(2.00) + 0.5(b_{Div.}) = 1.60; \quad b_{Div.} = 1.20.$

38. c. First, find the firm's beta coefficient:

$$k = R_F + b(k_M - R_F)$$
$$18\% = 12\% + b(5\%)$$
$$b = 1.20.$$

Now, find the beta of the G division:

$$1.20 = 0.8(1.00) + 0.2b_G$$
$$b_G = 2.00.$$

Finally, find the required rate of return for an asset with a beta of 2.00:

$$k = 12\% + 2.00(5\%) = 22\%.$$

The expected return of the asset is only 21 percent; thus, it should not be acquired.

CHAPTER 14

SECURITY VALUATION

Overview

The goal of financial management is to maximize the value of the firm. The value of any financial asset is the present value of the cash flows expected from that asset. Therefore, if the cash flows can be estimated, and a discount rate determined, the value of the financial asset can be calculated. Those financial assets such as bonds and constant growth stocks that have a regular cash flow have models that are easily solved. On the other hand, nonconstant growth stock valuation, though not difficult, requires a lengthy procedure.

Outline

I. First, it is necessary to define value.

    A. Liquidating value versus going-concern value.

        1. Liquidating value is the amount that could be realized by selling an asset or group of assets separately from the organization that has been using them.

        2. Going-concern value is the amount realized if the firm is sold as an operating business.

        3. Any excess of going-concern value over liquidating value represents the value of the organization and is referred to as goodwill or organization value.

    B. Book value vs. market value.

        1. Book value is the accounting value at which an asset is carried, usually its historical cost.

        2. Market value is the price at which an asset can be sold, generally the higher of going-concern or liquidating value.

        3. In the case of stock, book value is the firm's total common equity divided by shares outstanding, and market value is the price people will pay for a share of stock.

    C. The "fair" value of an asset is arrived at by estimating future net cash flows and discounting them at an appropriate capitalization rate to determine its present value.

    1. This capitalization-of-income method of valuation is the same as the present value of assets method used in capital budgeting.

    2. Fair value is also referred to as reasonable or intrinsic value.

II. The value of a bond is calculated as the present value of the stream of cash flows from the bond.

    A. It is necessary to know some key bond terms.

        1. A bond is a long-term promissory note.

        2. The par value is the stated face value of a bond, usually $1,000.

        3. The coupon payment is the dollar amount specified that the issuer will pay each year, or perhaps each six months. The coupon interest rate is obtained by dividing the annual coupon payment by the par value of the bond.

        4. The maturity date is the date when the par value is repaid to bondholders.

    B. Using these definitions, a basic bond valuation model can be constructed.

        1. Bonds with annual coupon payments represent an annuity of I dollars per year for n years, plus a final payment of M dollars at the end of n years.

        2. The present value of this payment stream determines the value of the bond.

        3. As an example, consider a 3-year, $1,000 bond paying $50 annually, when the appropriate interest rate, k_d, is 7 percent:

$$V_d = I(PVIFA_{k,n}) + M(PVIF_{k,n})$$

$$= \$50(2.6243) + \$1,000(0.8163) = \$947.52.$$

    C. A perpetual bond is a bond which never matures and pays a constant amount, C, forever.

        1. The value of a perpetuity is found as:

$$V_d = \frac{C}{k_d}.$$

        2. If the going rate of interest rises, the value of the perpetual bond will fall.

    D. Bond prices and interest rates are inversely related; that is, they tend to move in the opposite direction from one another.

        1. The longer a bond's maturity, the larger the price change in response to a given movement in market interest rates.

This means that the prices of long-term bonds are more sensitive to interest rate changes than are short-term bond prices.

2. The tendency of a bond's price to decline if interest rates rise is known as interest risk.

E. The bond valuation model must be adjusted when interest is paid semiannually:

$$V_d = (C/2)(PVIFA_{k_d/2, 2n}) + M(PVIF_{k_d/2, 2n}).$$

III. Preferred stock is valued as a perpetuity.

A. The cash flows from preferred stock generally consist of regular, fixed dividend payments, D_{ps}.

B. The value of preferred stock is found using the perpetuity formula:

$$V_{ps} = \frac{D_{ps}}{k_{ps}}.$$

IV. Common stocks are also valued by finding the present value of the expected cash flows.

A. Two factors complicate common stock valuation.

1. Future dividends, earnings, and stock prices cannot be forecasted with certainty.

2. Earnings and dividends are expected to grow, not remain constant, so annuity formulas cannot be used.

B. The present value of a common share for a 1-year holding period would be the present value of the dividend expected at year-end plus the present value of the expected selling price one year from now, or

$$P_0 = \frac{D_1 + P_1}{1 + k_s} = \frac{D_1 + P_0(1 + g)}{1 + k_s} = \frac{D_1}{k_s - g},$$

where g is the expected annual growth rate in earnings and dividends and $D_1 = D_0(1 + g)$.

1. Before using this valuation formula you must estimate the required return on the stock, k_s.

2. A stock with a required return of 12 percent which last paid a dividend of $1.90, and which has an expected growth rate that year of 5 percent, would be valued as follows:

$$P_0 = \frac{\$1.90(1.05)}{0.12 - 0.05} = \frac{\$1.995}{0.07} = \$28.50.$$

C. Multi-period stock valuation models are determined by discounting an infinite series of dividend payments.

Value of stock = P_0 = PV of expected future dividends

$$= \frac{D_1}{(1 + k_s)^1} + \frac{D_2}{(1 + k_s)^2} + \ldots + \frac{D_\infty}{(1 + k_s)^\infty}$$

$$= \sum_{t=1}^{\infty} \frac{D_t}{(1 + k_s)^t}.$$

D. For many companies, earnings and dividends are expected to grow at some "normal" or constant rate. Dividends in any future year t may be forecast as $D_t = D_0(1 + g)^t$, where D_0 is the last dividend paid and g is the expected rate of growth. For a company which last paid a \$2.00 dividend, and which has an expected 6 percent growth rate, the estimated dividend one year from now would be D_1 = (\$2.00)(1.06) = \$2.12; D_2 would be (\$2.00)(1.06)^2 = \$2.25, and the estimated dividend 4 years hence would be $D_t = D_0(1 + g)^t$ = \$2.00(1.06)^4 = \$2.52. Using this method of estimating future dividends, the current price, P_0, is determined as follows:

$$P_0 = \frac{D_1}{(1 + k_s)^1} + \frac{D_2}{(1 + k_s)^2} + \frac{D_3}{(1 + k_s)^3} + \ldots$$

$$= \frac{D_0(1 + g)^1}{(1 + k_s)^1} + \frac{D_0(1 + g)^2}{(1 + k_s)^2} + \frac{D_0(1 + g)^3}{(1 + k_s)^3} + \ldots$$

$$= \sum_{t=1}^{\infty} \frac{D_0(1 + g)^t}{(1 + k_s)^t}.$$

If g is constant, and if k_s is greater than g, this equation simplifies to

$$P_0 = \frac{D_1}{k_s - g}.$$

This valuation equation for a constant growth stock is the same as the equation developed for a stock expected to be held for only 1 year.

E. If expected dividend growth is zero ($g = 0$), the value of the stock (P_0) reduces to $P_0 = D_1/k_s$, or, solving for k_s, $k_s = D_1/P_0$. Therefore, a zero-growth stock is valued as a perpetuity, and the expected rate of return is simply the dividend yield. These equations are also applicable to preferred stock.

F. Firms typically go through periods of nonconstant growth, after which time their growth rate settles to a rate close to that of the economy as a whole. The value of such a firm is equal to the present value of its expected future dividends. To find the value of such a stock, we proceed in three steps:

1. Find the present value of the dividends during the period of nonconstant growth.
2. Find the price of the stock at the end of the nonconstant growth period and then, using k_s, discount this price back to the present.
3. Add these two components to find the present value of the stock, P_0.

G. A declining firm's return consists of a relatively high dividend yield combined with a capital loss yield; a no-growth firm's total return equals its dividend yield; a normal-growth firm provides both a dividend and a capital gains yield; and a firm experiencing a period of supernormal growth has a relatively low dividend yield and the highest capital gain yield expectation.

Definitional Questions

1. _____ value is the amount that a firm can realize by selling an asset or a group of assets.

2. The difference between going-concern value and liquidating value is _____ value or _____.

3. Market value is the price at which an asset can be _____, while _____ _____ reflects an asset's historical cost.

4. The _____ _____ is used to calculate the fair value of an asset.

5. A _____ is a long-term promissory note issued by a business firm or governmental unit.

6. The stated face value of a bond is referred to as its _____ value and it is usually set at $_____.

7. The "coupon interest rate" on a bond is determined by dividing the _____ _____ by the _____ _____.

8. The date at which the par value of a bond is repaid to each bondholder is known as the _____ _____.

9. A bond with annual coupon payments represents an _____ of C dollars per year for n years, plus a lump sum of M dollars at the end of n years, and its value, V, is the _____ _____ of this payment stream.

10. Market interest rates and bond prices move in _____ directions from one another.

11. To adjust the bond valuation formula for semiannual coupon payments, the _____ _____ and _____ _____ _____ _____ must be divided by 2, and the number of _____ must be multiplied by 2.

12. A _____ bond pays a constant amount forever.

13. Preferred stock can be viewed as a _____.

14. The income stream associated with a common stock consists of _____ and the expected future _____ _____.

15. Like other financial assets, the value of common stock is the _____ value of a future stream of income.

16. If the future growth rate of dividends is expected to be _____, the rate of return is simply the _____ yield.

Conceptual Questions

17. Changes in economic conditions cause interest rates and bond prices to vary over time.

    a. True   b. False

18. A 20-year bond with 1 year left to maturity has the same interest rate risk as a 10-year bond with 1 year left to maturity. Both bonds have the same coupon rate.

    a. True   b. False

19. According to the valuation model developed in this chapter, the value that an investor assigns to a share of stock is independent of the length of time the investor plans to hold the stock.

    a. True   b. False

20. Which of the following assumptions would cause the stock valuation model

$$P_0 = \frac{D_0(1 + g)}{k_s - g}$$

    to be invalid?

    a. The growth rate is negative.
    b. The growth rate is zero.
    c. The growth rate is less than the required rate of return.
    d. The required rate of return is above 30 percent.
    e. None of the above assumptions would invalidate the model.

Problems

21. Delta Corp. has a bond issue outstanding with a coupon rate of 10 percent per year and 6 years remaining until maturity. The par value of the bond is $1,000. Determine the current value of the bond if present market conditions justify a 14 percent rate of return. The bond pays interest annually.

    a. $1,126.42
    b. $1,000.00
    c. $844.45
    d. $841.15
    e. $735.07

22. Refer to Problem 21. Suppose the bond had a semiannual coupon. Now, what would be the current value?

    a. $1,126.42
    b. $1,000.00
    c. $844.45
    d. $841.15
    e. $735.07

23. Refer to Problem 21. Assume an annual coupon, but 20 years remaining to maturity. What is the current value under these conditions?

    a. $1,126.42
    b. $1,000.00
    c. $844.45
    d. $841.15
    e. $735.07

24. Bates Industries has a preferred stock issue outstanding which pays a coupon rate of 10 percent annually with a par value of $100. If the required rate of return on the preferred stock is 12 percent, what is the present value of the stock?

    a. $83.33
    b. $92.57
    c. $100.00
    d. $112.50
    e. $120.00

25. Stability, Inc., has maintained a dividend rate of $4 per share for many years. The same rate is expected to be paid in future years. If investors require a 12 percent rate of return on similar investments, determine the present value of the company's stock.

    a. $15.00
    b. $30.00
    c. $33.33
    d. $35.00
    e. $40.00

26. Your brother-in-law, a stockbroker at Securities Unlimited, Inc., is trying to sell you a stock with a current market price of $30. The stock's last dividend (D_0) was $3.00, and earnings and dividends are expected to increase at a constant growth rate of 10 percent. Your required return on this stock is 20 percent. From a strict valuation standpoint, you should:

    a. Buy the stock; it is fairly valued.
    b. Buy the stock; it is undervalued by $3.00.
    c. Buy the stock; it is undervalued by $2.00.
    d. Not buy the stock; it is overvalued by $2.00.
    e. Not buy the stock; it is overvalued by $3.00.

27. Lucas Laboratories' last dividend was $1.50. Its current equilibrium stock price is $15.75, and its expected growth rate is a constant 5 percent. If the stockholders' required rate of return is 15 percent, what is the expected dividend yield and expected capital gains yield for the coming year?

    a. 0%; 15%
    b. 5%; 10%
    c. 10%; 5%
    d. 15%; 0%
    e. 15%; 15%

28. The Forsythe Company has been hard hit by increased competition. Analysts predict that earnings (and dividends) will decline at a rate of 5 percent annually into the foreseeable future. If Forsythe's last dividend (D_0) was $2.00, and investors' required rate of return is 15 percent, what will be Forsythe's stock price in 3 years?

    a. $8.15
    b. $9.50
    c. $10.00
    d. $10.42
    e. $10.96

(The following information applies to the next three problems.)

The Club Auto Parts Company has just recently been organized. It is expected to experience no growth for the next 2 years as it identifies its market and acquires its inventory. However, Club will grow at an annual rate of 6 percent in the third year, and, beginning with the fourth year, should attain a 10 percent growth rate which it will sustain thereafter. The first dividend to be paid (D_1) is expected to be $0.60 per share. Investors require a 16 percent rate of return on Club's stock.

29. What is the current equilibrium stock price?

    a. $6.00
    b. $8.85
    c. $9.23
    d. $9.66
    e. $16.00

30. What will be Club's stock price at the end of the first year (P_1)?

    a. $6.00
    b. $8.85
    c. $9.23
    d. $9.66
    e. $16.00

31. You have just been offered a bond for $863.73. The coupon rate is 8 percent, payable annually, and interest rates on new issues with the same degree of risk are 10 percent. You want to know how many more interest payments you will receive, but the party selling the bond cannot remember. If the par value is $1,000, how many interest payments remain?

    a. 10
    b. 11
    c. 12
    d. 13
    e. 14

32. Dowling Corporation's stock is currently selling at $66.00 per share. The last dividend paid (D_0) was $3.00. Dowling is a constant growth firm. If investors require a return of 15 percent on Dowling's growth stock, what do they think Dowling's growth rate will be?

    a. 6%
    b. 7%
    c. 8%
    d. 9%
    e. 10%

Answers and Solutions

1. Liquidating

2. organization; goodwill

3. sold; book value

4. capitalization-of-income method

5. bond

6. par; 1000

7. coupon payment; par value

8. maturity date

9. annuity; present value

10. opposite

11. coupon payment; required rate of return; years

12. perpetual

13. perpetuity

14. dividends; selling price

15. present

16. zero; dividend

17. a. For example, if inflation increases, the required return will increase, resulting in a decline in price.

18. a. Both bonds are valued as 1-year bonds regardless of their original issue dates. Therefore, the interest rate risk is the same.

19. a. The model considers all future dividends. This produces a current value which is appropriate for all investors independent of the expected holding period.

20. e. The stock valuation model would be invalid if the growth rate equalled or exceeded the required rate of return.

21. c. $V = C(PVIFA_{k,n}) + M(PVIF_{k,n})$

   $= \$100(PVIFA_{14\%,6}) + \$1,000(PVIF_{14\%,6})$

   $= \$100(3.8887) + \$1,000(0.4556)$

   $= \$388.87 + \$455.60$

   $= \$844.47.$

Calculator solution = $844.45.

d. $V = (C/2)(PVIFA_{k/2,2n}) + M(PVIF_{k/2,2n})$

$\quad = \$50(PVIFA_{7,12}) + \$1,000(PVIF_{7,12})$

$\quad = \$50(7.9427) + \$1,000(0.4440)$

$\quad = \$397.14 + \$444.00$

$\quad = \$841.14.$

Calculator solution = \$841.15.

23. e. $V = C(PVIFA_{k,n}) + M(PVIF_{k,n})$

$\quad = \$100(PVIFA_{14,20}) + \$1,000(PVIF_{14,20})$

$\quad = \$100(6.6231) + \$1,000(0.0728)$

$\quad = \$662.31 + \$72.80$

$\quad = \$735.11$

Calculator solution = \$735.07.

24. a. $V_{ps} = \dfrac{D_{ps}}{k_{ps}}.$

$D_{ps} = \$100(0.10) = \$10$, and $k_s = 12$ percent.

Therefore, $V_{ps} = \dfrac{\$10}{0.12} = \$83.33.$

25. c. This is a zero-growth stock, or perpetuity:

$V = D_1/k_s = \$4.00/0.12 = \$33.33.$

26. b. $V = \dfrac{D_0(1 + g)}{k_s - g} = \dfrac{\$3.00(1.10)}{0.20 - 0.10} = \$33.00.$

Since the stock is currently selling for \$30.00, it is undervalued by \$3.00 and you should buy it.

27. c. Dividend yield $= \dfrac{D_1}{P_0} = \dfrac{D_0(1 + g)}{P_0} = \dfrac{\$1.50(1.05)}{\$15.75} = 0.10 = 10\%.$

Capital gains yield $= \dfrac{P_1 - P_0}{P_0} = \dfrac{P_0(1 + g) - P_0}{P_0} = g = 5\%.$

(Note that for a constant growth stock the dividend yield and capital gains yield are constant from year to year, and that the capital gains yield is equal to g.)

28. a. $P_0 = \dfrac{D_0(1 + g)}{k_s - g} = \dfrac{\$2.00(0.95)}{0.15 - (-0.05)} = \dfrac{\$1.90}{0.20} = \$9.50.$

$P_3 = P_0(1 + g)^3 = \$9.50(0.95)^3 = \$8.15.$

29. b.

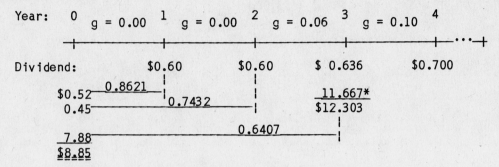

$$*P_3 = \dfrac{D_4}{k_s - g} = \dfrac{0.700}{0.16 - 0.10} = \$11.667.$$

30. d.   Since this is not a constant growth stock, $P_1 \neq P_0(1 + g)$. To find P_1, find the present value of Year 1 of all future expected dividends.   Note that D_1 does not contribute to the value of the stock at Year 1.

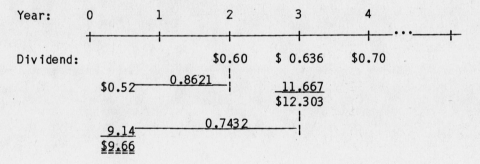

31. c. $V = C(PVIFA_{k,n}) + M(PVIF_{k,n})$

$\$863.73 = \$80(PVIFA_{10\%,n}) + \$1,000(PVIF_{10\%,n})$

Now use trial and error to find the value of n for which the equality holds.   For n = 12, $863.73 = 80(6.8187) + $1,000(0.3186) = $863.70.$

32. e. $P_0 = \dfrac{D_0(1 + g)}{k_s - g}$

$\$66.00 = \dfrac{\$3.00(1 + g)}{0.15 - g}$

$\$9.90 - \$66.00g = \$3.00 + \$3.00g$

$\$69.00g = \$6.90g$

$g = 10\%.$

CHAPTER 15

THE COST OF CAPITAL

Overview

This chapter describes how the cost of capital schedule is developed and then used in the capital budgeting process. First, the cost of capital must be determined for each component of the firm's capital structure. These components are normally debt, preferred equity, and common equity. The next task is to combine the component costs to form a weighted average cost of capital. The weights used are based on the firm's target capital structure, that capital structure which minimizes the firm's cost of capital. Finally, capital typically has a higher cost if the firm expands beyond certain limits. The break point concept is used to develop a step-function cost of capital schedule, which is then combined with the investment opportunity schedule to determine the optimal capital budget.

Outline

I. Determination of the cost of capital is an important aspect of financial management. The two primary uses of the cost of capital are in capital budgeting and in helping to establish the optimal capital structure. The cost of capital is also a necessary element in decisions regarding bond refunding, leasing, and working capital management.

   A. The appropriate cost of capital for most decisions is a weighted average cost.

   B. Capital components are items on the right-hand side of the balance sheet such as debt, preferred stock, common stock, and retained earnings.

   C. Each element of capital has a component cost which can be identified as follows:

      1. k_d = interest rate on new debt, before tax.

      2. $k_d(1 - T)$ = after-tax cost of debt, where t is the marginal tax rate.

      3. k_{ps} = component cost of preferred stock.

4. k_s = component cost of retained earnings; it is equal to the required rate of return on common stock.

5. k_e = cost of external capital obtained by issuing additional common stock; it must be distinguished from equity raised through retained earnings due to flotation costs of a stock issue.

6. k_a = the weighted average, or composite, cost of capital.

II. The cost of each capital component can be determined as follows:

A. The after-tax cost of debt, $k_d(1 - T)$, is defined as the interest rate that must be paid on new debt capital, reduced by $(1 - T)$ because interest payments are tax deductible.

1. For example, if Firm A has a tax rate of 46 percent and can borrow at a rate of 14 percent, then its after-tax cost of debt is k_d = 14%(1 - 0.46) = 14%(0.54) = 7.56%.
2. The tax deductibility of interest payments has the effect of causing the federal government to pay part of the interest charges.
3. k_d is applicable to new debt only, not to any previously outstanding debt.

B. The component cost of preferred stock, k_{ps}, is the preferred dividend, D_{ps}, divided by the issuance price net of flotation costs, P_n, or $k_{ps} = D_{ps}/P_n$. Note that no tax adjustment is made since preferred stock dividends are paid from after-tax earnings.

C. The cost of equity obtained by retaining earnings, k_s, is the rate of return stockholders require on the firm's common stock. There are three approaches used to determine k_s.

1. One approach is to use the Capital Asset Pricing Model (CAPM) as follows:
   a. Determine the riskless rate, R_F, usually based on U.S. Treasury securities.
   b. Use the stock's beta coefficient as an index of risk.
   c. Estimate the required rate of return on the market, or on an "average" stock, k_M.
   d. Determine the required rate of return on the firm's stock using the SML.
   e. If R_F = 10%, k_M = 15%, and the beta of Firm A is 1.3, then k_s = 10% + 1.3(5%) = 16.5%.
2. A simple but useful approach to determine k_s is to add a risk premium to the firm's own cost of long-term debt.
   a. Using this approach, k_s is found as follows:

$$k_s = \text{Bond rate} + \text{Risk premium.}$$

      b. A risk premium of from 2 to 4 percentage points is commonly used with this approach.

      c. If Firm A uses a risk premium of 3 percentage points, and their bond rate is 14 percent, then

$$k_s = 14\% + 3\% = 17\%.$$

3. The required rate of return, k_s, may also be estimated by the discounted cash flow (DCF) approach. This approach combines the expected dividend yield, D_1/P_0, with the expected future growth rate, g, of earnings and dividends, or

$$k_s = D_1/P_0 + g.$$

      a. The DCF approach assumes that stocks are normally in equilibrium and that growth is expected to be at a constant rate. If growth is not constant, then a nonconstant growth model must be used.

      b. The expected growth rate may be based on projections of past growth rates, if they have been relatively stable, or on expected future growth rates as estimated in some other manner.

      c. If Firm A last paid $4.00 in annual dividends which are expected to grow at a constant 10 percent per year, and Firm A's stock is selling for $63.00 per share, then

$$k_s = \frac{\$4(1.10)}{\$63} + 10\% = 16.98\%.$$

4. If Firm A cannot earn about 17 percent on reinvested equity capital, then it should pay its earnings to stockholders and let them invest directly in other assets that do provide this return. Thus, k_s is an opportunity cost.

5. It is recommended that all three approaches be used in estimating the required rate of return on common stock. When the methods produce widely different results, judgment must be used in selecting the best estimate.

D. The cost of new common stock, or external equity capital, k_e, is higher than the cost of retained earnings, k_s, because of flotation costs of new common stock.

1. To allow for flotation costs, F, we must adjust the DCF formula for the required rate of return as follows:

$$k_e = \frac{D_1}{P_0(1 - F)} + g.$$

2. If Firm A incurred flotation costs of 12 percent in issuing new common shares, the required rate of return would be as follows:

$$k_e = \frac{\$4.00(1.10)}{\$63.00(1 - 0.12)} + 10\% = 7.94\% + 10\% = 17.94\%.$$

3. If Firm A can earn 17.94 percent on investments financed by new common stock, then earnings, dividends, and the growth rate will be maintained, and the price per share will not fall. If it earns more than 17.94 percent, the price will rise; while if it earns less, the price will fall.

III. The proportions of debt and equity in a firm's target capital structure are used to calculate the weighted average cost of capital.

A. The calculation of the weighted average cost of capital is shown below for a firm which finances 30 percent with debt, 10 percent with preferred stock, and 60 percent with common equity and which has the following after-tax component costs:

Component	Weight x	After-tax Cost =	Weighted Cost
Debt	0.3	4.4%	1.32%
Preferred	0.1	12.0	1.20
Common	0.6	16.5	9.90
		$k_a =$	12.42%

B. In more general terms, and in equation format,

$$k_a = w_d(k_d)(1 - T) + w_{ps}(k_{ps}) + w_s(k_s \text{ or } k_e).$$

C. The capital structure that minimizes a firm's weighted average cost of capital also maximizes its stock price.

IV. The marginal cost of capital is defined as the cost of raising another dollar of new capital. In general, the marginal cost of any factor of production, including capital, will eventually rise as more and more of the factor is used.

A. As companies raise larger and larger sums during a given time period, the costs of both debt and equity components begin to rise. This causes an increase in the weighted average cost of each additional dollar of new capital.

B. The marginal cost of capital (MCC) schedule shows the relationship between the cost of each dollar raised, k_a, and the total amount of capital raised during the year. A graph of the relationship is shown by the following:

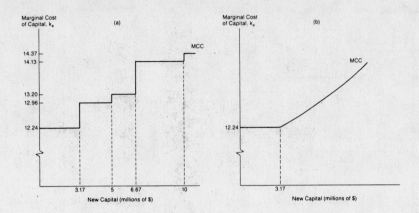

1. The schedule may appear as a step function (see Panel a in the above graph).
2. Realistically, the MCC schedule is probably smooth, curving upward after some amount of new capital has been raised (see Panel b in the above graph).

C. The optimal capital structure is the one that produces the lowest MCC schedule.

D. In general, a break will occur in the MCC schedule any time the cost of one of the components rises.

1. The break point is determined by the following equation:

$$\text{Break point} = \frac{\substack{\text{Total amount of lower-cost} \\ \text{capital of a given type}}}{\substack{\text{Fraction of this type of capital} \\ \text{in the optimal structure}}}.$$

2. If there are n such break points, there will be n + 1 different MCCs.

E. For ease in calculating the MCC schedule, first identify the points where breaks occur, then determine the cost of capital for each component in the intervals between breaks, and, finally, calculate the weighted averages of these costs.

V. The MCC schedule is used to determine the discount rate to be used in the firm's capital budgeting process.

A. The firm's investment opportunity schedule (IOS) and its MCC curve may be plotted on the same graph.

B. The intersection of these two curves determines the discount rate that should be used in the NPV ranking procedure. This intersection also determines the firm's optimal capital budget.

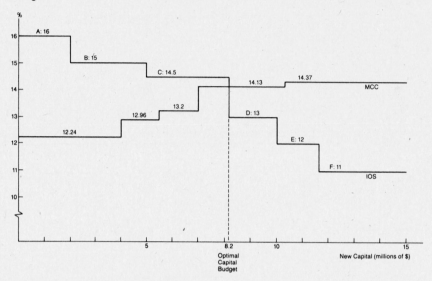

Here, Projects A, B, and C all have rates of return in excess of the cost of capital used to finance them. In the diagram above, the optimal capital budget would call for the company to invest 8.2 million dollars.

C. This cost of capital should be adjusted up or down to find the NPVs of projects with higher or lower risk.

VI. A number of difficult issues relating to the cost of capital are mentioned in the text to alert the reader to potential dangers. These topics are generally covered in more detail in advanced courses.

Definitional Questions

1. The firm should calculate its cost of capital as a _____ _____ of the after-tax costs of the various types of funds it uses.

2. Capital components are items on the right-hand side of the balance sheet such as (1) _____, (2) _____ _____, (3) _____ _____, and (4) _____ _____.

3. The cost of equity capital is defined as the _____ _____ _____ stockholders require on the firm's common stock.

4. There are _____ approaches that can be used to determine the cost of retained earnings.

5. Assigning a cost to retained earnings is based on the _____ _____ principle.

6. The cost of external equity capital is higher than the cost of retained earnings due to _____ _____.

7. Using the Capital Asset Pricing Model (CAPM), the required rate of return on common stock is found as a function of the _____ _____, the firm's _____ _____, and the required rate of return on an average _____.

8. The cost of common equity may also be found by adding a _____ _____ to the interest rate on the firm's own _____ _____.

9. The required rate of return may also be estimated as the _____ _____ on the common stock plus the expected _____ _____ in dividends.

10. The proportions of _____, _____ _____, and _____ _____ in the target capital structure should be used to calculate the _____ _____ cost of capital.

11. Minimizing the firm's weighted average cost of capital will tend to maximize the firm's _____ _____.

12. The _____ cost of capital is the cost of raising another dollar of capital.

13. The MCC schedule can be used to help determine the _____ _____ to be used in the capital budgeting process.

14. The _____ _____ _____ graphs a firm's capital projects in descending order of each project's _____ _____ _____ _____.

Conceptual Questions

15. If a firm obtains all of its common equity from retained earnings, its MCC schedule would be flat; that is, there will be no break points.

    a. True   b. False

16. The component costs of capital are based on historical, or embedded, costs.

    a. True   b. False

17. If there are n break points in the MCC schedule, there will be n + 1 different MCCs.

    a. True   b. False

18. Funds acquired by the firm through preferred stock have a cost to the firm equal to the preferred dividend divided by the price investors paid for one share.

    a. True   b. False

19. Which of the following statements <u>could</u> be true concerning the costs of debt and equity?

    a. The cost of debt for Firm A is greater than the cost of equity for Firm A.

    b. The cost of debt for Firm A is greater than the cost of equity for Firm B.

    c. The cost of retained earnings for Firm A is less than the cost of external equity for Firm A.

    d. The cost of retained earnings for Firm A is less than the cost of debt for Firm A.

    e. Statements b and c could both be true.

Problems

20. Roland Corporation's next expected dividend (D_1) is $2.50. The firm has maintained a constant payout ratio of 50 percent during the past 7 years. Seven years ago its EPS was $1.50. The firm's beta coefficient is 1.2. The required return on an average stock is 13 percent, and the risk-free rate is 7 percent. Roland's A-rated bonds are yielding 10 percent, and its current stock price is $30. Which of the following values is the most reasonable estimate of Roland's cost of retained earnings, k_s?

    a. 10%
    b. 12%
    c. 14%
    d. 20%
    e. 26%

21. The director of capital budgeting for See-Saw, Inc., manufacturers of playground equipment, is considering a plan to expand production facilities in order to meet an increase in demand. He estimates that this expansion will produce an IRR of 11 percent. The firm's target capital structure calls for a debt/equity ratio of 0.8.

    See-Saw currently has a bond issue outstanding which will mature in 25 years and has a 7 percent annual coupon rate. The bonds are currently selling for $804. The firm has maintained a constant growth rate of 6 percent. See-Saw's next expected dividend is $2 and its current stock price is $40. Its tax rate is 40 percent. Should it undertake the expansion? (Assume that there is no preferred stock outstanding and that any new debt will have a 25 year maturity.)

a. No; the expected return is 2.5 percentage points lower than the cost of capital.

b. No; the expected return is 1.0 percentage points lower than the cost of capital.

c. Yes; the expected return is 0.5 percentage points higher than the cost of capital.

d. Yes; the expected return is 1.0 percentage points higher than the cost of capital.

e. Yes; the expected return is 2.5 percentage points higher than the cost of capital.

22. Midterm Corporation's present capital structure, which is also its target capital structure, calls for 50 percent debt and 50 percent common equity. The firm has only one potential project, an expansion program with a 10.2 percent IRR and a cost of $20 million but which is completely divisible; that is, Midterm can invest any amount up to $20 million. Midterm expects to retain $3 million of earnings next year. It can raise up to $5 million in new debt at a before-tax cost of 8 percent, and all debt after the first $5 million will have a cost of 10 percent. The cost of retained earnings is 12 percent; Midterm can sell any amount of new common stock desired at a constant cost of new equity of 15 percent. The firm's marginal tax rate is 40 percent. What is Midterm's optimal capital budget?

a. $0 million
b. $5 million
c. $6 million
d. $10 million
e. $20 million

23. The management of Florida Phosphate Industries is planning next year's capital budget. FPI projects net income of $10,500, and its payout ratio is 40 percent. The company's earnings and dividends are growing at a constant rate of 5 percent; the last dividend, D_0, was $0.90; and the current equilibrium stock price is $8.59. FPI can raise up to $10,000 of debt at a 12 percent before-tax cost, the next $10,000 will cost 14 percent, and all debt after $20,000 will cost 16 percent. If FPI issues new common stock, a 10 percent flotation cost will be incurred on the first $16,000 issued, while flotation costs will be 20 percent on all new stock issued after the first $16,000. FPI is at its optimal capital structure, which is 40 percent debt and 60 percent equity, and the firm's marginal tax rate is 40 percent. FPI has the following independent, indivisible, and equally risky investment opportunities:

Project	Cost	IRR
A	$15,000	17%
B	20,000	14
C	15,000	16
D	12,000	15

What is FPI's optimal capital budget?

a. $62,000
b. $42,000
c. $30,000
d. $15,000
e. $0

24. Refer to Problem 23. Management neglected to incorporate project risk differentials into the analysis. FPI's policy is to add 2 percentage points to the IRR of those projects significantly less risky than average and to subtract 2 percentage points from the IRR of those which are substantially more risky than average. Management judges Project A to be of high risk, Projects C and D to be of average risk, and Project B to be of low risk. No projects are divisible. What is the optimal capital budget after adjustment for project risk?

a. $62,000
b. $50,000
c. $42,000
d. $30,000
e. $15,000

25. Gator Products Company (GPC) is at its optimal capital structure of 70 percent common equity and 30 percent debt. GPC's MCC and IOS schedules for next year intersect at a 14 percent marginal cost of capital. At the intersection, the IOS schedule is vertical and the MCC schedule is horizontal. GPC has a marginal tax rate of 40 percent. Next year's dividend is expected to be $2.00 per share, and GPC has a constant growth in earnings and dividends of 6 percent. The after-tax cost of equity used in the MCC at the intersection is based on new equity with a flotation cost of 10 percent, while the before-tax cost of debt is 12 percent. What is GPC's current equilibrium stock price?

a. $12.73
b. $17.23
c. $20.37
d. $23.70
e. $37.20

Answers and Solutions

1. weighted average

2. debt; preferred stock; common stock; retained earnings

3. rate of return

4. three

5. opportunity cost

6. flotation costs

7. risk-free rate (R_F); beta coefficient (b); stock (k_M)

8. risk premium; long-term debt

9. dividend yield; growth rate

10. debt; preferred stock; common equity; weighted average

11. stock price

12. marginal

13. discount rate

14. Investment Opportunity Schedule (IOS); internal rate of return (IRR)

15. b. The component cost of debt and/or preferred equity might increase, thus causing break points in the MCC schedule.

16. b. The costs reflect the costs of <u>future</u> borrowing, earnings retention, or stock sales and, thus, are market determined.

17. a.

18. b. Flotation costs must be subtracted from the investor's cost to get the net issuance price, which is then used to calculate the cost of preferred stock.

19. e. If Firm A has more risk than Firm B, Firm A's cost of debt could be greater than Firm B's cost of equity. Also, the cost of retained earnings is less than the cost of external equity because of flotation costs.

20. c. Use all three methods to estimate k_s.

(1) <u>CAPM</u>: $k_s = R_F + b(k_M - R_F) = 7\% + 1.2(13\% - 7\%) = 14.2\%$.

(2) <u>Risk Premium</u>: k_s = Bond yield + Risk premium
$$= 10\% + \text{approximately } 4\% = 14\%.$$

(3) <u>DCF:</u> $k_s = D_1/P_0 + g = \$2.50/\$30 + g$, where g can be estimated as follows:

$$\$0.75 = \$2.50(PVIF_{k,7})$$
$$PVIF_{k,7} = \$0.75/\$2.50 = 0.3000.$$

Thus k, which is the compound growth rate, g, is about 19%, or, using a calculator, 18.8%. Therefore, $k_s = 0.083 + 0.188 = 27.1\%$.

Roland Corporation has apparently been experiencing supernormal growth during the past 7 years, and it is not reasonable to assume that this growth will continue. The first two methods yield a k_s of about 14 percent, which appears reasonable.

21. e. Cost of equity = $k_s = \$2/\$40 + 0.06 = 0.11 = 11\%$.

Cost of debt = k_d = Yield to maturity on outstanding bonds based on current market price.

$$V = C(PVIFA_{k_d,n}) + M(PVIF_{k_d,n})$$

$$\$804 = \$70(PVIFA_{k_d,25}) + \$1,000(PVIF_{k_d,25}).$$

Solving by trial and error gives $k_d = 9\%$. In determining the capital structure weights, note that debt/equity = 0.8 or, for example, 4/5. Therefore, debt/assets is

$$\frac{D}{A} = \frac{Debt}{Debt + Equity} = \frac{4}{4 + 5} = \frac{4}{9}$$

and equity/assets = 5/9. Hence, the weighted average cost of capital is

$$k_a = k_d(1 - T)(D/A) + k_s(1 - D/A)$$
$$= 0.09(1 - 0.4)(4/9) + 0.11(5/9)$$
$$= 0.024 + 0.061 = 0.085 = 8.5\%.$$

The cost of capital is 8.5 percent, while the expansion project's IRR is 11.0 percent. Since the expected return is 2.5 percentage points higher than the cost, the expansion should be undertaken.

22. d. First, look only at debt:

Now, look only at equity:

Now, combine debt and equity and look at total capital:

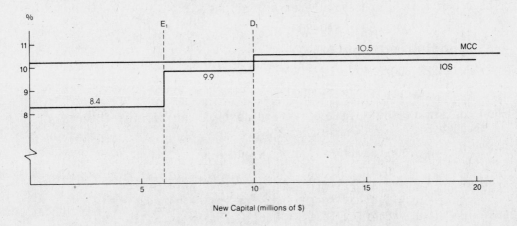

The break points are calculated as follows:

E_1 = $3,000,000/0.5 = $6,000,000.

D_1 = $5,000,000/0.5 = $10,000,000.

Now, determine the weighted average cost of capital for intervals A, B, and C:

$$k_a = w_d(k_d)(1 - T) + w_s(k_s \text{ or } k_e).$$
A = 0.5(8%)(0.6) + 0.5(12%) = 8.4%.
B = 0.5(8%)(0.6) + 0.5(15%) = 9.9%.
C = 0.5(10%)(0.6) + 0.5(15%) = 10.5%.

Finally, graph the IOS and MCC schedules.

Thus, the optimal capital budget is $10 million.

23. b. First, look only at debt:

Now, look only at equity:

Retained earnings are forecast to be $10,500(0.6) = $6,300. The cost of retained earnings is as follows:

$$k_s = \frac{D_0(1 + g)}{P_0} + g = \frac{\$0.90(1.05)}{\$8.59} + 0.05 = 0.16 = 16\%.$$

The cost of new equity is as follows:

$$k_{e1} = \frac{D_0(1 + g)}{P_0(1 - F)} + g = \frac{\$0.90(1.05)}{\$8.59(1 - 0.10)} + 0.05 = 0.1722 = 17.22\%.$$

$$k_{e2} = \frac{\$0.90(1.05)}{\$8.59(1 - 0.20)} + 0.05 = 0.1875 = 18.75\%.$$

Now, combine debt and equity and look at total capital:

$$\begin{array}{c}
\quad E_1 \quad B \quad D_1 \quad C \quad E_2 \quad D \quad D_2 \quad E \\
\hline
\$0 \quad \$10,500 \quad \$25,000 \quad \$37,167 \quad \$50,000
\end{array} \text{($ of capital)}$$

The break points are calculated as follows:

E_1 = $6,300/0.60 = $10,500.

D_1 = $10,000/0.40 = $25,000.

E_2 = $22,300/0.60 = $37,167.

D_2 = $20,000/0.40 = $50,000.

Now, determine the weighted average cost of capital for intervals A through E:

$$k_a = w_d(k_d)(1 - T) + w_s(k_s \text{ or } k_e)$$

A = 0.4(12%)(0.6) + 0.6(16.00%) = 12.48%.
B = 0.4(12%)(0.6) + 0.6(17.22%) = 13.21%.
C = 0.4(14%)(0.6) + 0.6(17.22%) = 13.69%.
D = 0.4(14%)(0.6) + 0.6(18.75%) = 14.61%.
E = 0.4(16%)(0.6) + 0.6(18.75%) = 15.09%.

Finally, graph the MCC and IOS schedules:

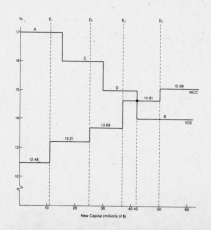

New Capital (millions of $)

Therefore, the optimal capital budget is $42,000.

24. b. First, determine the risk-adjusted IRRs:

Project	Cost	IRR	Risk	Risk-adjusted IRR
A	$15,000	17%	High	15%
B	20,000	14	Low	16
C	15,000	16	Avg.	16
D	12,000	15	Avg.	15

Now, regraph the IOS and MCC schedules:

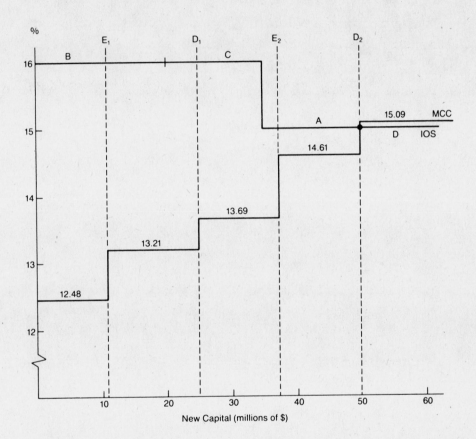

Note that Projects B and C are graphed first, and then the IOS can be ordered with A first or with D first. With A first, total cost of Projects B, C, and A is $50,000, which coincides with a break point. Clearly, Project D is not acceptable. Therefore, the optimal capital budget is $50,000.

25. c. At the intersection of the IOS and MCC schedules, k_a = 14%. Therefore,

$$w_d(k_d)(1 - T) + w_s(k_e) = k_a = 14\%$$
$$0.3(12\%)(0.6) + 0.7(k_e) = 14\%$$
$$k_e = 16.91\%.$$

Now, at equilibrium:

$$\hat{k}_e = k_e = \frac{D_1}{P_0(1 - F)} + g$$

$$0.1691 = \frac{\$2.00}{P_0(1 - 0.10)} + 0.06$$

$$0.1091 = \frac{\$2.222}{P_0}; \quad P_0 = \$20.37.$$

CHAPTER 16

CAPITAL STRUCTURE AND LEVERAGE

Overview

This chapter analyzes the effects of financial leverage on stock prices, earnings per share, and the cost of capital. The analysis suggests that some optimal capital structure exists which simultaneously maximizes stock price and minimizes the weighted average cost of capital. The use of debt tends to increase earnings per share, which will lead to a higher stock price. But at the same time, the use of debt also increases the riskiness to the stockholders, thereby lowering stock price. The optimal capital budget strikes a balance between risk and return. However, as a practical matter, it is difficult to determine the optimal capital structure with precision. Thus, firms tend to consider other factors such as interest coverage ratios, and the final target capital structure is arrived at judgmentally. Appendix 15A explains the interrelationship between financial and operating leverage.

Outline

I. Capital structure refers to the makeup of the entire right-hand side of the balance sheet. This includes short-term debt, long-term debt, preferred stock, and common equity.

   A. A firm's weighted average cost of capital depends on its capital structure.

      1. If the weights of the capital components change, the cost of capital will change and this could affect the set of acceptable projects.
      2. Changes in the capital structure also affect the riskiness of the firm's common stock and thus affect k_s, k_a, and P_0.

   B. Capital structure decisions involve a choice between risk and expected return.

      1. Additional debt increases the riskiness of the firm, but added leverage can result in higher returns.
      2. The optimal capital structure balances risk and return to maximize the stock price.

II. Financial leverage refers to the firm's use of fixed-charge securities such as debt and preferred stock, rather than common stock, in its capital structure.

A. The degree to which a firm has fixed financial charges-- interest and preferred dividends--will affect its expected earnings per share and the riskiness of these earnings.

B. EBIT is not affected by the firm's use of financial leverage.

C. Financial leverage will be "favorable" if the return on assets is greater than the cost of debt. However, the degree of risk associated with the firm will also increase as leverage increases.

D. As financial leverage increases, the cost of debt is also likely to rise due to the increased risk of not being able to meet the fixed charges.

E. Financial leverage increases the potential return to common stockholders, but it also increases the potential variability in earnings per share.

F. A firm should choose that capital structure which maximizes the price of its stock. This capital structure is called the target capital structure.

III. Changes in the use of financial leverage will affect EPS and stock price.

A. At first, EPS will rise as the use of debt increases. Interest charges rise, but the number of outstanding shares will fall as equity is replaced by debt.

B. At some point EPS will peak. Beyond this point interest rates rise so fast that EPS is depressed in spite of the fact that the number of shares outstanding is falling.

C. Risk, as measured by the standard deviation of EPS, rises continuously as the use of debt increases.

D. The expected stock price will at first increase with financial leverage. It will then reach a peak and decline as the firm's risk, and thus its required rate of return, increases with the use of debt.

1. The optimal capital structure is found when the expected stock price is maximized.
2. Management should set its target capital structure at this ratio of debt/assets.

E. The financial structure that maximizes EPS is usually higher than the one which results in the highest stock price for the firm.

IV. The pattern that the expected stock price follows with increasing financial leverage is due primarily to corporate income taxes and bankruptcy costs.

 A. Interest is tax deductible. So, with more debt in the capital structure, a greater proportion of operating income will flow through to the investor. This will increase the value of the firm and hence its stock price.

 B. On the other hand, higher debt ratios lead to greater bankruptcy risk. The increased risk of bankruptcy and the costs involved will cause the price of the stock to decline.

 C. In the absence of bankruptcy costs, the tax shelter effect would lead to a continuously increasing stock price. Without the tax shelter effect, the bankruptcy effect would cause the price of the stock to decrease continuously with leverage. When the two are combined, we see that the stock price initially rises, then peaks, and finally falls as the risk of incurring bankruptcy costs becomes very high.

 V. The capital structure that maximizes stock price is also the capital structure that minimizes the weighted average cost of capital. This is illustrated in the graphs on the following page.

VI. In many instances management is more concerned with the effects of financial leverage on the risk of bankruptcy than on maximizing share prices.

 A. Some of the reasons for this are as follows:

  1. It is extremely difficult to determine the relationships among financial leverage, P/E ratios, and equity capitalization rates (k_s). Therefore, it is frequently difficult to use this type of analysis to determine a target capital structure.
  2. Market prices are of reduced importance for small, closely held businesses.
  3. Established management teams are often conservative; they may be more interested in survival than in maximizing expected stock prices.
  4. Firms that provide vital services must put long-run viability above short-run stock price maximization.

 B. Because of these factors, management may place considerable emphasis on the times-interest-earned ratio and the fixed charge coverage ratio when establishing its financial structure. The higher these ratios, the less likely it is that a firm will be unable to meet all of its fixed charge obligations and thus face bankruptcy.

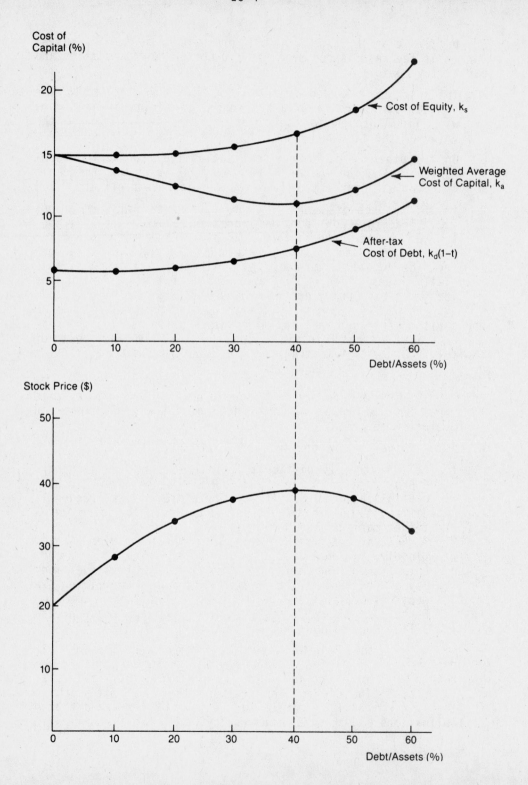

VII. A firm's capital structure can change because of merger activity.

   A. The acquiring firm may issue debt to purchase the target firm's stock.

   B. This action will change the combined firm's capital structure.

   C. This use of debt increases the value sufficiently to cover the premium offered for the stock and to provide a profit for the acquiring firm.

VIII. The following factors will all have some influence on the firm's choice of a target capital structure.

   A. Sales stability. If sales are stable, a firm will be more likely to take on increased debt and higher fixed charges.

   B. Types of assets (asset structure). Firms whose assets can readily be pledged as collateral for loans will tend to operate with a higher degree of financial leverage.

   C. Operating leverage. Lower operating leverage generally permits a firm to employ more debt.

   D. Growth rate. Firms that are growing rapidly generally need large amounts of external capital. The cost of financing with debt is generally less than with common stock, so more debt is sold.

   E. Profitability. A high degree of profitability would indicate the ability to afford a high level of fixed charges. However, many profitable firms are able to meet most of their financing needs with retained earnings.

   F. Taxes. Interest charges are tax deductible, while dividend payments are not. This factor favors the use of debt over equity.

   G. Control. Management may not wish to increase the shares of stock outstanding for fear of losing voting control of the company; thus, it might tend to finance with debt rather than with equity.

   H. Management attitudes. Managements vary in their attitudes toward risk. More conservative ones will use stock rather than debt for financing, while less conservative ones will use more debt.

   I. Lender and rating agency attitudes. This factor will penalize firms that go beyond the average for their industry in the use of financial leverage.

   J. Market conditions. At any point in time, securities markets may favor either debt or equity and make it impractical for firms to finance otherwise.

K. **Firm's internal condition.** Expected future earnings patterns and internal factors will influence management's choice of debt versus equity.

IX. There is wide variation in the use of financial leverage among both industries and the individual firms within each industry.

X. Appendix 15A describes the interrelationship between financial and operating leverage.

A. The degree of operating leverage (DOL) is defined as the percentage change in earnings before interest and taxes (EBIT) associated with a 1 percent change in sales volume.

1. The formula for DOL is as follows:

$$DOL = \frac{Q(P - v)}{Q(P - v) - F} = \frac{S - V}{S - V - F}.$$

Here, Q = units of output.
P = average sales price per unit.
v = variable cost per unit.
V = total variable costs.
S = sales in dollars.

2. The DOL varies with the level of sales.

B. The degree of financial leverage (DFL) is defined as the percentage change in earnings per share (EPS) associated with a 1 percent change in EBIT, and is given by

$$DFL = \frac{EBIT}{EBIT - I}.$$

C. The degree of total leverage, DTL, is defined as the percentage change in EPS associated with a 1 percent change in sales volume and is given by the following:

$$DTL = \frac{Q(P - v)}{Q(P - v) - F - I} = \frac{S - V}{S - V - F - I},$$

or

$$DTL = (DOL)(DFL).$$

Definitional Questions

1. The right-hand side of a firm's balance sheet is referred to as its _____ _____.

2. Determination of an _____ capital structure requires consideration of both _____ and _____.

3. A firm's _____ capital structure is generally set equal to the estimated optimal structure.

4. EPS _____ as the debt/assets ratio increases.

5. As financial leverage increases, the stock price will first begin to rise, then decline as financial leverage becomes excessive because of _____ _____.

6. Firms that have a high ratio of fixed to variable costs are said to operate with a high degree of _____ _____.

7. Operating leverage refers to the use of _____ _____.

8. Financial leverage refers to the use of _____ financing.

9. Difficulties in determining the relationship between _____ ratios, _____ capitalization rates, and the degree of _____ _____ have made some managers reluctant to rely heavily on implied stock price analysis.

10. Conservative financial managers may try to maintain a target _____ _____ that does not maximize the firm's _____ _____.

11. Some managers may be more concerned with _____ than with maximizing stock prices.

12. The _____ ratio and the _____ _____ _____ ratio give some indication of a firm's risk of default on its fixed charges.

13. External capital is particularly important to firms with a high _____ _____.

14. Debt has a _____ advantage over equity in that _____ is a deductible expense while _____ are not.

15. Management may prefer additional _____ as opposed to common stock in order to maintain _____ of the company.

Conceptual Questions

16. As a general rule, the capital structure that maximizes stock price also:

    a. Maximizes the weighted average cost of capital.
    b. Maximizes EPS.
    c. Maximizes bankruptcy costs.
    d. Minimizes the weighted average cost of capital.
    e. Minimizes the required rate of return on equity.

17. Higher financial leverage implies that:

    a. Earnings per share will be higher.
    b. The earnings stream will be riskier.
    c. Earnings per share will be lower.
    d. The earnings stream will be less risky.
    e. Operating leverage will be higher.

18. Normally, the standard deviation of expected earnings per share decreases as the debt ratio increases.

    a. True   b. False

19. In general, financial leverage is favorable whenever the return on assets exceeds the:

    a. Cost of capital.
    b. Cost of debt.
    c. Cost of common equity.
    d. Marginal cost of capital.
    e. Profitability index.

20. The degree of financial leverage is defined as:

    a. The percentage change in net operating income associated with a given percentage change in sales volume.
    b. The percentage change in earnings per share associated with a given percentage change in earnings before interest and taxes.
    c. The percentage change in earnings per share associated with a given percentage change in sales volume.
    d. The percentage change in net operating income associated with a given percentage change in breakeven sales quantity.
    e. The percentage change in breakeven sales volume associated with a given percentage change in debt level.

Problems

(The following information applies to the next two problems.)

The debt ratios of the Fischer Company and the Diamond Company are 50 percent and 30 percent, respectively. Both firms have assets totaling $100 million, a cost of debt of 16 percent, and an average tax rate of 40 percent.

21. If Fischer's return on assets before interest and taxes is 22 percent, what rate of return does Fischer earn on equity after interest and taxes?

    a. 7.0%
    b. 8.3%
    c. 9.6%
    d. 12.4%
    e. 16.8%

22. What rate of return must Diamond earn on assets before interest and taxes so that its return on equity after interest and taxes will equal Fischer's return on equity?

    a. 19.2%
    b. 22.0%
    c. 24.4%
    d. 26.6%
    e. 29.1%

23. The Morrow Company and the Davenport Company are identical except for their leverage ratios and the interest rate on debt. Each firm has $12 million in assets, each earned $3 million before interest and taxes in 1984, and each has a 40 percent corporate tax rate. Morrow, however, has a debt-to-total assets ratio of 30 percent and pays 18 percent on its debt, while Davenport has a 40 percent debt-to-total assets ratio and pays 20 percent interest on its debt. What are the rates of return on equity for Morrow and Davenport, respectively?

    a. 19.2%, 14.5%
    b. 16.8%, 17.0%
    c. 15.3%, 18.9%
    d. 12.2%, 17.2%
    e. 14.5%, 16.8%

24. Brown Products is a new firm just starting operations. The firm will produce backpacks which will sell for $22.00 apiece. Fixed costs are $500,000 per year, and variable costs are $2.00 per unit of production. The company expects to sell 50,000 backpacks per year, and its effective tax rate is 40 percent. Brown needs $2 million to build facilities, obtain working capital, and start operations. If Brown borrows part of the money, the interest charges will depend on the amount borrowed as follows:

Amount Borrowed	Percentage of Debt in Capital Structure	Interest Rate on Total Amount Borrowed
$ 200,000	10%	9.00%
400,000	20	9.50
600,000	30	10.00
800,000	40	15.00
1,000,000	50	19.00
1,200,000	60	26.00

Assume that stock can be sold at a price of $20 per share on the initial offering, regardless of how much debt the company uses. Then, after the company begins operating, its price will be determined as a multiple of its earnings per share. The multiple (or the P/E ratio) will depend upon the capital structure as follows:

Debt/Assets	P/E	Debt/Assets	P/E
0.0%	12.5	40.0%	8.0
10.0	12.0	50.0	6.0
20.0	11.5	60.0	5.0
30.0	10.0		

What is Brown's optimal capital structure as measured by the debt/assets ratio?

a. 10%
b. 20%
c. 30%
d. 40%
e. 50%

(The following four problems apply to Appendix 16A material.)

25. Refer to Problem 24. What is Brown's degree of operating leverage at the expected level of sales?

a. 1.00
b. 1.08
c. 2.00
d. 2.16
e. 3.00

26. Refer to Problem 24. What is Brown's degree of financial leverage at the optimal capital structure?

a. 1.00
b. 1.08
c. 2.00
d. 2.16
e. 3.00

28. Refer to Problem 24. What is Brown's degree of total leverage at the expected level of sales and optimal capital structure?

a. 1.00
b. 1.08
c. 2.00
d. 2.16
e. 3.00

29. Bicycles, Inc., currently sells 75,000 units annually. At this sales level, its net operating income (EBIT) is $4 million and the degree of total leverage is 2.0. The firm's debt consists of $20 million in bonds with a 10 percent coupon. Bicycles is considering a new assembly line which would entail an increase in

fixed costs, resulting in a degree of operating leverage of 1.8. However, the firm desires to maintain the degree of total leverage at 2.0. Assuming that EBIT remains at $4 million, what dollar amount of bonds must be retired to accomplish adding the assembly line yet retain the old degree of total leverage?

a. $10 million
b. $12 million
c. $14 million
d. $16 million
e. $18 million

Answers and Solutions

1. capital structure

2. optimal; risk; return

3. target

4. increases

5. bankruptcy costs

6. operating leverage

7. fixed assets

8. fixed-charge

9. P/E; equity; financial leverage

10. capital structure; stock price

11. survival

12. times-interest-earned; fixed charge coverage

13. growth rate

14. tax; interest; dividends

15. debt; control

16. d.

17. b.

18. b. As the debt ratio increases, the standard deviation of expected EPS increases because the earnings stream has become riskier.

19. b.

20. c.

21. e.
$$\begin{array}{lll}\text{Debt} & 50\% = & \$ \ 50 \text{ million} \\ \text{Equity} & \underline{50\%} = & \underline{50 \text{ million}} \\ & 100\% & \$100 \text{ million}\end{array}$$

EBIT	= $100(0.22)$	= \$22.0 million
Less: Interest	= $100(0.5)(0.16)$ =	8.0 million
Taxable income		$14.0 million
Taxes (@ 40%)		5.6 million
Net income		$ 8.4 million

Return on equity = $8.4 million/$50 million
= 16.8%.

22. c.
$$\begin{array}{lll}\text{Debt} & 30\% = & \$ \ 30 \text{ million} \\ \text{Equity} & \underline{70\%} = & \underline{70 \text{ million}} \\ & 100\% & \$100 \text{ million}\end{array}$$

Net income	= $70(0.168)$	= \$11.76 million
Plus: Taxes	= $(\$11.76/0.6)(0.4)$ =	7.84 million
Taxable income	= $(\$11.76/0.6)$	$19.60 million
Plus: Interest	= $(\$30)(0.16)$	4.80 million
EBIT		$24.40 million

Return on assets = $24.40 million/$100 million
= 24.4%.

   Note that since Diamond has less leverage, it must earn a higher rate on total assets to earn the same rate of return on equity as Fischer.

23. b. Morrow: D/TA = 30%.

EBIT	$3,000,000
Less: Interest = $(0.18)(\$12,000,000)(0.30)$	648,000
EBT	$2,352,000
Taxes = $(\$2,352,000)(0.40)$	940,800
Net income	$1,411,200

Return on equity = $1,411,200/(($12,000,000)(0.70))
= $1,411,200/$8,400,000
= 16.8%.

Davenport D/TA = 40%.

EBIT	$3,000,000
Less: Interest = $(0.20)(\$12,000,000)(0.40)$	960,000
EBT	$2,040,000
Taxes = $(\$2,040,000)(0.40)$	816,000
Net income	$1,224,000

Return on equity = $1,224,000/(($12,000,000)(0.60))
= $1,224,000/$7,200,000
= 17.0%.

24. The first step is to calculate EBIT:

Sales in dollars [50,000($22)]	$1,100,000
Less: Fixed costs	500,000
Variable costs [50,000($2)]	100,000
EBIT	$ 500,000

The second step is to calculate the EPS at each debt/assets ratio using the formula

$$EPS = \frac{(EBIT - I)(1 - T)}{Shares\ outstanding}$$

Recognize (1) that I = interest charges = (dollars of debt)(interest rate at each D/A ratio), and (2) that shares outstanding = (assets - debt)/initial price per share = ($2,000,000 - debt)/$20.00.

D/A	EPS	D/A	EPS
0%	$3.00	40%	$3.80
10	3.21	50	3.72
20	3.47	60	2.82
30	3.77		

Finally, the third step is to calculate the stock price at each debt/assets ratio using the following formula: price = (P/E)(EPS).

D/A	Price	D/A	Price
0%	$37.50	40%	$30.40
10	38.52	50	22.32
20	39.91	60	14.10
30	37.70		

Thus, a debt/assets ratio of 20 percent maximizes stock price. This is the optimal capital structure.

25. c. $DOL = \dfrac{PQ - vQ}{PQ - vQ - F} = \dfrac{\$22(50,000) - \$2(50,000)}{\$22(50,000) - \$2(50,000) - \$500,000} = 2.00.$

26. b. $DFL = \dfrac{EBIT}{EBIT - I} = \dfrac{\$500,000}{\$500,000 - \$38,000} = 1.08.$

27. d. $DTL = \dfrac{PQ - vQ}{PQ - vQ - F - I} = \dfrac{\$1,000,000}{\$462,000} = 2.16,$

or

$DTL = (DOL)(DFL) = (2.00)(1.08) = 2.16.$

28. d. DOL $= \dfrac{PQ - vQ}{PQ - vQ - F} = 1.8$. But, $PQ - vQ - F = EBIT = \$4$ million.

Therefore,

$$\frac{PQ - vQ}{\$4 \text{ million}} = 1.8$$

$$PQ - vQ = \$7.2 \text{ million}.$$

Now,

$$DTL = \frac{PQ - vQ}{PQ - vQ - F - I} = 2.0$$

$$\frac{\$7.2 \text{ million}}{\$4.0 \text{ million} - I} = 2.0$$

$$I = \$0.40 \text{ million}.$$

Therefore, the interest required is $0.40 million. The current interest payment is 0.10($20 million) = $2.0 million. Thus, the interest payment must be reduced by $1.60 million by retiring bonds. This would require that $1.60/0.10 = $16 million of bonds be retired.

CHAPTER 17

DIVIDEND POLICY

Overview

Dividend policy involves the decision whether to pay out earnings or to retain them for reinvestment in the firm. Any change in dividend policy has both favorable and unfavorable effects on the firm's stock price. Higher dividends mean higher immediate cash flows to investors, which is good, but lower future growth, which is bad. The optimal dividend policy balances these opposing forces and maximizes stock price. Because of the large number of factors involved, it is impossible to develop a precise model for use in establishing dividend policy. However, Chapter 17 does identify a number of factors that influence dividend policy. This chapter also describes the residual theory of dividends, dividend payment policies, and stock splits and stock dividends and discusses stock repurchases as an alternative to dividends.

Outline

I. Firms which follow a regular dividend policy will usually pay them on a quarterly basis in accordance with the following payment procedures:

A. On the declaration date directors declare the dividends and set the payment date and the holder-of-record date.

B. On the holder-of-record date the stock transfer books are closed. If the company is notified of the sale and transfer of stock on or before the holder-of-record date, the new owner receives the dividend.

C. The ex-dividend date is set four business days prior to the holder-of-record date. This practice is a convention of the brokerage business which allows sufficient time for stock transfers to be made on the books of the corporation. Shares purchased after the ex-dividend date are not entitled to the dividend.

D. The company mails checks to the holders of record on the payment date.

II. A firm's dividend policy is influenced by legal considerations and its own circumstances.

   A. Legal rules require that dividends be paid from current earnings or earnings retained from past years.

     1. The net profits rule states that dividends must be paid from present and/or past retained earnings.

     2. The capital impairment rule states that dividends cannot be paid out of invested capital.

     3. The insolvency rule states that no dividends can be paid while a firm is insolvent (when liabilities exceed assets).

   B. The cash or liquidity position of a firm influences its ability to pay dividends. A firm may have sufficient retained earnings, but if they are invested in physical assets, cash may not be available to make dividend payments.

   C. The need to repay debt also influences the availability of cash flow to pay dividends.

   D. Restrictions in debt contracts may specify that dividends be paid only out of earnings generated after signing the loan agreement and only when net working capital is above a specified amount. Also, preferred stock agreements often specify that preferred dividends take precedence over common stock dividends.

   E. A high rate of asset expansion creates a need for the firm to retain funds rather than to pay out dividends.

   F. A high rate of return on new investments makes it desirable to retain and invest earnings rather than to pay them out.

   G. Stability of earnings will allow a high payout ratio which can be maintained even during difficult economic times.

   H. A firm's access to capital markets will be influenced by the age and size of the firm; therefore, a well-established firm will have easier access to capital markets than a new, small, or venturesome firm. A firm which can obtain funds easily in the capital markets can have a higher payout ratio than a firm with limited access to capital markets.

   I. Control considerations may influence dividend policy, since the amount of additional external financing needed is influenced by the dividend payout. If the owners rely on internal financing to maintain control, the dividend payout will be reduced.

J. The <u>tax position of stockholders</u> also affects dividend policy.

1. Corporations owned largely by taxpayers in high income tax brackets tend to have lower dividend payouts because the tax rate on capital gains is lower than the personal tax rate applied to dividends.
2. Corporations owned by small investors tend to have high dividend payouts.
3. Sometimes there may be a conflict between stockholders in high income tax brackets and stockholders in lower tax brackets.
   a. The dividend policy may be a compromise--an intermediate payout ratio.
   b. If one group dominates, the members of the other group are likely to sell their shares. Therefore, a firm's dividend policy dictates the type of stockholders it has, and vice versa. This is called the <u>clientele effect</u>.

K. In addition, the <u>tax position of the corporation</u> affects its dividend policies. The threat of penalties for excessive accumulation of retained earnings may induce firms to maintain higher payout ratios than they otherwise might.

III. Corporations tend to follow one of three procedures in the payment of dividends.

A. <u>Steady, or steadily increasing, dividends per share.</u> This procedure suggests to shareholders that a regular dividend will be maintained and that earnings will be sufficient to pay it.

1. Dividends are increased only when earnings have increased and seem stable enough to maintain the new dividend level.
2. Dividend payments will be maintained, at least temporarily, even if earnings fall below the level of the dividend payment.
3. Most corporations attempt to follow this type of policy.
   a. Stable dividends or a stable dividend growth rate will tend to stabilize a firm's stock price movements.
   b. Investors who rely on dividends for income normally prefer a stable dividend policy.
   c. A stable dividend policy used to be required for legal listing of a company's stock.
   d. A stable growth rate policy confirms investors' estimates of the growth rate of the stock and may enhance its price.

B. <u>Constant payout ratio</u>. A few firms pay out a constant percentage of earnings.

    1. Earnings fluctuate; therefore, the dollar amount of dividends fluctuates.

    2. This policy is not likely to maximize the value of the firm's stock, since it results in an unpredictable dividend.

C. <u>Low regular dividend plus extras</u>. This is a compromise policy between the first two policies. This policy is often followed by firms with rather volatile earnings from year to year. The low regular dividend can usually be maintained even when earnings decline, and "extras" can be paid when excess funds are available.

IV. Many firms have instituted "dividend reinvestment plans" whereby stockholders simply reinvest their dividends in additional shares of the corporation. Income taxes must be paid on the amount of the dividends even though stock rather than cash is received.

V. The residual theory of dividends is based on the premise that investors prefer to have a firm retain and reinvest earnings rather than to pay them out in dividends if the rate of return the firm could earn on reinvested earnings exceeds the rate of return investors can obtain for themselves on other investments of comparable risk. A firm using the residual theory would follow these four steps:

A. Determine the optimal capital budget as discussed previously in Chapters 12 and 13.

B. Determine the amount of equity required to finance the optimal capital budget, recognizing that the funds used will consist of both equity and debt to preserve the optimal capital structure.

C. To the extent possible, use retained earnings to supply the equity required.

D. Pay dividends only if more earnings are available than are needed to support the optimal capital budget.

VI. Miller and Modigliani have argued that dividend policy has no effect on either stock price or cost of capital; that is, dividend policy is irrelevant.

A. They prove their position in a theoretical sense under the assumptions that there are no taxes and no flotation costs.

B. Since these assumptions are clearly not true, dividend policy probably is relevant in the sense that it influences stock price and the cost of capital.

VII. Stock dividends and stock splits are often used to lower a firm's stock price and, at the same time, to conserve its cash resources.

A. A stock dividend simply involves a bookkeeping transfer from the retained earnings to the paid-in capital account.

1. The dividend is paid in shares of stock instead of cash.
2. Total net worth remains unchanged, and the number of shares is increased.
3. The par, or stated, value of the stock is unchanged by the stock dividend.
4. The stock dividend increases the paid-in capital account and reduces retained earnings.

B. The effect of a stock split is an increase in the number of shares outstanding and a reduction in the par, or stated, value of the shares. For example, if a firm had 1,000 shares outstanding with a par value of $100 per share, a 2-for-1 split would reduce the par value to $50 and increase the number of shares to 2,000.

1. The split does not involve any cash payment, only additional certificates representing new shares.
2. The total net worth of the firm remains unchanged.
3. A stock split does not affect a change in the paid-in capital account.

C. A stock split or stock dividend will influence the value of the firm in several ways.

1. The effect on the market price of the stock depends on prospective changes in underlying earnings power reflected in current or announced changes in dividend payouts.
   a. If stock dividends are associated with a cash dividend increase, the value of the firm's stock should rise.
   b. If the stock dividend is not accompanied by a cash dividend increase, the dilution of EPS and dividends per share will cause the value of the stock to fall.
2. Cash conservation is accomplished to a degree. However, the total amount paid out for dividends will increase if the effective dividend rate is increased for the larger number of shares.
3. The number of shareholders may be increased by reducing the price per share of the stock to a more popular trading range.

VIII. Stock repurchases per share are an alternative to dividends.

A. Stock repurchased by the issuing firm is called treasury stock.

B. Advantages of a repurchase to the stockholder include:
 1. Profits earned on repurchases are taxed at the capital gains rate, whereas dividends are not.
 2. The stockholder is given a choice of whether to sell or to not sell his stock to the firm.
 3. The repurchase can remove a large block of stock overhanging the market.

C. Advantages of repurchase from management's point of view include:

 1. If an increase in cash flow is temporary, the cash can be distributed to stockholders as a repurchase rather than as a dividend which could not be maintained in the future.
 2. It may be cheaper to use repurchased stock rather than newly issued stock for acquisitions or when stock options are exercised.
 3. If directors hold the firm's stock, they may favor repurchases for tax purposes.
 4. Repurchases can be used to raise the debt ratio quickly.
 5. Treasury stock can be resold when the firm needs more funds.

D. Disadvantages of repurchase from the stockholders' point of view include:

 1. Repurchases are not as dependable as cash dividends; therefore, the price of the stock may benefit more from cash dividends. A dependable repurchase program is not practical due to the improper accumulation tax.
 2. Selling stockholders may not be aware of all the implications of the repurchase; therefore, repurchases are usually announced in advance.
 3. If a firm pays too high a price for the repurchased stock, it is to the disadvantage of the remaining stockholders.

E. Disadvantages of repurchase from management's point of view include:

 1. A repurchase program is often considered an indicator that management cannot locate any other good investments.
 2. If the repurchase is deemed primarily for the avoidance of taxes, the firm may be penalized under the improper accumulation of earnings provision in the tax code.

F. Therefore, while repurchases on a regular basis do not appear feasible due to various uncertainties, occasional repurchases do offer some significant tax advantages over dividends, and repurchases can be valuable in making a significant change in capital structure within a short period.

Definitional Questions

1. An increase in dividends will _____ the amount of funds available for _____ and thus may lower the expected _____ _____ of earnings.

2. The "cost" of retained earnings is an _____ cost that reflects the rate of return available to stockholders on investments of comparable risk.

3. A firm's dividend policy may be constrained by bond _____ provisions and the availability of _____ to actually pay the dividend.

4. A company may be forced to increase its _____ ratio in order to avoid a tax on retained earnings deemed to be unnecessary for the conduct of the business.

5. Some stockholders prefer dividends to _____ _____ because of a need for current _____.

6. The policy of using "extra" dividends is most appropriate for a firm with _____ earnings.

7. The stock transfer books of a corporation are closed on the _____ date, and _____ are paid to shareholders as of that date.

8. The _____ date occurs four days prior to the _____ date and provides time for stock transfers to be recorded on the books of the firm.

9. Actual payment of a dividend is made on the _____ date as announced by the _____.

10. Many firms have instituted _____ _____ plans whereby stockholders can purchase additional shares of the company's stock.

11. A stock _____ requires that an accounting transfer be made from _____ _____ to the _____ _____ and _____ _____ accounts.

12. A stock split involves a reduction in the _____ _____ of the common stock, but no accounting transfers are made between accounts.

13. Stock repurchased by the firm which issued it is called _____ _____.

Conceptual Questions

14. An increase in cash dividends will result in an increase in the price of the common stock because D_1 will increase in our stock valuation model.

    a. True   b. False

15. A stock dividend with a par value will affect which of the following balance sheet accounts?

    a. Common stock
    b. Paid-in surplus
    c. Retained earnings
    d. Cash
    e. The accounts in a, b, and c will all be affected.

16. A stock split will affect which of the following balance sheet accounts?

    a. Common stock
    b. Paid-in surplus
    c. Retained earnings
    d. Cash
    e. None of the above accounts

17. The residual theory of dividends asserts that:

    a. Total dividend payments should be constant and residual earnings invested internally.
    b. Dividend payout ratio should be constant and residual earnings invested internally.
    c. Dividends should be paid out of residual earnings after investment needs have been met.
    d. Dividends are a constant percentage of the residuals from a regression analysis.
    e. No dividends should be paid if the firm's earnings will not meet its capital budgeting requirements.

18. One rationale for paying out a stable amount of dividends is that fluctuations in the amount of dividends may cause:

    a. Increased uncertainty about the level of future dividends.
    b. Higher corporate income tax for the firm.
    c. Higher personal income tax rates for shareholders.
    d. A decrease in expected future earnings.
    e. Investors to place a higher value on the firm's stock.

Problems

19. The Butler Corporation's expected net income for next year is $1.0 million. The company's target, and current, capital structure is 40 percent debt and 60 percent common equity. The optimal capital budget for next year is $1.2 million. If Butler uses the residual theory of dividends to determine next year's dividend payout, what is the expected payout ratio?

    a. 0%
    b. 10%
    c. 28%
    c. 42%
    e. 56%

20. Amalgamated Shippers has a current, and target, capital structure of 30 percent debt and 70 percent equity. This past year Amalgamated, which uses a residual theory dividend policy, had a dividend payout ratio of 47.5 percent and net income of $800,000. What was Amalgamated's capital budget?

    a. $400,000
    b. $500,000
    c. $600,000
    d. $700,000
    e. $800,000

Answers and Solutions

1. reduce; reinvestment; growth rate

2. opportunity

3. indenture; cash

4. payout

5. capital gains; income

6. volatile

7. holder-of-record; dividends

8. ex-dividend; holder-of-record

9. payment; directors

10. dividend reinvestment

11. dividend; retained earnings; common stock; paid-in capital

12. par value

13. treasury stock

14. b. A dividend increase could be perceived by investors as leading to lower growth in future earnings, thus, reducing g in the valuation model. The net effect on stock price is uncertain.

15. e.

16. e.

17. c. The firm should finance its capital budgeting projects according to its optimal capital structure, and any residual earnings should then be paid out as dividends.

18. a.

19. c. The $1,200,000 capital budget will be financed using 40 percent debt and 60 percent equity. Therefore, the equity requirement will be 0.6($1,200,000) = $720,000. Since the expected net income is $1,000,000, $280,000 will be available to pay as dividends. Thus, the payout ratio is expected to be $280,000/$1,000,000 = 0.28 = 28%.

20. c. Of the $800,000 in net income, 0.475($800,000) = $380,000 was paid out as dividends. Thus, $420,000 was retained in the firm for investment. This is the equity portion of the capital budget, or 70 percent of the capital budget. Therefore, the total capital budget was $420,000/0.7 = $600,000.

CHAPTER 18

CAPITAL MARKETS AND COMMON STOCK FINANCING

Overview

Capital markets present a range of alternatives to a firm formulating financing decisions. This chapter begins with an examination of the broad categories of sources of funds available to the firm and the role of investment banking in funds acquisitions. Next, the legal rights and privileges of common stockholders, and the market for common stock, are described. Chapter 18 concludes by discussing the implications of security laws. Appendix 18A examines the use of rights in financing.

Outline

I. There are three primary sources of funds available to corporations.

   A. Internal cash flows provide over 70 percent of funds for business corporations.

   B. External long-term financing provides 15-20 percent of total sources.

   C. Short-term external financing fluctuates in response to changes in the state of the economy.

II. Sources of direct financing include term loans and private placements.

   A. Direct financing has three major advantages over public financing.

      1. Direct financing arrangements can be made more quickly than public offerings, which may take months to prepare.
      2. A borrower can renegotiate the terms of a direct loan more easily than the terms of a public offering.
      3. Direct financings are generally less expensive to arrange than public offerings because direct financings are not subject to SEC registration requirements.

   B. Term loans are direct business loans with a maturity of more than one year but usually less than 15 years.

1. Repayment provisions of term loans generally provide for amortization, or systematic repayment over the life of the loan.
2. Maturities of term loans differ depending on the liability structure of the lender.
   a. Banks tend to have shorter-term liabilities; therefore, bank term loans usually run three to five years.
   b. Insurance companies have longer-term liabilities, and their term loans usually run between five and 15 years.
3. Banks require collateral on about 90 percent of the number of term loans they make.
4. In addition to fixed interest charges, institutional investors have increasingly taken compensation in the form of options to buy common shares. These options usually are in the form of detachable warrants permitting the purchase of the shares at stated prices over designated periods of time.
5. Because term loans represent long-term fixed commitments, restrictive provisions are generally included in the contract or agreement for the protection of the lender.
   a. The borrower must usually maintain a specified current ratio, and a specified minimum level of net working capital.
   b. Additional long-term borrowing, pledging of assets, assumption of contingent liabilities, and the signing of long-term leases are limited.
   c. An effort is made to insure the continuity of management.
   d. Payment of dividends is usually restricted to earnings made subsequent to the loan.
   e. Periodic financial statements and budgets are required by the lender.
6. The costs of term loans vary with the size of the loan and the strength of the borrowing firm.

III. The financial manager must have a knowledge of the investment banking process, the process by which new securities are issued to the public.

A. Investment banking institutions serve as financial intermediaries, making private savings available to business firms. The investment banker does this by purchasing and distributing the securities of individual companies, performing the following functions:
   1. Underwriting. The investment banker purchases the new security issue, pays the issuer, and markets the securities. The banker bears, or underwrites, the risk of

price fluctuations from the time of purchase to the time that the issue is distributed. Thus, investment bankers are sometimes called underwriters.

2. Distribution. The investment banker maintains a sales staff which performs the marketing function more efficiently and economically than if it were done by the individual firm.

3. Advice and counsel. The experience of the investment banker enables him to advise the issuer regarding the characteristics of the issue to insure successful flotation.

B. The process of issuing securities to the public follows these steps:

1. Preunderwriting conferences are held between the issuing firm and the investment banker to discuss alternative forms of financing and to reach the decision to sell securities.

2. An underwriting investigation is made by the underwriters into the firm's prospects. Specialists are called in to examine legal, accounting, engineering, and other aspects of the firm.

3. The underwriting agreement is formulated and specifies all underwriting terms except the actual price of the securities.

4. A registration statement is filed with the Securities and Exchange Commission. A waiting period of 20 days is usually required before clearance by the Securities and Exchange Commission is received. The underwriter can make no sales during this time but can distribute preliminary prospectuses.

5. The offering price of securities is negotiated between the firm and its investment banker.

   a. When a company "goes public" for the first time, the investment banker and the firm negotiate the price in accordance with valuation principles.

   b. When additional offerings are involved, the underwriter agrees to buy the securities at a prescribed number of points below the closing price on the day before the offering.

   c. Generally, the investment banker prefers a low price and a high yield, while the issuer of the securities naturally wants the opposite.

   d. Competition usually forces investment bankers to price close to market-determined levels.

6. An underwriting syndicate is formed as a temporary association to handle the purchase and distribution of the

securities issue, with the investment banking house which set up the deal as the lead, or managing, underwriter.

   a. The syndicate is formed to reduce the risk to the managing underwriter and to permit an economy of selling effort and encourage nationwide distribution.

   b. A selling group, consisting of 300 to 600 dealers, is formed for the purpose of distributing the securities.

   c. The operations of the selling group are governed by the selling group agreement which: (1) describes the issue, (2) sets the selling group's commission, and (3) limits the duration of the selling group, usually to 30 days.

   d. After the selling group has been formed, the actual offering takes place. The formal public offering is called opening the books.

   e. During the offering period, the price of the security is pegged by placing orders to buy at a specified price in the market. This is done to prevent a cumulative downward movement in the price.

C. The costs of a public securities issue are termed flotation costs.

   1. These costs include the underwriting investigation, preparation of the registration statement, legal fees, and compensation to the investment banker.

   2. Flotation costs depend on the type of security issued and the size of the issue. Costs as a percentage of the proceeds of the issue are greater for small issues than for large issues. Fixed expenses are high because the selling job and risks are greater for the securities of small firms than for large firms.

   3. Flotation costs are generally highest for common stock and lowest for debt.

      a. The distribution job is harder for stock than for bonds because it is usually bought in smaller blocks.

      b. Underwriting risks are higher with stock because the price is more volatile.

IV. The theory of efficient capital markets questions whether financial managers can "beat the market" through the timing and selection of financing sources.

A. Weak-form efficiency holds that excess returns cannot be earned on the basis of historical price or returns patterns.

B. Semistrong-form efficiency holds that excess returns cannot be achieved on the basis of publicly available information.

   1. Existing prices reflect all the information currently known to the market.

       2. Prices will change only when new information arrives.

  C. Strong-form efficiency holds that excess returns cannot be earned on the basis of internal information. In other words, corporate insiders cannot benefit from privileged information which they receive before the general public.

  D. Empirical evidence appears to be consistent with the weak and semistrong forms of capital efficiency, but this evidence does not support strong-form efficiency.

  E. Capital market efficiency has implications for investors and financial managers.

       1. Since superior forecasting is unlikely, efforts to gain from the timing of financing decisions will not achieve above-average results.

       2. The need for regulation is reduced because opportunities for manipulative gain are limited.

V. Common stock represents the ownership of an incorporated business. Stock ownerships confer both rights and responsibilities to the stockholders.

  A. Common stockholders are usually given certain collective rights, including the right to:

       1. Amend the charter of the corporation if the changes are approved by state officials.
       2. Adopt and amend the bylaws.
       3. Elect the corporate directors.
       4. Authorize the sale of fixed assets.
       5. Approve mergers.
       6. Change the amount of authorized common stock.
       7. Authorize issuance of preferred stock, debentures, bonds, and other securities.

  B. Each stockholder also has specific rights as an individual owner enabling him to:

       1. Vote as prescribed by the corporate charter.
       2. Sell his or her stock to another party.
       3. Inspect the books of the corporation.
       4. Share in the residual assets of the corporation in the case of dissolution.

  C. Two important positive considerations of stock ownership are income and control.

       1. Common stockholders are the recipients of the residual income of the corporation.
       2. Through the right to vote, holders of common stock have legal control of the corporation.

D. Another consideration of equity ownership is risk.

1. Common equity provides a cushion for creditors if losses occur on dissolutions. The equity-to-total assets ratio is an indicator of the degree by which the amounts realized on the liquidation may decline from stated book values before creditors suffer losses.

2. Common stockholders have limited liability in case of loss--their loss is limited to the amount of their investment.

E. Each stockholder has the right to cast one vote in the annual stockholders' meeting for each share of stock owned.

1. A proxy is a temporary transfer of the right to vote.

2. The use of proxies is supervised by the Securities and Exchange Commission to prevent:
   a. Self-perpetuation of management.
   b. Small stockholder groups from gaining special advantages.

3. The preemptive right gives the existing equity owners the first option to purchase any additional issues of common stock.
   a. The preemptive right is designed to protect the power of control of present stockholders.
   b. The preemptive right maintains the pro rata share of earnings for the present stockholders and, thus, prevents the value of the stock from being diluted by new issues.

F. Firms use different forms of common stock to meet their special needs.

1. Firms sometimes issue two classes of stock, where the class sold to the public pays dividends, and the class retained by the organizers of the firm does not pay dividends until the earning power of the corporation has been established. This allows a small company to acquire external funding without sacrificing income.

2. A firm which has just gone public may issue founder's shares which carry sole voting rights for a number of years, but pay no dividends until the firm's earnings are established. Founder's shares allow the organizers of the firm to maintain complete control during the firm's developmental period.

VI. In reaching a decision as to whether to issue common stock, the financial manager should consider several factors.

A. Common stock offers several advantages over other forms of financing.

1. The firm is under no legal obligation to pay dividends, so no continuing fixed charges are incurred.
2. Common stock has no maturity date.
3. The creditworthiness of the firm is increased because the firm has more equity to protect against losses to creditors.
4. At times, common stock may be sold more easily than debt.
   a. It carries a higher expected return than does preferred stock or debt.
   b. It may provide the investor with a better hedge against inflation.
5. Returns from common stock, in the form of capital gains, are subject to lower personal income tax rates.

B. The disadvantages of common stock to the issuing firm include the following:

1. The control of the firm must be shared with the new shareholders.
2. Earnings and dividends must be shared with an increased number of owners.
3. Flotation costs are relatively high.
4. The required return on stock is normally higher than the required return on debt.
5. Dividends are not deductible from income for tax purposes.

C. From a social viewpoint, common stock is a desirable form of financing.

1. Common stock financing renders the firm less vulnerable to the consequences of declines in sales and earnings.
2. Stock financing may tend to amplify cyclical fluctuations in investment because of wide swings in equity prices.

VII. The United States has a highly developed market for buying and selling common stocks. Institutional investors have long dominated the bond market, and in recent years they have become a major factor in the stock market. Pension funds and other institutional investors now own about 35 percent of the stock of large, publicly held firms, and they represent about 75 percent of the trading volume in stocks.

A. The stocks of smaller companies are generally owned by management groups and are referred to as closely held, or privately owned, corporations. The stocks of larger firms are generally held by a large number of investors. These companies are publicly held corporations.

B. Stock market transactions may be separated into three distinct categories.

    1. The secondary market deals with trading in previously issued, or outstanding, shares of established, publicly owned companies. The company receives no new money on these sales.

    2. The primary market handles additional shares sold by established, publicly owned companies. Companies can raise additional capital by selling in this market.

    3. The primary market also handles new public offerings of shares in firms that were formerly closely held. Capital for the firm can be raised by going public, and the market is often termed the new issue market.

VIII. Most businesses begin life as proprietorships, partnerships, or closely held corporations. However, if the business prospers and grows, at some point the decision must be made as to whether to go public. This decision is made by considering the relative advantages and disadvantages.

A. Going public has the following advantages:

    1. The owners are able to diversify their holdings by selling some of their stock in a public offering.

    2. Public ownership increases the liquidity of the stock.

    3. New corporate cash is more easily raised by a public offering.

    4. Going public establishes the firm's value in the marketplace.

B. Going public has the following disadvantages:

    1. A publicly owned company must file quarterly and annual reports with various governmental agencies.

    2. Publicly owned firms must disclose operating and ownership data.

    3. The opportunities for owner/managers to engage in questionable, but legal, self-dealings are reduced.

    4. If the publicly held firm is very small, the shares will be traded very infrequently, and a liquid market will not really exist.

IX. Stocks traded on organized exchanges are called listed stocks. While the decision to go public is significant, the decision to list is not a major event. In order to have a listed stock, a company must apply to an exchange, pay a relatively small fee, and meet the exchange's minimum requirements.

A. The company will have to file a few new reports with an exchange.

B. The firm will have to abide by the rules of the exchange.

C. Firms benefit from listing their stock by gaining status and free publicity. If the prestige and reputation of the firm are enhanced, the value of its stock will also be increased.

X. The securities markets, including the organized exchanges, brokers, investment bankers, and dealers, are regulated by the federal government through the Securities and Exchange Commission (SEC).

A. The financial manager should be aware of the federal laws regulating issuance and trading of securities because they influence his liability and affect financing costs.

B. The Securities Act of 1933 relates to the marketing of new issues. It seeks to provide full disclosure of information, a record of representations, and penalties for violations. The major provisions are:

1. The Act applies to public interstate offerings in amounts of $1.5 million or more.

2. It requires registration 20 days in advance of the offering to the public. A prospectus describing the company and the securities to be offered must be sent to prospective purchasers of the new issue.

3. It allows purchasers who suffer loss due to misrepresentation or omission of material facts to sue for damages.

C. The Securities Exchange Act of 1934 extends the disclosure principle to the trading of existing issues. Its major provisions are:

1. The Act established the SEC (Securities and Exchange Commission).

2. It requires registration and regulation of the national securities exchanges.

3. It requires corporate insiders to file monthly reports of changes in ownership of stock of the corporation and provides legal redress for stockholders.

4. It gives the SEC power to prohibit manipulations through wash sales, pools, and pegging operations except during stock flotations.

5. It gives the SEC control over proxy machinery and devices.

6. It gives the Federal Reserve System control over the flow of credit (margin credit) that may be used in purchasing securities.

D. The security industry realizes the importance of stable markets, sound brokerage firms, and the absence of stock manipulation. Therefore, the various exchanges and trade organizations work closely with the regulatory agencies to police the markets and protect customers.

E. The purpose of regulation is to insure that adequate and accurate information is available concerning securities offered to the public, and to prevent fraud. Regulation cannot insure that investments will be successful or that investors will exercise good judgment.

XI. Appendix 18A discusses the use of rights in financing.

A. A right is an option to buy a share of newly issued stock at a specified price during a designated period of time.

  1. A rights offering involves the sale of additional stock to existing stockholders and is mandatory if the preemptive right exists for the firm in question.
  2. Each stockholder is issued a right, which contains the terms of the option, for each share of stock owned.

B. Several questions face the financial manager in a rights offering.

  1. How many rights will be required to purchase a share of the new stock?
  2. What should be the value of each right?
  3. What effect will the rights offering have on the price of existing stock?
  4. What will be the subscription price of the stock?

C. If a stockholder exercises his rights, a rights offering does not affect the value of his stock.

D. The use of rights in common stock financings provide several advantages to the firm.

  1. The stock is offered first to existing stockholders which increases the likelihood of a favorable reception.
  2. The flotation costs associated with a rights offering may be lower than the costs of a public offering.
  3. The price of the stock is usually lowered by the offering, and the new stock price might make the stock attractive to a larger group of investors.

E. Rights offerings will complicate the sale of the securities and raise the flotation costs if present stockholders are not willing to buy more stock and, thus, sell their rights.

Definitional Questions

1. Direct financing are generally quicker, more _____, and less _____ to arrange than public offering.

2. _____ _____ are direct business loans having maturities of 1 to 15 years.

3. Term loan agreements generally include _____ _____ designed to protect the lender over the life of the loan.

4. Investment bankers perform the tasks of _____ and distributing security issues and _____ issuing firms regarding the characteristics of the issues.

5. By underwriting a security issue, an investment banker bears the risks of fluctuations in the _____ of the stock.

6. An _____ _____ specifies the terms of the security issue.

7. In order to spread the risk of underwriting a sizeable common stock issue, investment bankers will form an _____ _____.

8. Setting the _____ price for an issue of stock may present a conflict of interest between the issuer and the _____ _____.

9. The theory of _____ _____ _____ holds that financial managers cannot forecast security prices better than the market and, thus, cannot earn excess returns based on the timing and selection of financing sources.

10. If a stockholder cannot vote in person, participation is still possible at the annual meeting through a _____.

11. The preemptive right protects stockholders against loss of _____ of the corporation as well as _____ of market value from the sale of new shares at a low price.

12. Firms may find it desirable to separate the common stock into different _____. Generally, this classification is designed to differentiate stock in terms of the right to receive _____ and to _____.

13. The trading of previously issued shares of a corporation takes place in the _____ market, while new shares are sold in the _____ market.

14. _____ _____ refers to the sale of shares of a closely held business to the general public.

15. Going public establishes the firm's _____ in the marketplace.

16. Securities traded on the organized exchanges are known as _____ securities.

17. Before an interstate issue of stock amounting to $1.5 million or more can be sold to the public, it must be _____ with and approved by the _____.

18. If the preemptive right exists for a firm, any new issue of stock must be offered for sale first to the existing stockholders through a _____ _____.

Conceptual Questions

19. The stockholder assignment to management of their right to vote is called:

    a. A privilege.
    b. A preemptive right.
    c. An ex right.
    d. A proxy.
    e. A prospectus.

20. A firm may go public yet not receive any additional funds in the process.

    a. True   b. False

21. Flotation costs are generally higher for issuing bonds than for issuing stocks.

    a. True   b. False

22. A preliminary prospectus distributed prior to approval of the registration statement is called a:

    a. Final offer.
    b. Blue sky paper.
    c. Proxy.
    d. Red herring.
    e. Bid appeal.

23. When new shares are being sold, if it appears that the investment banker will be unable to sell the entire issue at the initial offering price, the only way the entire issue can be sold is to lower the price.

    a. True   b. False

Problems

(The following information applies to the next two problems.)

Harmonic Recording Company
Balance Sheet

	Accounts payable	$ 32,000
	Notes payable	36,000
	Long-term debt	72,000
	Common stock (30,000 shares authorized, 20,000 shares outstanding)	180,000
	Retained earnings	150,000
Total assets $470,000	Total liabilities and equity	$470,000

23. What is the book value per share of Harmonic's common stock?

   a. $15.25
   b. $16.50
   c. $17.00
   d. $17.75
   e. $18.50

24. Suppose the firm sold the remaining authorized shares and netted
   $13.50 per share from the sale. What is the new book value per
   share?

   a. $13.00
   b. $13.50
   c. $14.50
   d. $15.50
   e. $16.50

Answers_and_Solutions

1. flexible; expensive

2. Term loans

3. restrictive provisions

4. underwriting; advising

5. price

6. underwriting agreement

7. underwriting syndicate

8. offering; investment banker

9. efficient capital markets

10. proxy

11. control; dilution

12. classes; dividends; vote

13. secondary; primary

14. Going public

15. value

16. listed

17. registered; SEC

18. rights offering

19. d.

20. a.   An example, that of the Ford Foundation selling stock to the general public, is given in the text.

21. b. The investment banker normally must expend greater effort in selling stocks, thus must charge a higher fee.

22. d.

23. b.   The investment banker can increase the demand for the stock by "promoting" the issue.

24. b. Total equity = Common stock + Retained earnings
$$= \$180,000 + \$150,000$$
$$= \$330,000.$$

Book value per share = Total equity/Shares outstanding
$$= \$330,000/20,000$$
$$= \$16.50.$$

25. d.   The firm now sells the remaining 10,000 shares and nets $13.50 per share for a total of $135,000.   Thus, the new total equity is $330,000 + $135,000 = $465,000, and 30,000 shares are outstanding.   The new book value per share is $465,000/30,000 = $15.50. Note that selling new shares below book value results in a lower book value on all shares.

CHAPTER 19

DEBT AND PREFERRED STOCK

Overview

Most firms find it desirable to use long-term debt financing, and some also use preferred stock. This chapter first discusses the many types of long-term debt securities--secured and unsecured, convertible and nonconvertible, zero coupon and normal coupon, and so on--and then discusses the process by which managers choose among alternative forms of financing. The variety of types of financing stems from the fact that different groups of investors favor different types of securities, and their tastes change over time. The astute financial manager knows how to "package" securities at a given point in time to attract the greatest number of potential investors, thereby keeping the firm's cost of capital to a minimum. Appendix 19A discusses bond refunding operations.

Outline

I. A bond is a long-term contract under which a borrower agrees to make a series of payments of interest and principal to the holder of the bond. There are several types of bonds and some bond terminology with which the finance student should be familiar.

    A. A <u>mortgage</u> is a pledge of real assets as security for a loan.

    B. A <u>debenture</u> is unsecured long-term debt.

    C. An <u>indenture</u> is a document which contains the details of the long-term contractual relationship between the issuing corporation and the bondholders. The SEC approves the indenture and makes sure that all indenture provisions are met before a company is allowed to sell new securities to the public. The indenture includes:

        1. The form of the bond.

        2. A description of any pledged property.

        3. The authorized amount of the issue.

        4. Protective clauses or covenants such as limitations on indebtedness, restrictions on dividends, or the minimum current ratio requirement during the period of indebtedness.

        5. Provisions for redemption or call privileges.

D. The <u>trustee</u> is an agent of the bondholders, but he is appointed by the issuer before the bonds are sold.

   1. Any legal person is competent to act as a trustee, but typically the duties of the trustees are handled by a department of a commercial bank.
   2. The trustee has three main responsibilities.
      a. To certify the issue of the bonds.
      b. To police the behavior of the corporation in its performance of the responsibilities set forth by the indenture.
      c. To represent the interests of the bondholder in the event of default.

E. A <u>restrictive covenant</u> is a provision in a bond indenture that requires the issuer to finance the firm's operations in a manner that will maintain the quality of the bonds after they have been issued. The trustee is responsible for making sure that the covenants are not violated.

F. A <u>call provision</u> gives the issuing corporation the right to call the bond for redemption.

   1. If it is used, the company must pay a call premium over and above the par value of the bond.
   2. This provision is valuable to the firm but potentially detrimental to an investor, especially when interest rates are cyclically high.

G. A <u>sinking fund</u> facilitates the orderly retirement of a bond issue or preferred stock issue.

   1. Typically, the firm is required to buy and retire a portion of the bond issue each year.
   2. Failure to meet a sinking fund payment usually constitutes a default on the bond issue.
   3. The sinking fund may be used to call a certain percentage of the bonds at a stipulated price, with bonds selected by lottery from serial numbers, or the sinking fund payment may be used to buy bonds on the open market. The firm will choose the method that results in the required reduction of indebtedness for the smallest outlay.
   4. The call provision of the sinking fund can work to the detriment of bondholders, since the call is generally at par while the bond may have been purchased well above par.
   5. Since a sinking fund provides additional protection to investors, bonds that have them are likely to carry lower yields than comparable bonds with no sinking fund provisions.

H. <u>Funded debt</u> is simply long-term debt.

I. Secured long-term debt can be classified on three bases.

    1. The priority of claims means that a _senior mortgage_ has first claim on assets and earnings, and a _junior mortgage_ is subordinate to it. _Subordinated debt_ is unsecured debt, which is paid only after designated debt senior to it has been paid.

    2. A bond can be classified with respect to the right to issue additional securities which are secured by property pledged to the bond.

        a. A _closed-end mortgage_ specifies that no additional bonds may be sold which have a lien on the property specified in the original mortgage.

        b. An _open-end mortgage_ exists if the bond indenture fails to mention additional bond issues. Therefore, the property can be repledged.

        c. A _limited open-end mortgage_ allows the sale of a specified amount of additional bonds.

    3. Bonds can be classified with respect to the scope of their liens.

        a. A specific lien specifies certain designated property.

        b. A blanket mortgage pledges all real property owned by the company.

J. Unsecured long-term bonds are called debentures. Debentures provide no lien on any specific property as security for the debt.

    1. The use of debentures depends on the firm's general credit strength and the nature of its assets.

    2. A _subordinated debenture_ is an unsecured bond that has a claim on assets after senior debt in the event of liquidation.

        a. Second mortgage bonds are subordinate to first mortgage bonds. Also, subordinated debentures may be subordinated to designated notes payable, or to all other debt.

        b. The use of subordinated debentures is stimulated by periods of tight money because such debentures provide an equity cushion for loans from commercial banks or other senior debt.

    3. _Income bonds_ are bonds which pay interest only if income is earned by the company.

K. _Original issue deep discount bonds_ (OIDs) and _zero coupon discount bonds_ are offered at a substantial discount below their par values.

1. The advantages to the issuer are that (1) no cash flows are required on zero coupon bonds until maturity, (2) OIDs and zero coupon bonds often have lower required rates of return than coupon bonds, and (3) the issuer receives an annual tax deduction.
2. The advantages to the investor are that (1) there is little danger of a call and (2) zero coupon bonds guarantee a "true" yield to maturity since there is no reinvestment rate risk.
3. OIDs and zero coupon bonds are most attractive to tax-exempt institutions, which do not have to pay taxes each year on the implicit interest from the bonds.

L. Bond issues are normally assigned quality ratings by both Moody's Investors Service and Standard & Poor's Corporation. These ratings reflect the probability that a bond issue will go into default. Aaa and AAA are the highest ratings. Bonds in default are rated D.

1. Bond ratings influence investors' perceptions of risk and therefore have an impact on the interest rate paid and on the firm's cost of capital.
2. Institutions are generally limited to investing in investment-grade securities, that is, those rated BBB or Baa, or higher. It is important, therefore, that a firm maintain a good quality rating on its bond issues.
3. Rating assignments are based on qualitative and quantitative factors, including the firm's debt/assets ratio, TIE, and fixed charge coverage ratio.

II. Long-term debt offers both advantages and disadvantages to the issuer and the bondholder.

A. From the viewpoint of the bondholder, debt is good with regard to risk, has limited advantages with regard to income, and is weak with regard to control.

1. Debt is favorable because it gives the holder priority in both earnings and liquidation. It also has a definite maturity and protective covenants.
2. The bondholder generally receives a fixed return, which is not dependent on the issuer's earnings or the state of the economy.
3. The bondholder may exercise no control except in the case of default.

B. The advantages of debt to the issuer include:

1. Debt has a limited cost, which is lower than the cost of common or preferred stock.
2. Stockholders retain voting control.

       3. Interest expense is tax deductible.
       4. Call provisions add flexibility to the financial structure of the firm.

  C. The disadvantages to the issuer are:

       1. A fixed interest commitment is made.
       2. Higher risk may result in lowering the value of common stock outstanding.
       3. A definite maturity date exists requiring repayment or refunding.
       4. Stringent indenture provisions may be imposed.
       5. Generally accepted financial standards limit the amount of debt in the financial structure.

  D. Debt is favorable to the issuer when the following conditions exist.

       1. Sales and earnings are relatively stable.
       2. A rise in profits or the general price level is expected.
       3. The existing debt ratio is relatively low.
       4. The common stock price is temporarily depressed.
       5. Control considerations are important.

III. Corporate bonds are traded much less frequently than stocks.

  A. Over 95 percent of the bond trading which does occur takes place in the OTC market.

  B. Information on OTC market bond trades is not published, but a representative group of bonds is listed on the NYSE, and these trades are often reported.

IV. Preferred stock is by nature a hybrid security. It is classified as debt or equity depending upon the analysis being made.

  A. Preferred stock is like debt in that it does not carry voting rights.

  B. Preferred stock is like equity in that failure to pay dividends does not cause default on the obligation.

  C. Bondholders view preferred stock as equity because it produces an additional equity base and reduces the risks of loss to bondholders. On the other hand, stockholders view preferred stock as a leverage-inducing security similar to debt.

V. Preferred stock represents an equity investment in a firm, but it has many of the characteristics associated with a bond issue.

  A. Preferred stock has priority ahead of common stock with regard to the assets and earnings of the firm.

B. Preferred stock usually has a par value, normally $25 or $100; however, most recent issues have no par value.

1. Preferred stockholders must consent to a subsequent sale of securities having a prior or equal claim on earnings.
2. A minimum level of retained earnings is required before common stock dividends are allowed.

C. Most preferred stock dividends are cumulative. This means that all past preferred dividends must be paid before common dividends can be paid.

D. About 40 percent of the preferred stock issued in recent years has been convertible into common stock.

E. Some other provisions are encountered occasionally.

1. Voting rights--preferred stockholders are sometimes given the right to vote for a minority of directors.
2. Participating--occasionally, a type of preferred stock is issued that participates with the common stock in sharing the firm's earnings.
3. Sinking fund--some preferred issues require the firm to purchase and retire a given percentage of the preferred stock each year.
4. Maturity--a sinking fund provision in effect creates a maturity date for preferred stock.
5. Call provision--a call provision allows the company to call in the preferred stock for redemption by paying the par value plus a call premium.

VI. There are advantages and disadvantages associated with preferred stock financings.

A. The advantages to the issuer of selling preferred stock are:

1. The obligation to make fixed payments is avoided.
2. The firm obtains higher earnings for its original owners if the use of additional leverage is successful.
3. The firm avoids the provision of equal participation in earnings by the new stockholders.
4. Preferred stock usually does not dilute existing control of the firm.
5. Since it usually has no maturity date and no sinking fund, preferred stock is more flexible than bonds.
6. The use of preferred stock enables the firm to conserve mortgageable assets.

B. The disadvantages to the issue are:

1. Preferred stock sells at a higher yield than bonds.
2. Dividends are not an expense for tax purposes.

3. Many preferred issues are convertible into common stock, which allows preferred stockholders to participate in higher earnings should they materialize.

C. From the viewpoint of the investor, preferred stock offers the following advantages.

1. It provides reasonably steady income.
2. Preferred stockholders have priority over common stockholders in the event of liquidation.
3. Corporations often like to hold preferred stock as an investment since 85 percent of the dividends received are not taxable.

D. The disadvantages of preferred stock to investors are these.

1. The returns are limited.
2. The stock has no legally enforceable right to dividends.
3. Accrued cash dividends are seldom paid off in full.

VII. Since it is a hybrid security, the use of preferred stock is favored by conditions that fall between those favoring the use of common stock and those favoring the use of debt.

A. If profit margins are adequate, the firm will gain from the additional leverage provided by preferred stock.

B. Relative costs of alternative sources of financing are important considerations when choosing among preferred stock and alternative forms of financing.

C. When the use of debt involves excessive risk and the issuance of common stock poses control problems, preferred stock may be a good compromise.

VIII. Many different classes of securities may be issued by a firm so that it can appeal to the risk-return tradeoff preferences of as many investors as possible. Also, different types of securities may be appropriate at different times.

IX. When choosing among alternative forms of financing, the financial manager must consider the risks involved with each type of financing as well as the returns to investors. The relative costs of financing should be evaluated by considering the effects of each financing alternative on the market value of common stock, the cost of capital, and the control of the firm.

X. Appendix 19A discusses refunding operations.

A. If a company sold bonds or preferred stock at a time when interest rates were relatively high, and if the issue were callable, the company could sell a new issue of low-yielding securities if interest rates fell and use the proceeds to retire the high-rate issue. This is called a refunding operation.

B. Refunding operations involve two separate questions.

    1. Is it profitable to recall an outstanding bond in the current period and replace it with a new issue?

    2. Even if refunding is currently profitable, would it be even more profitable if postponed to a later date?

C. The decision to refund a security issue is analyzed in a manner similar to a capital budgeting decision.

Definitional Questions

1. Long-term debt is sometimes referred to as _____ debt.

2. A _____ is a long-term contract under which the issuer agrees to make a series of _____ payments and to repay the _____ amount borrowed.

3. The legal document setting forth the terms and conditions of a bond issue is known as the _____.

4. The _____ represents the bondholders and sees that the terms of the indenture are carried out.

5. A bond secured by real estate is known as a _____ bond.

6. In meeting its sinking fund requirements, a firm may generally exercise the _____ provision or purchase bonds on the _____ _____.

7. Except when the call is for sinking fund purposes, when a bond issue is called, the firm must pay a _____ _____, or an amount in excess of the _____ value of the bond.

8. A restrictive _____ is a provision in the bond's _____ which requires the issuer to meet certain stated conditions.

9. _____ debt is junior to other debt and can be paid off only after _____ debt has been paid.

10. _____ _____ is a hybrid security which can be viewed as debt or equity.

11. If a preferred stock is _____, then any preferred dividend _____ must be paid before dividends can be paid to common stockholders.

12. The _____ provision of preferred stock issues allows preferred stockholders to participate in the higher earnings of the firm.

13. Preferred stocks are attractive to _____ investors because of favorable tax treatment (the 85 percent exclusion).

14. When selecting a method for financing investments, the financial manager must tradeoff the _____ and _____ of each financing alternative.

15. The analysis of a bond refunding decision is similar to a _____ _____ decision.

Conceptual Questions

16. There is a direct relationship between bond ratings and the required rate of return of bonds; that is, the higher the rating, the higher the required rate of return.

    a. True   b. False

17. Which of the following would tend to increase the coupon interest rate on a bond to be issued?

    a. Sinking fund
    b. Restrictive covenant
    c. Call provision
    d. Change in bond rating from Aa to Aaa
    e. Both a and c above

18. From the investor's viewpoint, rank the following securities, all issued by the same firm, in order of increasing risk:

    1. Preferred stock
    2. Debentures
    3. Convertible preferred stock
    4. Mortgage bonds

    a. 1, 2, 3, 4
    b. 4, 1, 2, 3
    c. 4, 1, 3, 2
    d. 4, 2, 1, 3
    e. 4, 2, 3, 1

19. Zero coupon bonds have become quite popular over the last several years. These bonds are advantageous to the <u>issuer</u> because:

   a. The bond is, in effect, not callable.
   b. These bonds generally have a higher yield to maturity than normal coupon bonds.
   c. The bond's cash outflows are spread over the life of the bond.
   d. The bonds are initially sold above par value.
   e. None of the above statements are correct.

20. In general, a decision to refund a bond issue is made when:

   a. Interest rates have risen.
   b. Interest rates have fallen.
   c. The issue is convertible.
   d. The debt ratio is below the industry norm.
   e. The firm's liquidity position has improved.

Problems

21. T.J. Stone is planning to issue a zero coupon bond. The bond has a par value of $1,000, matures in 10 years, and will be sold at an 80 percent discount, or for $200. The firm's marginal tax rate is 40 percent. What is the annual after-tax cost of debt to Stone on this issue?

   a. 9.59%
   b. 10.00%
   c. 11.62%
   d. 14.79%
   e. 17.46%

22. The Henner Company has an issue of 9 percent cumulative preferred stock outstanding on which it has paid no dividends during the past 3 years. Sales and profits have increased, so that Henner would like to begin paying dividends again. Earnings after taxes but before preferred dividends are $540,000. Henner has 10,000 shares of $100 par preferred stock and 100,000 shares of common stock outstanding. What is the largest common dividend Henner can pay this year?

   a. $2.50 per share
   b. $2.10 per share
   c. $1.80 per share
   d. $0.40 per share
   e. Henner cannot pay a common dividend this year.

Answers and Solutions

1. funded

2. bond; interest; principal

3. indenture

4. trustee

5. mortgage

6. call; open market

7. call premium; par

8. covenant; indenture

9. Subordinated; senior

10. Preferred stock

11. cumulative; arrearages

12. convertibility

13. corporate

14. risks; returns

15. capital budgeting

16. b.   The higher a bond's rating, the lower its required rate of return.   A higher bond rating indicates that the bond is less risky; thus, investors will accept a lower return on it.

17. c.   A call provision will increase the interest rate on a bond, while a sinking fund, restrictive covenants, and an increase in bond ratings all make the bond more attractive to investors and lower the interest rate.

18. d.   Convertible preferred is more risky than straight preferred because a portion of the investor's expected return is based on stock price appreciation.   Granted, the dividend yield is lower on convertible issues, but the total required rate of return is higher.

19. e.

20. b.

21.   a.   Look at the cash flows to the firm.   At Year 0, the firm receives $200.   At Year 10, the firm must pay out $1,000.   For each of the 10 years, Stone is declaring a ($1,000 - $200)/10 = $80 interest expense, even though it is not actually paying interest in the interim period.   The tax benefit of that expense is 0.40($80) = $32.   Putting these cash flows on a time line, we get the following:

The cost of debt to the firm is that discount rate which equates the present values of the cash inflows and outflows, or the IRR. This can be solved by trial and error.   The calculator solution is 9.59 percent.

22.   c.

| Preferred dividend arrearages | = ($100)(0.09)(10,000)(3 years) = $270,000 |

| Current preferred dividend | = ($100)(0.09)(10,000) | = 90,000 |

Preferred dividends due = $360,000

Earnings after taxes   = $540,000
Preferred dividends due   = 360,000
Earnings available for common dividend = $180,000

Maximum dividends per share = $180,000/100,000
                            = $1.80.

CHAPTER 20

WARRANTS, CONVERTIBLES, AND OPTIONS

Overview

Thus far, the discussion of long-term financing has concentrated on common stock, preferred stock, and various types of debt. This chapter describes how the use of warrants and convertibles can make a company's securities attractive to an even broader range of investors. Both convertibles and warrants are used as "sweeteners." They make it possible for small companies to sell debt or preferred stock that otherwise could not be sold. For large companies, warrants and convertibles result in lower costs of the securities sold. Partly because of investors' interest in warrants and convertibles, a new market in pure options was created in the 1970s. Chapter 20 concludes with a brief description of options and the options markets.

Outline

I. The use of warrants and convertible securities adds flexibility to the firm's financing operations, and using these securities may result in a lower overall cost of capital and a higher value of the firm's stock.

II. A warrant is an option to buy a stated number of shares of stock at a specified price called the exercise price or option price.

   A. Often warrants are attached to debt instruments as an incentive for investors to buy the combined issue at a lower interest rate than would otherwise be the case. Additionally, warrants may eliminate the need for extremely restrictive indenture provisions.

   B. The "formula" or "exercise" value of a warrant is calculated as follows:

$$\begin{pmatrix} \text{Formula or} \\ \text{exercise} \\ \text{value} \end{pmatrix} = \begin{pmatrix} \text{Market price} \\ \text{of common} - \begin{matrix} \text{Option} \\ \text{price} \end{matrix} \\ \text{stock} \end{pmatrix} \begin{pmatrix} \text{Number of shares} \\ \text{each warrant entitles} \\ \text{owner to purchase} \end{pmatrix}.$$

   C. Warrants generally sell in the market at prices above their formula values.

1. The premium of a warrant's market value over its formula value decreases as the price of the common stock increases.
2. This decline in premium is due to (1) declining leverage impact and (2) greater loss potential as the stock price increases.

D. Warrants have generally been used as "sweeteners" by small, risky firms to make their bonds or preferred stocks more attractive.

E. Warrants generate additional equity capital when they are exercised.

1. The option price is generally set 10 to 30 percent above the market price of the stock at the time the warrant is issued.
2. If the market price is above the option price, and the warrants are about to expire, holders will exercise their options and purchase stock.
3. Since warrants pay no dividends, holders will be inclined to exercise them and obtain common stock as the common dividend is increased.
4. A stepped-up option price will also induce holders to exercise their warrants.

F. Most warrants are detachable and can be traded separately from the bond or preferred stock with which they were issued.

G. Warrants generally produce needed funds as the company grows and as the stock price increases over the exercise price.

III. Convertible securities are bonds or preferred stocks that are exchangeable into common stock at the option of the holder and under specified terms and conditions.

A. Conversion of a bond or preferred stock, unlike exercise of a warrant, does not produce additional funds for the firm. However, conversion does lower the debt ratio.

B. The conversion ratio, or rate, specifies the number of common shares that will be received for each bond or share of preferred stock that is converted.

C. The conversion price, P_c, is the effective price paid for the common stock when conversion occurs. For example, if a bond is issued at its par value of $1,000 and can be converted into 40 shares of common stock, the conversion price would be

$$P_c = \frac{\$1,000}{40} = \$25 \text{ per share.}$$

Someone buying the bond and then converting it would, in effect, be paying $25 per share for the stock.

D. Like that of a warrant, the conversion price of a bond is typically set at about 10 to 30 percent above the market price of common stock when the bond is sold. Thus, if the common stock is selling for $20.83 at the time the convertible is issued, the conversion price might be set at 1.2($20.83) = $25, with a conversion ratio of 40.

   1. Sometimes a convertible bond will have a stepped-up conversion price, which results in the conversion price increasing a number of times during the life of the bond.
   2. The conversion price of a bond will change if the firm pays a stock dividend or splits its stock. This feature protects convertibles from dilution.

E. Convertible issues have certain advantages and disadvantages to the issuing corporation.

   1. By giving investors an opportunity to realize capital gains, a firm can sell debt with a lower interest rate.
   2. The sale of a convertible issue has the effect of selling common stock at the time the convertible is issued.
      a. If the stock price does not increase, investors will not convert and the company will be stuck with debt rather than equity in its capital structure, but the interest rate on this debt will be comparatively low.
      b. If the stock price does rise, the company can force conversion by including a call feature in the bond's indenture.
   3. However, if the firm's stock price rises sharply, it may have been a disadvantage to sell the convertible instead of waiting to sell common shares at higher prices.

F. The actual market price of a convertible bond will always be equal to or greater than the higher of its straight debt value or its conversion value.

G. The expected rate of return on a company's convertible should lie between its cost of straight debt and its cost of common stock.

H. Firms with warrants or convertible securities outstanding can theoretically report earnings per share in two ways.

   1. Primary EPS. Earnings available are divided by the average number of shares that would be outstanding if only those warrants and convertibles likely to be exercised or converted had actually been exercised or converted.
   2. Fully diluted EPS. This shows EPS as if all warrants and convertibles had been exercised or converted prior to the reporting date regardless of the likelihood of this occurring.

I. For firms with large amounts of warrant securities or convertible securities or both outstanding, there can be a substantial difference between EPS calculations. Therefore, the SEC requires that primary and fully diluted earnings be shown.

IV. An option is a contract giving the holder the right to buy or sell an asset at a predetermined price within a specified time period.

A. Warrants and executive stock options are options created and given up by a company in exchange for something of value to the firm (low interest rate debt or better executive performance).

B. Options created by individuals are traded on a number of stock exchanges.

C. An option to buy stock is a call option.

D. An option to sell stock is a put option.

E. Corporations on whose stock options are written have nothing to do with the options market, thus do not raise money in this market nor have any direct transactions in it.

Definitional Questions

1. Warrants and convertible securities may make a company's securities more attractive to a broader range of _____ and lower its _____ _____ _____.

2. A _____ is an option to buy a stated number of shares of _____ _____ at a specified _____.

3. Warrants are often attached to a _____ issue in order to make it saleable at a relatively low _____ rate.

4. Warrants have both a _____ value and a market price.

5. The "formula" value of a warrant equals the _____ price minus the _____ price times the number of shares each warrant entitles the owner to purchase.

6. A warrant's premium above the formula value will decline as the _____ of the common stock _____.

7. This decline in premium is due to reduced _____ and increased _____ as the stock price increases.

8. The _____ price of a warrant is generally set at about _____ to _____ percent above the market price of the stock.

9. When they are exercised, warrants add additional _____ _____ to a firm's capital structure.

10. Warrants will certainly be exercised if the stock price is above the _____ price and the warrant is about to _____.

11. Holders of warrants will have an extra incentive to convert to _____ _____ as the company increases the _____ on its common shares.

12. Almost all warrants are _____ and can be traded separately from the debt or preferred stock with which they were issued.

13. Convertible bonds or preferred stocks may be exchanged for _____ _____ at the option of the _____.

14. The _____ _____ specifies the number of shares of common stock that will be received for each bond that is converted.

15. The _____ _____ is the effective price paid for the common stock upon conversion.

16. When a convertible bond is issued, the conversion price is determined by dividing the _____ _____ of the bond by the number of shares received on conversion.

17. Selling a convertible issue may have the effect of selling _____ _____ at a price higher than the market price prevailing at the time the convertible is issued.

18. If a firms' stock price does increase, the company can force _____ of the convertible bonds by including a _____ _____ in the bond indenture.

19. It may be unwise for a firm to sell a convertible issue if it anticipates that its _____ _____ will increase rapidly in the near future.

20. In reporting its earnings, a firm with warrants and convertible securities must report both _____ EPS and _____ _____ EPS.

Conceptual Questions

21. The coupon interest rate on convertible bonds is generally higher than the rate on nonconvertible bonds of the same quality.

    a. True   b. False

22. Primary EPS shows what EPS would have been if all warrants and convertibles had been converted prior to the reporting date.

    a. True   b. False

23. Investors are willing to accept lower interest (or dividend) yields on convertible securities in the hopes of later realizing capital gains.

    a. True   b. False

24. The conversion of a bond replaces debt with common equity on a firm's balance sheet, but it does not bring in any additional capital.

    a. True   b. False

25. The market price of a warrant may be substantially above its formula value.

    a. True   b. False

Problems

26. The Clayton Corporation has warrants outstanding that permit the holder to purchase one share of common stock per warrant at a price of $30. Calculate the formula value of Clayton's warrants if the common stock is currently selling at $20 per share.

    a. -$20
    b. -$10
    c. $5
    d. $10
    e. $20

27. Refer to Problem 26. Calculate the formula value if the common stock is now selling at $40 per share.

    a. -$20
    b. -$10
    c. $0
    d. $10
    e. $20

28. White Corporation has just sold a bond issue with 10 warrants attached to each bond. The bonds have a 20 year maturity, an annual coupon interest rate of 12 percent, and they sold at the $1,000 initial offering price. The current yield to maturity on bonds of equal risk, but without warrants, is 15 percent. What is the value of each warrant?

    a. $22.56
    b. $21.20
    c. $20.21
    d. $19.24
    e. $18.78

(The following information applies to the next four problems.)

Central Food Brokers is considering issuing a 20-year convertible bond that will be priced at its par value of $1,000 per bond. The bonds have a 12 percent annual coupon interest rate, and each bond could be converted into 40 shares of common stock. The stock currently sells at $20 per share, has an expected annual dividend of $3.00, and is growing at a constant 5 percent per year. The bonds are callable after 10 years at a price of $1,050, with the price declining by $5 per year. If, after 10 years, the conversion exceeds the call price by at least 20 percent, management will probably call the bonds.

29. What is the conversion price?

    a. $20
    b. $25
    c. $33
    d. $40
    e. $50

30. If the yield to maturity on nonconvertible bonds of similar risk is 16 percent, what is the straight-debt value?

    a. $1,000.00
    b. $907.83
    c. $812.22
    d. $762.85
    e. $692.37

31. What is the conversion value in Year 10?

    a. $800
    b. $1,000
    c. $1,148
    d. $1,222
    e. $1,303

32. If an investor expects the bond issue to be called in Year 10, and he plans on converting it at that time, what is his expected rate of return on his bond upon conversion?

    a. 12.0%
    b. 12.2%
    c. 13.6%
    d. 14.4%
    e. 15.3%

Answers and Solutions

1. investors; cost of capital

2. warrant; common stock; price

3. debt; interest

4. "formula"

5. market; option

6. price; increases

7. leverage; risk

8. option; 10; 30

9. common equity

10. option; expire

11. common stock; dividend

12. detachable

13. common stock; holder

14. conversion ratio

15. conversion price

16. par value

17. common stock

18. conversion; call provision

19. stock price

20. primary; fully diluted

21. b. The coupon interest rate is lower because investors expect some capital gains return upon conversion.

22. b. Primary EPS includes only those shares from warrants and convertibles likely to be converted in the near future.

23. a. However, the investor is including the expected capital gain as part of his required return, so the total required return on convertibles is higher than on the straight security.

24. a.

25. a.

26. b. Formula value = FV = (Market price of common stock - Option price)(Number of shares purchased per warrant). When P_0 = \$20, then

$$FV = (\$20 - \$30)(1) = -\$10,$$

Note that negative prices cannot actually exist, so the formula value could also be considered to be zero.

27. d. When P_0 = \$40, then FV = (\$40 - \$30)(1) = \$10.

28. e. First, find the straight-debt value:

$$V = C(PVIFA_{k,n}) + M(PVIF_{k,n})$$
$$= \$120(PVIFA_{15\%,20}) + \$1,000(PVIF_{15\%,20}) = \$812.22.$$

Thus, the value of the attached warrants is $1,000 - $812.22 = $187.78. Since each bond has 10 warrants, each warrant must have a value of $18.78.

29. b. P_c = Par value/Shares received

= $1,000/40 = $25.00.

30. d. $V = C(PVIFA_{k,n}) + M(PVIF_{k,n})$

= $120(PVIFA_{16\%,20}) + $1,000(PVIF_{16\%,20})$

= $762.85.

31. e. $C_t = P_t R$; $C_{10} = P_{10} R = $20(1.05)^{10}(40) = $1,303.12 \approx $1,303.$

32. c. This is solved by finding the value of k_c in the equation:

Price paid = $C(PVIFA_{k_c,n})$ + Expected market value$(PVIF_{k_c,n})$.

Therefore, find the value of k_c for the following:

$1,000 = $120(PVIFA_{k_c,10}) + $1,303(PVIF_{k_c,10})$

$k_c = 13.6\%.$

CHAPTER 21

LEASING

Overview

Firms generally own fixed assets and report them on their balance sheets, but it is the use of the fixed assets that is important, not their ownership. One way of obtaining the use of facilities and equipment is to buy them, but an alternative is to lease them. This chapter describes the three major types of leases, then discusses the effects of leasing on a firm's balance sheet. Next, a simple analysis technique is presented for evaluating lease proposals from the standpoint of the lessee. Chapter 21 concludes with a discussion of additional factors that affect leasing decisions and the use of leveraged leases.

Outline

I. The ownership of assets is not as important as the ability to use them in a profitable manner. Leasing provides the same ability to use capital assets as outright ownership.

   A. Historically, land and buildings were the types of assets most often leased, but today it is possible to lease almost any kind of fixed asset.

   B. There are three common types of leasing arrangements.

      1. Sale and leaseback. In this type of lease, a firm owning an asset sells the property to a financial institution and simultaneously leases it back for a specified period at specific terms.
         a. The sale-and-leaseback arrangement is an alternative to simply borrowing against the property on a mortgage loan basis.
         b. The seller receives the purchase price but retains the use of the property in exchange for rental payments.
         c. The lease payments are sufficient to return the purchase price to the investor plus provide a stated return on the investment.
      2. Operating leases. These leases include both financing and maintenance services.

       a. Operating leases ordinarily call for the lessor to maintain the equipment; the cost of maintenance is built into the lease payments.

       b. The lease contract is written for less than the useful life of the equipment; that is, the lease is not fully amortized.

       c. The lessor expects to recover the cost of the equipment through renewal payments or through disposal of the leased equipment.

       d. Operating leases often contain a cancellation clause to protect the lessee against obsolescence.

  3. <u>Financial, or capital, leases.</u> These leases are fully amortized; however, they do not provide for maintenance and are not cancellable.

       a. They differ from a sale-and-leaseback in that equipment is new.

       b. Equipment is purchased from a manufacturer rather than from the lessee.

II. Lease payments are deductible expenses for income tax purposes providing the IRS does not challenge the lease as simply being an installment sale in another form.

  A. The IRS considers an agreement to be a sale if the following conditions exist.

    1. The payments made by the lessee over a relatively short period of time approximately equal the price at which the asset could have been bought.

    2. The lessee is permitted to continue using the asset over its entire life by making relatively nominal renewal payments.

  B. These restrictions prevent a company from using a lease arrangement to depreciate equipment over a much shorter period than its useful life.

III. Using lease financing rather than borrowing to purchase assets can have a substantial impact on a firm's balance sheet.

  A. Leasing is referred to as "off balance sheet" financing because often neither assets nor lease liabilities appear on the firm's balance sheet.

  B. A firm with extensive lease arrangements would have both its assets and its liabilities understated in comparison with a firm which borrowed to purchase assets. The firm that leases would show a lower debt ratio.

  C. FASB #13 requires firms to "capitalize" certain financial leases and to restate their balance sheets.

       1. Leased assets must be reported under "fixed assets."
       2. The present value of future lease payments must be shown as "debt."

  D. Lease financing is comparable to debt financing in that a specified series of payments is to be made and failure to meet these payments may result in bankruptcy.

IV. Several unique factors are important in analyzing lease proposals.

  A. Estimated residual value refers to the value of the property at the end of the lease term.

       1. A high residual value may favor ownership of the property rather than a lease arrangement.
       2. Obsolescence of the equipment may greatly reduce its real value at the end of the lease term.
       3. Competition among lessors will force residual values to be fully reflected in the lease payments.

  B. Increased credit availability means that firms may be able to lease equipment under more liberal terms than they could borrow funds to purchase the asset.

       1. Since some leases do not appear on the balance sheet, a firm that leases may seem less highly leveraged than one which borrows.
       2. This point is not as significant as it was before FASB #13 was issued because FASB #13 now requires the capitalization of many leases.

  C. Leasing arrangements may make it possible for marginally profitable firms to take advantage of the investment tax credit and accelerated depreciation.

       1. These credits are available only if a firm's profits and taxes exceed a certain level.
       2. Leasing enables those firms which cannot use the tax credit to pass it on to the lessor, who responds with a reduction in the lease charges.
       3. Accelerated depreciation works in the same manner.

  D. The lease proposal must be analyzed by both parties. The lease agreement must be profitable to both the lessee and the lessor.

V. When the owner-lessor borrows funds in order to purchase the property which he leases to the lessee, the lease is called a leveraged lease.

A. Wealthy individuals seeking tax shelters often act as owner-lessors.

B. Whether or not a lease is leveraged is unimportant from the lessee's standpoint.

Definitional Questions

1. Conceptually, leasing is similar to _____, and it provides the same type of financial _____.

2. Under a _____ arrangement, the seller receives the purchase price of the asset but retains _____ of the property.

3. _____ leases include both financing and maintenance arrangements.

4. A financial, or capital, lease is similar to a _____ arrangement, but financial leases generally apply to the purchase of _____ equipment directly from a manufacturer.

5. The use of lease financing may understate both the _____ and _____ on a firm's balance sheet.

6. FASB #13 requires that firms _____ certain financial leases and restate their _____ _____.

7. Capitalizing a lease requires that the asset be listed under _____ _____, and that the _____ _____ of the future lease payments be shown as _____.

8. The value of an asset at the end of the lease term is referred to as its _____ _____.

9. _____ among leasing companies will tend to force leasing rates down to the point where _____ values are fully reflected in the lease rates.

10. Since some leases do not appear on the _____ _____, a firm may be able to use more _____ than if it did not lease.

11. Leasing may permit a firm to take effective advantage of the investment _____ _____ when it would not otherwise have been able to do so.

12. A firm with low profits may be able to pass along the tax credit and be compensated in the form of lower _____ _____.

Conceptual Questions

13. Capital leases include both financing and maintenance arrangements.

    a. True   b. False

14. When one is evaluating a lease proposal, cash flows should be discounted at a relatively high rate because those flows are fairly certain.

    a. True   b. False

15. Generally, operating leases are fully amortized, and the lease is written for the expected life of the asset.

    a. True   b. False

16. A firm which uses extensive lease financing may have a substantially lower debt ratio than a firm which borrows to finance its assets.

    a. True   b. False

17. Firms have the option whether or not to capitalize a financial lease.

    a. True   b. False

Problem

18. Treadmill Trucking Co. is negotiating a lease for five new tractor/trailer rigs with International Leasing. Treadmill has received its best offer from Betterbilt Trucks for a total price of $1 million. The terms of the lease offered by International Leasing call for an 8 percent return to the lessor for the 5 year term of the lease. As an alternative to leasing, the firm can borrow from a large insurance company and buy the trucks. The $1 million would be borrowed on an amortized term loan at a 10 percent interest rate for 5 years. Under both alternatives, the trucks will be depreciated by the ACRS method and will have an expected salvage value of $100,000 at the end of 5 years. Maintenance costs are expected to be $10,000 per year. Treadmill plans to buy the trucks at the salvage value at the end of the fifth year if it chooses to lease. International Leasing has a 60 percent marginal tax rate, while Treadmill Trucking has a lower tax rate of 20 percent. Should Treadmill lease or buy the trucks?

    a. Buy, since the net advantage is $5,576.
    b. Buy, since the net advantage is $11,032.
    c. The firm is indifferent between buying and leasing.
    d. Lease, since the net advantage is $11,032.
    e. Lease, since the net advantage is $5,576.

Answers and Solution

1. borrowing; leverage

2. sale-and-leaseback; use

3. Operating

4. sale-and-leaseback; new

5. assets; liabilities

6. capitalize; balance sheets

7. fixed assets; present value; debt

8. residual value

9. Competition; residual

10. balance sheet; leverage

11. tax credit

12. lease payments

13. b. Operating leases include both financing and maintenance arrangements. Capital leases provide financing arrangements only.

14. b. The cash flows are fairly certain, so they should be discounted at a relatively low rate.

15. b. Operating leases are frequently not fully amortized. The lessor expects to recover all costs either in subsequent lease renewals or through the sale of the used equipment.

16. a. Since some leases do not appear on the balance sheet, a firm which leases may have a lower debt ratio than a firm which borrows and purchases assets.

17. b. FASB #13 spells out in detail the conditions under which leases must be capitalized.

18. e. To work this problem it is necessary to complete a lease versus purchase analysis as presented on Page 21-7.

Year (1)	Loan Payment (2)	Interest (3)	Amortization Payment (4)	Remaining Balance (5)	Maintenance Cost (6)	ACRS Depreciation (7)	(3)+(6)+(7)= Tax Deductible Expense (8)	(0.20)x(8)= Tax Savings (9)	(2)+(6)-(9)= Cash Outflow if Owned (10)	(1 - 0.2)x (Lease Cost)= After-tax Lease Cost (11)	PVIFs for 8% (12)	(10)x(12)= Present Value of the Cost of Owning (13)	(11)x(12)= Present Value of the Cost of Leasing (14)
1	$ 263,797	$100,000	$163,797	$836,203	$10,000	$ 150,000	$260,000	$52,000	$221,797	$200,366	0.9259	$205,362	$185,519
2	263,797	83,620	180,177	656,026	10,000	220,000	313,620	62,724	211,073	200,366	0.8573	180,953	171,774
3	263,797	65,603	198,194	457,832	10,000	210,000	285,603	57,121	216,676	200,366	0.7938	171,997	159,051
4	263,797	45,783	218,014	239,818	10,000	210,000	265,783	53,157	220,640	200,366	0.7350	162,170	147,269
5	263,797	23,982	239,815	3[a]	10,000	210,000	243,982	48,796	225,001	200,366	0.6806	153,136	136,369
5	---	---	---	---	---	---	---	---	---	100,000[b]	0.6806	---	68,060
Totals:	$1,318,985	$318,988	$999,997			$1,000,000						$873,618	$868,042

[a]This non-zero balance is due to rounding errors.

[b]Purchase of assets for the $100,000 salvage value. Net advantage to leasing = $873,618 - $868,042 = $5,576.

NOTE: All figures have been rounded to the nearest dollar.

CHAPTER 22

MERGERS AND HOLDING COMPANIES

Overview

A merger involves the consolidation of two or more firms. Mergers can provide economic benefits through economies of scale, but they also have the potential for reducing competition, and for this reason mergers are carefully regulated by governmental agencies. This chapter begins by describing the types of mergers, the reasons for mergers, the forecasting of expected growth, and the estimation of the postmerger stock price. Next, merger terms and the effects of accounting practices on the consolidated financial statements are discussed. In a merger, one firm disappears. However, an alternative is for one firm to buy a majority of the common stock of another and to run the acquired firm as an operating subsidiary. When this occurs, the acquiring firm is said to be a holding company. Chapter 22 concludes by discussing the advantages and disadvantages of holding companies.

Outline

I. While most corporate growth occurs through internal expansion, the most dramatic growth is often the result of corporate merger activity.

  A. There are four primary types of mergers.

   1. <u>Horizontal</u>. This occurs when one firm combines with another in the same line of business.
   2. <u>Vertical</u>. A vertical merger exists when firms combine in a producer-supplier relationship.
   3. <u>Congeneric</u>. This type of merger involves related enterprises other than horizontal or vertical mergers.
   4. <u>Conglomerate</u>. When unrelated enterprises combine, a conglomerate merger occurs.

  B. In most mergers, one company, the target company, is acquired by another, the acquiring company.

   1. In a friendly merger, the managements of both of the companies approve the merger and recommend it to their stockholders.

      a. Under these circumstances a suitable price is deter-
mined and the acquiring company will buy the target
company's shares.

      b. Payment will be made either in cash or in shares of
the acquiring company.

  2. A hostile merger is one in which the target firm's management resists the takeover. The target management may
either feel the price offered is too low or simply want
to remain independent.

      a. Under these circumstances, the acquiring company may
make a tender offer for the target company's shares.
This is a direct appeal to the target firm's stockholders, asking them to exchange their shares for
cash or for stock in the acquiring firm.

      b. The number of tender offers has increased greatly
during the past several years.

C. Empirical studies have identified four specific reasons for
mergers.

  1. The stockholders of acquired firms receive significant
gains from mergers. These gains may arise from economies
of scale, complementary resources, better use of excess
cash or unused debt capacity, and increased R&D capacity.

  2. A firm may find that it is cheaper to expand capacity by
purchasing an existing company than to purchase new
assets needed for additional production.

  3. Firms which desire to expand capacity may be able to
obtain financing more easily to buy an existing company
than to purchase new physical assets.

  4. Nearly one-third of all mergers have been stimulated by
tax considerations. Often, a merger will allow a
profitable firm to take advantage of its unprofitable
merger partner's tax loss carry forwards.

II. While merger analysis may appear simple, there are a number of
complex issues involved.

A. The cash flow benefits, measured in terms of earnings per
share, must be estimated.

B. The impact of the merger on the combined firm's required rate
of return and on its P/E ratio must be determined.

C. The acquiring and target firms managers and stockholders must
agree on the terms of the merger.

D. From a financial standpoint, there are two basic types of
mergers.

1. Operating mergers are mergers in which the operations of two companies are combined in hopes of synergistic gains.
   a. Synergy is said to exist whenever the value of the combined firms is greater than the value of the two taken separately.
   b. Operating mergers may result in economies of scale in production or distribution which will lead to synergistic benefits.
2. Financial mergers are mergers where the two operations are not combined and no operating economies are expected.

E. The primary benefit from an operating merger is higher expected total profits. Financial mergers may result in improved leverage, greater liquidity for the stock, or a matching of capital needs and resources.

III. Estimating future operating income is a key element in the analysis of any proposed merger.

A. In a financial merger, the expected cash flows are the sum of the independent cash flows of the two companies.

B. If the combination is an operating merger, cash flow projections are more difficult, but essential to the merger analysis.

1. Synergistic effects will result in greater cash flows than would have been achieved by summing the cash flows of the two independent companies.
2. Economies of scale may result in lower operating costs per unit of production.

C. The postmerger market price of the combined firm's stock will depend on the postmerger earnings per share and the P/E ratio applied to those earnings.

IV. The terms of a merger include two important elements.

A. Postmerger control of the firm. This is of great interest to managers due to their concern for their jobs and their ability to maintain operating control of the firm after the merger.

B. Price to be paid. The second key element, price, is paid in either cash or in stock of the acquiring company.

1. A cash payment should be approximately equal to the discounted value of the incremental earnings expected from the merger.
2. If an exchange of stock is involved, the exchange ratio determines the number of shares paid for each share of the target firm's stock.

3. The following three factors influence the exchange ratio.
   a. <u>Current earnings</u>. For example, if a firm earning $2.00
      per share were to acquire a firm earning $1.00, the exchange ratio, ER, might be $1/$2 = 0.5, or one share of the acquiring firm for every two shares of the target company.
   b. <u>Projected future earnings</u>. This will be important if there are significant differences in growth rates of the two firms or if substantial synergism is expected. In the latter case, a minimum acceptable ER for the target firm and a maximum acceptable ER for the acquiring firm can be calculated.
   c. <u>Current market values</u>. The ratio of the two firms' market values will be an important determinant of the exchange ratio. This ratio will have to be adjusted if the target firm's synergistic value has not been accounted for in its price.

V. There are some additional points of interest regarding the acquisition of firms.

A. If a high P/E firm acquires a low P/E firm and the ER is based on current market price, then the acquiring firm will obtain an immediate increase in EPS. Of course, if the opposite occurs, the acquiring firm will obtain an immediate decrease in EPS.

B. The postmerger market price will reflect the final EPS, which is determined by the exchange ratio and synergistic effects, and will also reflect the final P/E ratio, which will depend on investors' appraisal of the prospects of the combined firm.

C. The target firm should be acquired only if the acquisition will raise the acquiring firm's stock price.

VI. Mergers are handled either as a pooling of interests or as a purchase.

A. In pooling, the consolidated balance sheet is simply the sum of the individual balance sheets of the merged companies.

B. In a purchase, the acquiring firm is assumed to have bought the acquired company.

   1. If the price paid is equal to the net asset value of the acquired firm, then the consolidated balance sheet resembles that under pooling.
   2. If the price paid exceeds net asset value, then assets are increased to reflect the price actually paid.

3. If the price paid is less than the net asset value, then assets are written down when preparing a consolidated balance sheet.

C. There can be significant differences in reported profit under the two methods.

D. There are six conditions which must be met before a pooling can occur.

VII. Holding companies may be used to obtain some of the same benefits that could be achieved through mergers and acquisitions. However, the holding company device has some unique disadvantages as well as unique advantages.

A. The advantages of holding companies include the following:

1. Control with fractional ownership. Effective control of a company may be achieved with far less than 50 percent ownership of the common stock.

2. Isolation of risks. Claims on one unit of the holding company are not liabilities to the other units. Each element of the holding company organization is a separate legal entity.

3. Approval not required. The holding company may purchase stock in and take effective working capital of the acquired firm without the permission or approval of the acquired firm's stockholders.

B. Disadvantages of holding companies include the following:

1. Partial multiple taxation. Consolidated tax returns may be filed only if the holding company owns 80 percent or more of the voting stock of the subsidiary. Otherwise, intercorporate dividends will be taxed, but 85 percent of the dividends received by the holding company may be deducted from taxable income.

2. Ease of enforced dissolution. It is much easier for the Justice Department to require disposal of a stock position than to demand the separation of an integrated business operation.

3. Risks of excess leverage. The holding company device can be used to control large amounts of assets with a relatively small equity investment. The substantial leverage involved in such an operation may result in high returns but also involves a high degree of risk.

Definitional Questions

1. A _____ merger takes place when two firms in the same business combine, while the combination of a steel company with a coal company would be an example of a _____ merger.

2. The merger of two completely unrelated enterprises is referred to as a _____ merger.

3. A firm which seeks to take over another company is commonly called the _____ company, while the firms it seeks to acquire are referred to as _____ companies.

4. A merger may be described as "friendly" or "hostile" depending upon the attitude of the _____ of the target company.

5. A _____ _____ is a request by the acquiring company to the target company's _____ to submit their shares in exchange for a specified price or a specified number of shares of stock.

6. If the value of two firms, in combination, is greater than the sum of their separate values, then _____ is said to exist.

7. An _____ merger combines the business activity of the two firms with the expectation of _____ benefits.

8. _____ mergers do not combine the business operations of two firms, and no operating economies are expected.

9. The three factors which influence the exchange ratio are (1) _____ _____, (2) _____ _____, and (3) _____ _____.

10. Earnings, growth rates, and synergistic effects may be reflected in the _____ _____ of the target company.

11. Unless a holding company owns at least _____ percent of the shares of a subsidiary company, it may be subject to multiple _____ on a portion of any intercorporate _____.

Conceptual Questions

12. In a financial merger, the expected cash flows are the sum of the cash flows of the separate companies.

    a. True   b. False

13. The estimation of the postmerger market price of the combined firms' stock is based on the postmerger earnings per share and dividend payout ratio.

    a. True   b. False

14. The consolidated balance sheet is the same under purchase accounting and pooling of interests if:

    a. The price paid is exactly equal to the gross asset value.
    b. The price paid is exactly equal to the net asset value.
    c. The price paid is exactly equal to the total assets minus liabilities value.
    d. The price paid is exactly equal to the goodwill account.
    e. Statements b and c above are both correct.

15. The income statement of the postmerger firm will be the same regardless of the accounting method used.

    a. True   b. False

16. The holding company device can be used to take advantage of the principle of financial leverage. Thus, the holding company can control a great deal of assets with limited debt.

    a. True   b. False

Problems

(The following information applies to the next five problems.)

A national hardware chain, American Hardware, is considering a merger with a smaller chain, Eastern Hardware. American executives feel that if they were to offer a "fair" exchange ratio, the merger proposal would be received favorably by Eastern's stockholders and management. The following table presents some data on the two companies:

	P_0	D_0	EPS	g	Total Earnings	Number of Shares of Common Stock
American	$36.00	$1.85	$3.00	10%	$12,000,000	4 million
Eastern	9.00	0.75	1.50	5	1,500,000	1 million

17. Calculate the exchange ratio in shares of American per share of Eastern based on current EPS.

    a. 0.250
    b. 0.400
    c. 0.444
    d. 0.500
    e. 1.000

18. Calculate the exchange ratio in shares of American per share of Eastern based on EPS in 5 years.

    a. 0.250
    b. 0.400
    c. 0.444
    d. 0.500
    e. 1.000

19. Calculate the exchange ratio in shares of American per share of Eastern based on current market values.

    a. 0.250
    b. 0.400
    c. 0.444
    d. 0.500
    e. 1.000

20. Calculate the exchange ratio in shares of American per share of Eastern that will maintain American's present EPS, assuming there will be a synergistic increase in earnings of $1,500,000.

    a. 0.250
    b. 0.400
    c. 0.444
    d. 0.500
    e. 1.000

21. Calculate the exchange ratio in shares of American per share of Eastern that will maintain Eastern's current EPS, again assuming a $1,500,000 synergistic increase in earnings.

    a. 0.250
    b. 0.400
    c. 0.444
    d. 0.500
    e. 1.000

(The following information applies to the next two problems.)

Jensen Electric is considering a merger with the Shady Lamp Co. A significant amount of synergy is expected. In the past year Jensen had earnings of $2,500,000 while Shady Lamp earned $1,200,000. Synergistic earnings after the merger are anticipated to be about $500,000. At this time the acquiring firm has 1,000,000 shares outstanding. The target firm has 750,000 shares outstanding.

22. What is the maximum ER that Jensen's management can accept without causing a dilution of their EPS?

    a. 0.533
    b. 0.833
    c. 0.906
    d. 1.205
    e. 1.420

23. How low can the ER go without diluting the EPS of Shady Lamp's current stockholders?

    a. 0.533
    b. 0.833
    c. 0.906
    d. 1.205
    e. 1.420

Answers and Solutions

1. horizontal; vertical

2. conglomerate

3. acquiring; target

4. management

5. tender offer; stockholders

6. synergy

7. operating; synergistic

8. Financial

9. current earnings; future earnings; market values

10. market price

11. 80; taxation; dividends

12. a. In a financial merger, no synergistic effects are anticipated.

13. b. It is based on the postmerger EPS and P/E ratio.

14. e.

15. b. Goodwill generated under purchase accounting is amortized, thus reducing the reported net income.

16. b. The assets are controlled with only a small amount of equity, but considerable debt.

17. d. Let ER = exchange ratio. $ER = EPS_E/EPS_A = \$1.50/\$3.00 = 0.50$ shares of American.

18. b. $ER = [EPS_E(1 + g_E)^n]/[EPS_A(1 + g_A)^n]$

    $= [1.50(1.05)^5]/[3.00(1.10)^5]$

    $\simeq 0.40$ shares of American.

19. a. $ER = P_E/P_A = \$9.00/\$36.00 = 0.25$ shares of American.

20. e. First, establish an exchange ratio such that new EPS_A = old EPS_A.

    $$\text{Old EPS} = \$3 = E_A/N_A = \$12,000,000/4,000,000.$$

    New EPS will be equal to the new total earnings divided by the new shares. New total earnings, defined as TE, may be estimated as follows:

    $$TE = E_A + E_E + S$$
    $$= \$12,000,000 + \$1,500,000 + \$1,500,000$$
    $$= \$15,000,000$$

where E_A and E_E are American's and Eastern's original total earnings, and S is the synergistic earnings. The new EPS may be found as follows:

$$EPS_{New} = \$15,000,000/\text{New total shares.}$$

The new total shares (N) will be equal to the old American shares (N_A) plus the shares given up to Eastern stockholders (N_E), which will be equal to $N = N_A + N_E(ER)$. Finally, combine the above equations and then solve for ER to establish the required exchange ratio:

$$EPS_{Old} = EPS_{New} = \$3 = \frac{\$15,000,000}{N_A + N_E(ER)} = \frac{\$15,000,000}{4,000,000 + 1,000,000ER}$$

$$\$12,000,000 + \$3,000,000ER = \$15,000,000$$

$$\$3,000,000ER = \$3,000,000$$

$$ER = \$3,000,000/\$3,000,000 = 1.0.$$

Therefore, given synergistic earnings of $1.5 million, American could exchange shares with Eastern on a 1-for-1 basis and still maintain its old EPS.

21. c. In this case set an exchange ratio such that the holder of 1 share of Eastern will have the same earnings after the merger as before. Each share of Eastern will receive one-half share of American stock. Thus, to maintain the old Eastern earnings of $1.50 per share, we must have $ER(EPS_A) = \$1.50$, where EPS_A refers to the new EPS of American after the merger. Therefore, $EPS_A = \$1.50/ER$.

In the solution above using $EPS_A = EPS_{new}$, EPS_A was determined to be:

$$EPS_A = \frac{\$15,000,000}{N_A + N_E(ER)}$$

Now set $EPS_A = \$1.50/ER$ and solve for ER:

$$\frac{\$1.50}{ER} = \frac{\$15,000,000}{4,000,000 + ER(1,000,000)}$$

$$(\$1.50)(4,000,000)$$
$$+ (\$1.50)(ER)(1,000,000) = \$15,000,000ER$$

$$\$13,500,000ER = \$6,000,000$$

$$ER = 0.444.$$

To check the answer:

$$\text{EPS}_A \text{ if ER is 0.444:} \quad \frac{\$15,000,000}{4,000,000 + 0.444(1,000,000)} = \$3.38.$$

Earnings per old Eastern share: $0.444(3.38) = \$1.50$.

Thus, except for a rounding error, the owner of 1 share of Eastern would receive 0.444 shares of American, and that this fractional share would have earnings of \$1.50. (Of course, fractional shares might not be issued, but the owner of 1,000 shares of Eastern would receive 444 shares of American.)

22. c. $\quad \text{ER} = \dfrac{\text{TE} - \text{EPS}_J(N_J)}{\text{EPS}_J(N_S)}$

$\qquad = \dfrac{\$4,200,000 - \$2.5(1,000,000)}{\$2.5(750,000)}$

$\qquad = 0.906$ shares of Jensen for one share of Shady Lamp.

23. a. $\quad \text{ER} = \dfrac{\text{EPS}_S N_J}{\text{TE} - N_S \text{EPS}_S}$

$\qquad = \dfrac{\$1.60(1,000,000)}{4,200,000 - 750,000(\$1.60)}$

$\qquad = 0.533.$

CHAPTER 23

BANKRUPTCY AND REORGANIZATION

Overview

Thus far, the text has dealt with issues faced by growing, successful enterprises. However, many firms encounter financial difficulties, and some actually fail. Chapter 23 discusses the causes of business failures and their possible remedies. These remedies range from the informal procedures of extension and composition to the formal, legal procedures of reorganization and liquidation provided for under the Bankruptcy Reform Act of 1978. A careful understanding of the remedies available should allow financial managers, not only of distressed firms but also of their creditors, to minimize losses should failure be imminent.

Outline

I. Understanding the causes of business failure and the possible strategies for dealing with it is important to all financial managers.

  A. There are several definitions of "failure."

   1. Economic failure. Failure that occurs when a firm's revenues do not cover its total costs, including its cost of capital.
   2. Business failure. This is a term used by Dun & Bradstreet to designate any business that has terminated with a resultant loss to creditors.
   3. Technical insolvency. A firm is considered technically insolvent if it cannot meet its current obligations as they fall due.
   4. Insolvency in bankruptcy. This occurs when a firm's total liabilities exceed the fair market value of its assets.
   5. Legal bankruptcy. This is a legal procedure carried out under special courts of law for liquidating or reorganizing a business.

B. The great majority of financial failures are caused by management incompetence.

C. A significant number of businesses fail each year, but they are a small percentage of the total business population.

D. Bankruptcy is much more frequent among smaller firms, partly because merger or government intervention is used to rescue larger firms.

E. Bankruptcy is generally a last resort to solving business problems because of its cost and complexity, the disruption of the community, and the erosion of confidence in the business community.

II. If a firm is fundamentally sound, creditors generally prefer to work out temporary financial difficulties with the company rather than resort to legal bankruptcy proceedings. This often involves restructuring the debt of the troubled firm.

A. An extension involves a "stretching out" or delay of payments beyond the required payment period. It is generally preferred by creditors because it provides for payment in full.

B. A composition involves a percentage settlement of all creditors' claims as full settlement of the debt; creditors get less than 100 cents on the dollar.

C. Three conditions are necessary to make debt restructuring feasible.

1. The debtor must be a good moral risk.
2. The debtor must show an ability to recover.
3. General business conditions must be favorable to recovery.

D. Often a settlement will include both an extension and a composition in an effort to keep a debtor from bankruptcy.

E. Voluntary settlements generally provide the greatest return to creditors because legal, investigative, and administrative expenses are minimized. They may take a loss, but a smaller one than would be incurred under formal bankruptcy proceedings.

III. Reorganization is a formal, court-approved effort to solve a failing company's financial problems by changing its capital structure. Debts will be converted to equity, and debt maturities lengthened, to produce a situation where the firm can meet its reduced debt service obligations.

A. Regardless of the legal procedure followed, reorganization processes have certain common characteristics.

1. Some modifications in the nature or the amount of the firm's obligations must be made.
2. New funds must be raised to increase working capital and to rehabilitate property.
3. The causes of operating and financial problems must be identified and eliminated.

B. All reorganizations must provide for two conditions.

1. The adjustment of creditor claims must be fair to all parties (fairness).
2. There must be a reasonably high probability of recovery and successful future operations (feasibility).

IV. Federal Bankruptcy laws establish provisions for reorganization and liquidation of insolvent firms.

A. The issues addressed in the bankruptcy statutes are as follows:

1. Is the firm's problem permanent or temporary?
2. If the situation is permanent, who will bear the losses?
    a. The absolute priority doctrine adheres strictly to the priority of each claim.
    b. The relative priority doctrine, being more flexible, takes into account the consequences to each claimant.
3. Is the value of the firm greater if it is liquidated or if it is rehabilitated?
4. Should existing management or a trustee be in control while the firm is being liquidated or reorganized?

B. The Bankruptcy Reform Act of 1978 represents a major effort to speed up and streamline legal proceedings.

1. The Act represents a shift from the absolute priority doctrine towards the relative priority doctrine.
2. Chapter 11 of the new code provides more flexibility and more scope for informal negotiation among creditors, stockholders, and the company.
    a. A petition to the bankruptcy court can be voluntary or involuntary.
    b. A court appointed committee of unsecured creditors negotiates a reorganization.
    c. A trustee is appointed by the court if existing management is deemed incompetent.
    d. Liquidation will occur if no fair and feasible reorganization can take place.

V. Whether a firm is liquidated or reorganized depends upon which action will result in the greatest value of the firm. The procedure that promises higher returns to creditors and owners will be selected. The courts (with advice from the SEC if very large firms are involved) are responsible for determining the fairness and feasibility of any proposed plan of reorganization.

A. The basic doctrine of fairness states that claims must be recognized in the order of their legal and contractual priority. Common stockholders are in the weakest position as there may be little or no residual value for them as owners of the company.

B. The primary test of feasibility in a reorganization is whether the fixed charges after reorganization will be adequately covered by earnings. This usually requires that operating income be increased, fixed charges be reduced, or both. This is normally accomplished through one or more of the following actions:

1. Debt maturities are usually lengthened, and some debt is usually converted into equity.
2. When the quality of management has been substandard, a new team must be given control of the company.
3. Obsolete and depleted inventories must be replaced.
4. Sometimes the plant and the equipment must be modernized before the firm can compete successfully on a cost basis.
5. Reorganization may also require an improvement in production, marketing, advertising, and other functions.
6. It is sometimes necessary to develop new products or markets to enable the firm to move from areas where economic trends are poor into areas with more potential for growth or stability.

VI. When a firm cannot be effectively reorganized, it is liquidated.

A. Liquidation may take place through an assignment, which is a procedure that does not involve the courts.

1. Assignment results in title to the debtor's assets being transferred to a third party, known as an assignee or trustee.
2. The assignee will sell the assets and distribute the proceeds on a pro rata basis to the creditors.
3. Assignment is generally preferred to a more formal liquidation procedure because of the reduced time, formality, and expense.

B. Liquidation may occur through bankruptcy which is a legal procedure carried out under the jurisdiction of a special court. The Federal Bankruptcy Act is designed to achieve three objectives.

1. It provides safeguards against fraud during liquidation.
2. It provides for equitable distribution of the debtor's assets among the creditors.
3. It enables insolvent debtors to discharge their obligations and start new businesses unhampered by previous debts.

C. The order of priority of claims in bankruptcy is as follows:

1. Secured creditors have first claim against the proceeds of the sale of specific property pledged as security. If the proceeds do not fully satisfy the secured creditor's claims, the remaining balance is treated as a general creditor claim.
2. Trustee's costs to administer and operate the bankrupt firm have next priority.
3. Next comes the expenses incurred after an involuntary case has begun but before a trustee is appointed.
4. Wages due workers (accrued wages) have next priority. However, these wages must have been earned within three months prior to the filing of the bankruptcy petition and cannot exceed $2,000 for any worker.
5. Workers also have claims for unpaid contributions to employee benefit plans. These claims, plus wages due, cannot exceed $2,000 for any worker.
6. Claims for customer deposits, not to exceed $900 per claimant, have next priority.
7. Next are taxes due the United States, state, county, and any other government agency.
8. Unfunded pension plan liabilities have a claim above that of the general creditors for an amount up to 30 percent of the common and preferred equity. Any remaining unfunded pension claims are treated as general creditor claims.
9. General or unsecured creditors come next. Trade credit, unsecured loans, the unsatisfied portion of secured loans, and debentures are classified as general creditors. Holders of subordinated debt also fall into this category, but they must turn over required amounts to senior debtholders.
10. Next are preferred stockholders.
11. Finally, any funds remaining are distributed to the common stockholders.

Definitional Questions

1. A firm is technically _____ when it is unable to meet its obligations as they come due.

2. A firm is not legally _____ unless it fails according to certain criteria established by the Federal _____ _____.

3. The most predominant cause of business failure is _____ _____.

4. Bankruptcy is more common among smaller firms because _____ and _____ _____ generally keep larger firms from failing.

5. In order to make extension or composition feasible, the debtor must be a good _____ _____ and show the ability to _____.

6. A firm's creditors will normally prefer _____ over _____ because it provides for full payment.

7. A formal, court approved arrangement to keep a company going by changing its capital structure is known as a _____.

8. Any reorganization must meet the standards of _____ and _____ before it will be approved by the court.

9. If an acceptable plan of reorganization cannot be worked out, the firm will be _____.

10. According to the doctrine of _____, claims must be recognized in order of their legal _____.

11. The _____ of a reorganization plan is measured in part by the earnings coverage of _____ _____.

12. In order to improve the coverage ratio, the _____ of debt may have to be lengthened, or _____ may have to be converted to _____.

13. The liquidation of a business may occur through an _____ or through formal _____ proceedings.

14. Under an _____, title to the debtor's _____ is transferred to a third party, known as an _____ or _____.

15. The assignee or trustee liquidates the assets and distributes the proceeds among the _____ on a _____ _____ basis.

16. The Federal Bankruptcy Act provides safeguards against _____ by the debtor and provides for an equitable distribution of the firm's _____.

17. In liquidation, _____ creditors of the bankrupt firm have the _____ priority of claims.

Conceptual Questions

18. Informal settlements such as extensions and composition tend to be more expensive than more formal settlements.

    a. True   b. False

19. In a composition, the payment received is only a percentage of the amount due, but it is accepted as full settlement of the obligation.

    a. True   b. False

20. Liquidation by assignment is carried out under the jurisdiction of a bankruptcy court.

a. True   b. False

21. List the following creditors in descending order of claim priority (highest priority to lowest):

1. Common stockholders
2. Taxes due
3. Wages due
4. Secured creditors
5. General creditors

a. 1, 2, 3, 4, 5
b. 4, 2, 3, 5, 1
c. 2, 4, 3, 5, 1
d. 3, 4, 2, 5, 1
e. 4, 3, 2, 5, 1

Problem

22. You are given the following balance sheet:

Balance Sheet
Crown Electronics Corporation
December 31, 1984
(Millions of Dollars)

Cash	$ 0.10	Accounts payable	$ 16.00
Accounts receivable	1.00	Notes payable	
Inventories	8.90	(to bank, 8%)	10.00
Total current		Wages payable	1.50
assets	$ 10.00	Taxes payable	0.50
Net plant	40.00		
Net equipment	50.00		
		Total current	
		liabilities	$ 28.00
		First mortgage bonds, 6%*	20.00
		Subordinated debentures	
		(to N/P), 8%	20.00
		Preferred stock ($100	
		par), 10%	15.00
		Common stock ($1 par)	25.00
		Additional paid-in capital	15.00
		Retained	
earnings	(23.00)		
Total Assets	$100.00	Total Claims	$100.00

*The first mortgage bonds are secured by the plant but not by the equipment.

A substantial portion of Crown's current liabilities will soon be due and payable, and the firm's liquidity is in such poor condition that it cannot cover these obligations. Furthermore, Crown's treasurer is unable to raise additional funds from the capital market. Fearing that it may be forced into bankruptcy, management has filed for reorganization under Chapter 11 of the Federal Bankruptcy Act. The table below presents the expected proceeds from the sale of assets through liquidation if no suitable reorganization plan can be worked out:

	Expected Proceeds
Plant	$16,000,000
Equipment	13,000,000
Accounts receivable	500,000
Inventories	2,400,000
Cash	100,000
Total proceeds	$32,000,000

Assume that the firm was liquidated. If the associated legal and administrative costs were $2,000,000, what would be the final allocation to the notes payable holders?

a. $10,000,000
b. $7,200,000
c. $5,000,000
d. $3,600,000
e. $0

Answers and Solutions

1. insolvent

2. bankrupt; Bankruptcy Act

3. management incompetence

4. mergers; government intervention

5. moral risk; recover

6. extension; composition

7. reorganization

8. fairness; feasibility

9. liquidated

10. fairness; priority

11. feasibility; fixed charges

12. maturity; debt; equity

13. assignment; bankruptcy

14. assignment; assets; assignee; trustee

15. creditors; pro rata

16. fraud; assets

17. secured; highest

18. b. They tend to be relatively inexpensive since legal and administrative expenses are low.

19. a.

20. b. Assignment is an informal procedure that does not require a bankruptcy court.

21. e.

22. b. First, look at the priority claims:

Proceeds from sale of assets		$32,000,000
Less:		
Proceeds from sale of plant to secured creditors	$16,000,000	
Legal and administrative fees	2,000,000	
Wages due	1,500,000	
Taxes due	500,000	20,000,000
Available for unsecured creditors		$12,000,000

At this point, there are total remaining claims by creditors of $50,000,000. Therefore, each dollar of remaining credit would get $12,000,000/$50,000,000 = $0.24 in the initial allocation. Then, the holders of the subordinated debentures must turn over their initial allocation to notes payable until notes payable are satisfied or the debentures' initial allocation is exhausted.

Remaining Claims	Unsatisfied Portion of Claims	Initial Allocation (24%)	Final Allocation	Percent of Claim Satisfied
First mortgage bonds	$ 4,000,000	$ 960,000	$ 960,000	85%
Notes payable (to bank)	10,000,000	2,400,000	7,200,000	72
Accounts payable	16,000,000	3,840,000	3,840,000	24
Subordinated debentures	20,000,000	4,800,000	0	0
Totals	$50,000,000	$12,000,000	$12,000,000	24%

Note that the claims of preferred and common stockholders would be completely wiped out.

CHAPTER 24

INTERNATIONAL FINANCIAL MANAGEMENT

Overview

As the world economy becomes more integrated, the role of multi-national firms is ever increasing. Although the same basic principles of financial management apply to multinational corporations as well as to domestic ones, the financial managers of multinational firms face a much more complex task. Chapter 24 presents some of the issues that must be considered by multinational financial managers. The primary problem, from a financial standpoint, is the fact that the cash flows must cross national boundaries. These flows may be constrained in various ways, and, equally important, their values in dollars may rise or fall depending on exchange rate fluctuations. This means that the multinational financial manager must be constantly aware of the many complex interactions among national economies and their effects on multinational operations.

Outline

I. U.S. manufacturing firms have invested 25 percent of their assets overseas, primarily because of the higher rates of return available on foreign investments. A similar percentage of their income is obtained from foreign sources.

   A. Most multinational corporations have a base in one country and operate branches or subsidiaries in other countries.

   B. U.S. firms have been far more aggressive in making foreign investments than have firms based in other countries.

   C. Multinational financial management must take into account not only such traditional topics as capital budgeting and cost of capital but also international differences in financial markets and institutions.

II. There are four specific reasons why companies move into international operations.

A. A good many of the present multinational firms commenced their international operations because raw materials were located abroad.

B. Other firms expanded overseas to obtain an outlet for their finished products.

C. Still other firms have moved their manufacturing facilities overseas to take advantage of low production costs in cheap labor areas.

D. Finally, banks and other service corporations have expanded overseas to better serve their primary customers and to take advantage of profitable new investment opportunities.

III. Currencies of the various countries are related through a complex system of foreign exchange.

A. The exchange rate specifies the amount of one currency required to purchase one unit of another currency.

B. The International Monetary Fund (IMF) was the center of a fixed exchange rate system that operated for 25 years after World War II.

1. Under this system the U.S. dollar was the base currency, and the relative value of all other currencies to the dollar was controlled within narrow limits.

2. Currency fluctuations depend on supply and demand, capital movements, and the activities of international speculators, which were kept within limits by the actions of the various central banks that bought or sold currency to maintain a specific price.

3. If a country devalued its currency, then fewer units of another currency would be required to buy one unit of the devalued currency. Its "price" would be reduced, making the country's goods cheaper and thus stimulating exports and discouraging imports. A country could devalue its currency only with the approval of the IMF.

C. In the early 1970s, the fixed exchange rate system was replaced by a system under which the U.S. dollar was permitted to "float."

1. A floating exchange rate system is one under which currency prices are allowed to reach their own levels without government intervention.

2. The present managed floating system permits currencies' rates to move without any specific limits, but central banks do buy and sell currencies to smooth out rather than reverse exchange rate fluctuations.

D. The foreign exchange market is made up of brokers and banks in New York and other financial centers around the world.

E. The rate paid for delivery of currency two days after the day of trade is called the spot rate.

F. When currency is bought or sold and is to be delivered at a later date, the forward exchange rate is used.

   1. If the forward rate is above the spot rate, it is said to be at a premium.
   2. A forward rate below the spot rate is said to be at a discount.

G. The forward market provides protection against future changes in exchange rates.

IV. Relative interest rates and exchange rates influence a multinational corporation's financing and its profitability.

A. A foreign currency on average will depreciate at a percentage rate approximately equal to the amount by which its inflation rate exceeds our own.

B. Countries experiencing higher rates of inflation tend to have higher interest rates.

C. Gains from borrowing in countries with low interest rates can be offset by losses from currency appreciation in those countries.

V. There are several important differences in the analysis of foreign versus domestic investment opportunities.

A. Cash flow analysis is much more complex for overseas investments.

   1. Usually a firm will organize a separate subsidiary in each foreign country in which it operates.
   2. Any dividends or royalties repatriated by the subsidiary must be converted to the currency of the parent company, and thus are subject to exchange rate fluctuations.
   3. Dividends and royalties are normally taxed by both foreign and domestic governments.
   4. Some governments place restrictions, or exchange controls, on the amount of cash that may be remitted to the parent company in order to encourage reinvestment of earnings in the foreign country.

B. The cost of capital may be higher for foreign investments because they may be riskier.

   1. Exchange risk refers to the fact that exchange rates may fluctuate, increasing the uncertainty about cash flows to the parent company.

2. Sovereign risk refers to the possibility of expropriation and to restrictions on cash flows to the parent company.
3. The combination of exchange risk, sovereign risk, and the "regular" risk factors makes up the investment climate of a foreign country.
4. The more uncertain or unfavorable a country's investment climate, the higher the cost of capital must be for investments in that country.

VI. Funds to finance foreign projects can be obtained from several sources, in addition to common equity supplied by the parent company.

A. Selling common stock to residents of foreign countries has both advantages and disadvantages.

1. It can result in loss of control of the subsidiary if the parent company sells more than 50 percent of the shares. In fact, some countries require majority ownership by local residents.
2. However, some degree of local ownership may be a desirable feature in countries with less stable governments, since it provides an incentive for the local residents to exert pressure against the threat of expropriation or other interference.

B. Local borrowing is another means of funding foreign projects.

1. If the subsidiary is highly leveraged, and obtains this debt from local sources, expropriation will result in only minimal losses to the parent.
2. Additionally, borrowing locally may be advantageous if local sources of funds offer attractive interest rates. However, a borrower must be careful to take into account expected future changes in the exchange rate.

VII. Firms with substantial amounts of overseas investments encounter special problems in managing foreign assets.

A. Translation losses (or gains) may occur when financial statements are "translated" from a foreign currency to U.S. dollars.

B. The procedures for accounting for foreign currency translation are contained in FASB #52.

1. In preparing the parent company's consolidated balance sheet, all assets and liabilities are translated into U.S. dollars at the current exchange rate.
2. In preparing the income statement, revenues and expenses are translated at the average exchange rate that prevailed during the reporting period.

3. Balance sheet translations may result in an increase or decrease in net worth.
   a. If the subsidiary is self-contained and integrated into the foreign country, the change in net worth would appear only on the balance sheet with an accompanying note.
   b. However, if the subsidiary is not self-contained, the change in net worth must be shown on the income statement as a gain or loss, thus causing volatility of the parent company's reported net income.

C. The exposure to losses (or gains) due to changing exchange rates is called foreign exchange exposure. Multinational financial managers can, and do, take actions to reduce their foreign exchange exposure.

   1. A common method of hedging foreign exchange exposure is to use forward contracts in the foreign exchange market.
   2. Also, assets may be financed in either dollars or in foreign currency depending upon the expected movement in exchange rates.

VIII. Direct foreign investment by U.S. corporations is one way for U.S. citizens to invest in world markets. Another way is to purchase stocks, bonds, or various money market instruments issued in foreign countries. Such investments in foreign money and capital markets are known as portfolio investments as distinguished from direct investments in physical assets.

A. A Eurodollar is a U.S. dollar placed in a time deposit in a foreign (normally European) bank, including foreign branches of U.S. banks.

B. The Eurodollar market is essentially a short-term market--most loans and deposits are for less than 1 year. However, there are also two important types of international bond markets.

   1. Foreign bonds are bonds sold by a foreign borrower but denominated in the currency of the country in which the issue is sold.
   2. Eurobonds are bonds sold in a country other than the one in whose currency the bond issue is denominated.

Definitional Questions

1. The _____ _____ determines the number of units of one currency that can be exchanged for another.

2. International financial transactions were carried out under a _____ _____ _____ system from the end of World War II until 1971.

3. The organization which controlled the fixed exchange rate system was the _____ _____ _____, which served as a world central bank.

4. Under the fixed rate system, the relative values of various currencies were based on the _____ _____.

5. Countries such as West Germany with export surpluses and a strong currency might have to _____ their currencies upward.

6. In the early 1970s the _____ rate system was replaced by one that permitted the U.S. dollar to _____ against other currencies.

7. Evaluation of foreign investments involves the analysis of dividend and royalty cash flows that are _____ to the parent company.

8. Some foreign governments restrict the amount of income that may be repatriated to encourage _____ in the foreign country.

9. _____ risk refers to the possibility of restrictions on cash flows or the outright _____ of property by a foreign government.

10. Dollar deposits held by European banks are often called _____.

11. The difference between a multinational firm's foreign monetary assets and its debt denominated in a foreign currency is known as the firm's _____ _____ position.

12. Multinational firms may _____ their exposure to foreign exchange fluctuations by making use of _____ _____ in the foreign exchange market. Such contracts fix the _____ rate at some future date. Thus, the firms will not have to rely on the _____ rate in existence when they need funds in the future.

Conceptual Questions

13. When a central bank of a country buys and sells its currency to smooth out fluctuations in the exchange rate, the system is referred to as a managed float system.

    a. True   b. False

14. A foreign currency will, on average, appreciate at a percentage rate approximately equal to the amount by which its inflation rate exceeds the inflation rate in the United States.

    a. True   b. False

15. Which of the following statements concerning multinational cash flow analysis is not correct?

a. The relevant cash flows are the dividends and royalties repatriated to the parent company.
b. The cash flows must be converted to the currency of the parent company and, thus, are subject to future exchange rate changes.
c. Dividends and royalties are normally taxed only by the government of the country in which the subsidiary is located.
d. Foreign governments may restrict the amount of the cash flows that may be repatriated.
e. All of the above statements are correct.

16. The cost of capital is generally lower for a foreign project than for an equivalent domestic project since the possibility of exchange gains exists.

a. True   b. False

17. Under FASB #52, the net corporate translation gain or loss from all subsidiaries must be reported through the income statement.

a. True   b. False

Problems

18. The "spot rate" for Greek drachmas is 0.0313 U.S. dollars per drachma. What would the exchange rate be, expressed in drachmas per dollar?

a. 0.0313 drachmas per dollar
b. 3.1300 drachmas per dollar
c. 31.9489 drachmas per dollar
d. 319.4890 drachmas per dollar
e. 400.0000 drachmas per dollar

19. The U.S. dollar can be exchanged for 942.1432 Italian lira today. The Italian currency is expected to appreciate by 10 percent tomorrow. What is the expected exchange rate tomorrow expressed in lira per dollar?

a. 836.1935 lira per dollar
b. 841.3167 lira per dollar
c. 847.9289 lira per dollar
d. 958.2334 lira per dollar
e. 965.9813 lira per dollar

20. You are considering the purchase of a block of stock in Galic Steel, a French steel producer. Galic just paid a dividend of 10 francs per share; that is, D_0 = 10 francs. You expect the dividend to grow indefinitely at a rate of 15 percent per year, but because of a higher expected rate of inflation in France than in the United States, you expect the franc to <u>depreciate</u> against

the dollar at a rate of 5 percent per year. The exchange rate is currently 5 francs per U.S. dollar, but this ratio will change as the franc depreciates. For a stock with this degree of risk, including exchange rate risk, you feel that a 20 percent rate of return is required. What is the most, in dollars, that you should pay for the stock?

a. $20.90
b. $31.70
c. $46.00
d. $53.60
e. $60.34

21. Refer to Question 20. Now assume that the franc is expected to <u>appreciate</u> rather than depreciate against the dollar at the rate of 1 percent per year. All other facts are unchanged. Under these conditions, what should you be willing to pay for the stock?

a. $20.90
b. $31.70
c. $46.00
d. $53.60
e. $60.34

Answers and Solutions

1. exchange rate

2. fixed exchange rate

3. International Monetary Fund (IMF)

4. U.S. dollar

5. revalue

6. fixed; "float"

7. repatriated

8. reinvestment

9. Sovereign; expropriation

10. Eurodollars

11. net monetary

12. hedge; forward contracts; exchange; spot

13. a.

14. b. The foreign currency will depreciate if its inflation rate is higher than that of the United States.

15. c. Dividends and royalties are also taxed by the parent company's government, although the U.S. government does give the parent company a tax credit for taxes paid by the subsidiary.

16. b. The cost of capital is generally higher because of exchange risk and sovereign risk.

17. b. The gain or loss need only be reported through the income statement for those subsidiaries that do not operate in a self-contained manner.

18. c. The exchange rate for drachmas per dollar would be the reciprocal of the exchange rate of dollars per drachma: 1/(0.0313 dollars per drachma) = 31.9489 drachmas per dollar.

19. c. [(942.1432)(0.90)]/$1.00 = 847.9289 lira per dollar.

20. a. First, the valuation equation must be modified to convert the expected dividend stream to dollars:

$$D_t = D_0(1 + g)(ER),$$

where ER = exchange ratio. ER = 1/5 today, but if francs depreciate at a rate of 5 percent, it will take more francs to buy a dollar in the future. The value of ER at some future time (t) will be

$$ER_t = \frac{Dollars}{Francs} = \frac{1}{5(1.05)^t}$$

Therefore, D_t in dollars may be calculated as follows:

$$D_t \text{ (in dollars)} = (10 \text{ francs})(1 + g)^t(ER_t)$$

$$= \frac{10(1.15)^t}{5(1.05)^t}$$

$$= \frac{\$2(1.15)^t}{(1.05)^t}$$

$$= \$2(1.15/1.05)^t$$

$$= \$2(1.0952)^t.$$

Thus, if the dividend in francs is expected to grow at a rate of 15 percent per year, but the franc is expected to depreciate at a rate of 5 percent per year against the dollar, then the growth rate, in dollars, of dividends received will be 9.52 percent. We can now calculate the price of the stock in dollars:

$$P_0 = \frac{D_1}{k - g} = \frac{\$2(1.0952)}{0.20 - 0.0952} = \frac{\$2.1904}{0.1048} = \$20.90.$$

21. e. Solve the problem as above:

$$ER_t = \frac{(1)(1.01)^t}{5}.$$

$$D_t \text{ (in dollars)} = (10 \text{ francs})(1 + g)^t \frac{(1.01)^t}{5}$$

$$= \frac{10}{5} (1.15)^t (1.01)^t$$

$$= 2(1.1615)^t.$$

Thus, the franc dividend is expected to increase at a rate of 15 percent per year, and the value of these francs is expected to rise at the rate of 1 percent per year, so the expected growth rate of the dollar dividend is 16.15%. We can now calculate the stock price:

$$P_0 = \frac{D_1}{k - g} = \frac{\$2(1.1615)}{0.20 - 0.1615} = \frac{\$2.3230}{0.0385} = \$60.34.$$

FINANCIAL MANAGEMENT IN THE SMALL FIRM

Overview

Small business firms differ from large corporations in several respects. In particular, the goals of the small firm tend to reflect the objectives of the individual entrepreneur rather than the objectives of the investors. Also, the individual entrepreneur needs a broader range of skills than any individual executive in a corporation, and the entrepreneur has a smaller margin for error in decisions. Although many of the principles and analytical methods applicable to large firms are equally applicable to small firms, the latter do face unique problems. Chapter 25 describes the formation and growth of the small firm and some of the special problems the small firm faces in raising capital.

Outline

I. While the same general principles of financial management apply to small as well as large firms, small businesses face certain unique problems, and they are generally operated in a very personalized manner.

   A. Small businesses go through a life cycle which includes the following stages:

      1. Experimentation stage. Sales and profits grow slowly following the establishment of a firm.
      2. Exploitation period. The firm enjoys rapid growth of sales and high profitability as market acceptance of its products accelerates, and the firm expands to meet this increased demand.
      3. Maturity. Sales are dependent in large part on replacement demand, thus sales growth begins to slow.
      4. Decline. The firm faces new competition, technological and managerial obsolescence, and saturation of demand for its goods.

   B. Competent management will attempt to prolong the exploitation stage of the life cycle and to prevent the firm from entering the decline stage.

C. Each of the four stages of development of a business has its own financing pattern.

   1. In the formative stage, a new small firm must rely most heavily on personal savings, trade credit, and government agencies.
   2. During the rapid growth period, internal financing will become an important source of financing, although continued reliance will be placed on trade credit. Also, it may be possible at this stage to obtain bank credit to finance seasonal needs and, perhaps, even a term loan.
   3. While growing to maturity, it may become feasible to go public. In this stage, the firm has access to the broader money and capital markets.
   4. Finally, at maturity the firm must plan for the possibility of share repurchases, mergers, or other long-term strategies.

D. Some firms are small because of the nature of the industry, while other firms are small primarily because they are new companies. These two types of small businesses face fundamentally different situations, and they have vastly different problems and opportunities.

II. Traditional small businesses belong to industries whose nature may dictate that the size of operating units be relatively small due to diseconomies of scale beyond a fairly small size.

A. Such industries tend to be characterized by a localized market, low capital requirements, and relatively simple technology.

B. Reliance on the skills of one individual may cause a number of business problems.

   1. One individual may not possess all of the managerial skills required to operate the business.
   2. The span of responsibilities may be too much for one individual to control.
   3. Day-to-day pressures may interfere with long-range planning.
   4. Plans for management succession may be lacking.

C. Many small businesses are opened each year, despite the risks and hard work involved. The reasons generally given are profit potential, the freedom to make decisions, and the challenge of running a business.

D. The major capital markets are typically not available as a source of funds for small businesses.

   1. Trade credit is by far the most important source of short-term financing.

2. Real estate and equipment may be used as collateral for bank loans.

3. Financial ratio analysis is especially important to help measure the operating and managerial efficiency of small businesses.

4. Because the typical small firm has limited liquidity, working capital management is a critical function.

    a. Inventories generally represent a high proportion of assets and must be carefully controlled.

    b. A competitive credit policy may be required, but excessive accounts receivable should not be permitted to endanger liquidity.

5. There is a much greater reliance on internal financing than is true of larger firms.

E. Some traditional small businesses are moving toward franchise operations.

1. Franchises display the following characteristics:

    a. Training and experience in a particular line of business are supplied to a proprietor on a rental contract basis.

    b. A valuable name may be provided to a proprietor.

    c. Bulk buying made available by the franchise may lower costs to the proprietor.

2. The major potential disadvantage of a franchise is the excessive price a franchisee may be required to pay for the trademark, specialty inputs, supplies, and managerial advice.

III. The second type of small business is the new firm with growth potential. Typically, such a firm has developed a new product or service.

A. The experimentation period is one of planning for future growth and of establishing the firm in the market.

1. Planning for future growth must be based on the realization that growth will result from increased market share or industry expansion.

2. The techniques necessary for success must be identified.

3. Knowledge of the administrative tools must be obtained.

    a. The importance of financial planning and control must be recognized.

    b. Ratio analysis should be used to isolate problems and to plan the broad outlines of the firm's financial structure.

    c. Breakeven analysis can be used to measure how changing sales levels will affect the firm's risk and return characteristics.

B. The high-growth period is one of rapid growth in both sales and profits.

   1. Cash flows and working capital management become increasingly important during the exploitation stage.

   2. There may be a critical need for external financing at this stage.

      a. Equity capital is still very difficult to raise through regular financial markets.

      b. Venture capital firms may be an important source of needed funds.

      c. Larger business firms may also be willing to provide equity capital for investment purposes.

      d. Another important source of capital for small businesses are the Small Business Investment Companies (SBICs), private companies licensed by the SBA to provide capital and management counsel to small business.

C. A growing firm may at some point need to "go public" in order to raise large amounts of capital as well as to provide a market for the stock of the original owners.

   1. Going public brings about a number of changes in the manner in which a firm is operated.

      a. More formal controls and financial planning techniques are required.

      b. Information must be reported to outside investors on a timely basis.

      c. Additional management personnel are required for the expanded level of operations.

      d. A board of directors should be formed to develop sound plans and policies.

   2. Establishing a price for the stock when a firm goes public is particularly difficult.

      a. The cost of equity capital is hard to estimate.

      b. The required rate of return for small, risky firms is high.

      c. Tax considerations for the original owners are important.

   3. The timing of the issue is critical, as variations in money market conditions may have an important impact on the success of the issue.

IV. Specialized venture capital firms have been created to meet the financing needs of small firms with growth potential.

A. Venture capital firms can be organized either as partnerships or as formal corporations called <u>investment development companies</u>.

        1. Venture capitalists are often wealthy individuals who are interested in receiving income as capital gains and, thus, are in a position to take larger risks.

        2. In recent years, large established business firms have taken an increasing interest in venture capital financing.

    B. Venture capital companies generally take an equity position in the firms they finance, but they may also provide debt capital.

    C. Typically, venture capital firms do not require voting control, but they do maintain continuous contact with the firm, providing management counsel and monitoring the firm's progress.

    D. Another important source of venture capital is the Small Business Investment Company (SBIC) sponsored by the Small Business Administration.

V. The Small Business Administration operates a number of programs designed to assist the financing and development of small businesses.

        1. The SBA licenses, regulates, and supports the SBICs.

        2. The SBA's Business Loan Program provides funds directly to small businesses when they are unable to obtain funds from private sources on reasonable terms.

           a. In a direct loan, the SBA simply makes a loan to the small business borrower.

           b. In a participation loan, the SBA lends part of the funds, while a private lender advances the balance. A portion of the funds provided by the private lender may be guaranteed by the SBA.

VI. An employee stock ownership plan (ESOP) is a pension or profit-sharing which is allowed to invest in the securities of the employer company.

    A. The company makes an annual, tax-deductible contribution to the plan.

        1. The ESOP represents a pool of untaxed dollars which allows the firm to carry out financial transactions at a lower cost.

        2. ESOPs provide liquidity and equity capital, as well as control over the timing of financing.

3. Some possible disadvantages of ESOPs should also be noted.
    a. Stock ownership may be diluted unless the stock purchased is nonvoting.
    b. Earnings will be reduced by the amount of the contribution, which could result in lower stock prices.
4. If an ESOP is structured carefully, the disadvantages can be minimized, resulting in a plan which is beneficial to all parties involved.

Definitional Questions

1. Like most firms, the development pattern of a small business seems to follow a _____ _____.

2. The _____ stage of this life cycle is likely to be initiated by the invention of a new _____ or _____.

3. The most rapid growth in sales and profits is likely to occur during the _____ stage.

4. During the maturity phase of the life cycle, growth is largely dependent upon _____ demand.

5. The period of _____ is characterized by the appearance of substitutes, technological obsolescence, and _____ of markets.

6. Small businesses predominate in industries that are characterized by _____ markets, _____ technology, and low _____ requirements.

7. Individual owners may not have the _____ skills necessary for the efficient operations of an expanding business.

8. In addition to profits, the motivation for establishing a small business may include personal _____ to make decisions and the challenge of performing a _____ of tasks.

9. Bank loans may be available if the firm has _____ _____ or _____ that can be used as collateral.

10. Rapidly growing firms in the exploitation stage of the life cycle have a difficult time in raising _____ capital.

11. Federally sponsored _____ _____ _____ _____ are one source of funds for the rapidly growing new business.

12. The primary reasons for "going public" are to raise _____ for the firm to use in its expansion program and to help the firm's founders _____ their own financial assets.

13. _____ costs for a new issue of common stock by a small firm are very high in comparison with the issuance of additional shares of larger, well-established firms.

14. Specialized firms created for the purpose of supplying funds to small firms with growth potential are called _____ _____ companies.

15. The Small Business Administration may make _____ or _____ loans to assist the growth of a small business.

16. An _____ _____ _____ _____ is a pension or profit-sharing plan which invests in the _____ of the employer company.

17. An ESOP is a pool of _____ _____ which lower the costs of financial transactions to the firm.

Conceptual Questions

18. One critical problem of many small businesses is that of management succession.

    a. True   b. False

19. Working capital management is much less important for the management of a small business than for that of a large corporation.

    a. True   b. False

20. Rapidly growing firms in the exploitation stage of the life cycle generally have great appeal to the average equity investor.

    a. True   b. False

21. The industry segments in which small businesses predominate exhibit all of the following characteristics: (1) a localized market, (2) low capital requirements, and (3) complex technology.

    a. True   b. False

22. Small businesses typically have no access to the regular capital markets as a source of funds.

    a. True   b. False

23. The sale of stock in a closely held business to the general public is known as a decision to list stock.

    a. True   b. False

Answers

1. life cycle

2. experimentation; product; service

3. exploitation

4. replacement

5. decline; saturation

6. localized; simple; capital

7. managerial

8. freedom; variety

9. real estate; equipment

10. equity

11. Small Business Investment Companies (SBICs)

12. capital; diversify

13. Flotation

14. venture capital

15. direct; participation

16. employee stock option plan; securities

17. untaxed dollars

18. a.

19. b. Since small businesses generally have limited liquidity, and inventories represent a large proportion of assets, working capital management is a critical function.

20. b. Firms in the exploitation stage are typically entering new areas about which little information is available. They may have great potential, but large risks are involved. Thus, the average equity investor will not invest in small businesses at this stage.

21. b. Generally, small businesses have relatively simple technology.

22. a.

23. b. This is going public. Listing stock is placing the stock on an organized exchange.